Architecture Constructed

Frontispiece. *Rear view of a building mockup, Watertown MA, 2022, Builder Unknown, Photo by Mark Jarzombek.*

Architecture Constructed

Notes on a Discipline

MARK JARZOMBEK

BLOOMSBURY VISUAL ARTS
LONDON • NEW YORK • OXFORD • NEW DELHI • SYDNEY

BLOOMSBURY VISUAL ARTS
Bloomsbury Publishing Plc
50 Bedford Square, London, WC1B 3DP, UK
1385 Broadway, New York, NY 10018, USA
29 Earlsfort Terrace, Dublin 2, Ireland

BLOOMSBURY, BLOOMSBURY VISUAL ARTS and the Diana logo are trademarks of
Bloomsbury Publishing Plc

First published in Great Britain 2023

Cover design: Eleanor Rose
Cover image: Roof Framing Plan, Plate 50, *The Carpenter and Joiner's Companion
in the Geometrical Construction of Working Drawings*, Peter Nicholson, 1826.
Digitally recreated by Mark Jarzombek, 2022

A catalogue record for this book is available from the British Library.

A catalog record for this book is available from the Library of Congress.

ISBN: HB: 978-1-3503-2612-5
        PB: 978-1-3503-2611-8
        ePDF: 978-1-3503-2613-2
        eBook: 978-1-3503-2614-9

Typeset by RefineCatch Limited, Bungay, Suffolk
Printed and bound in India

To find out more about our authors and books visit www.bloomsbury.com
and sign up for our newsletters.

To Nancy

CONTENTS

ACKNOWLEDGMENTS

This work came about over the years in a class I teach called *4.607, Thinking about Architecture*, and so I would like to thank the legions of students for their conversations and prompts as well as those who have prompted me for clarity. I would also like to acknowledge the larger community of colleagues and friends who have taken an interest in my work. Among the various colleagues who read the manuscript in its early stages and discussed it with me, I would like to thank in particular Franz Oswald, Michael Osman, Hadas Steiner, Jordan Kauffman, and Mark Dorian. I would like to thank Aidan Flynn for his help with the manuscript and images.

FOREWORD

In Paul Valéry's *Eupalinos ou l'architecte* (1921), Socrates and Phaedrus encounter each other in Hades where their conversation takes them to the subject of architecture. Socrates tells Phaedrus that as a youth when he was once walking along a beach he came across a mysterious object that had washed ashore. When he studied it more closely, he could not tell whether it was a product of nature or of human artifice. This uncertainty compelled him to reflect upon a number of themes about the nature of form and about the act of making. A difficult choice presented itself to the young Socrates who experiences a "strange hesitation between souls," between becoming a philosopher or an architect. Eventually he decided on the former though he acknowledged: "There was within me an architect whom circumstances did not fashion forth."[1]

Had Valéry's Socrates decided to become an architect, he would have gone through a rather brutal awakening to discover that his ancient historical self along with his posthumous incarnation in Plato's dialogues had already shaped the discipline in ways that they could never have anticipated back then. Socrates—that beloved icon of wisdom for most of us—and his student Plato, as it turns out were responsible for the proverbial split between architecture and building. Socrates' ennobling and much vaunted demand "Know thyself" was meant for the young, well-healed, slave-owning intelligentsia of Athens and not for artisans whom Socrates called dismissively *banausos*. The *banausos* were seen as too busy at their work to develop the societal awareness ostensibly necessary for "elevated" self-reflection. Plato took it one step further and assumed that the main job of the *banausos* was to take orders. Stated simply, Greek philosophy created a class of people who were at the get-go defined as unable to participate in the making of mind's narrative of self, with Western philosophy basically preserving this imprint into the modern age. Even though the *banausos* were certainly important contributors to society, they were condemned by their occupationality; it is the misfortune of architecture to still carry the traces of that ancient division and its structural incompletion into the contemporary world. And yet, so much of recent theory and practice in architecture sees the history of that ancient division as just some bad dream. So how do we understand that incompletion as its own theoretical project?

PART ONE

CHAPTER ONE

Preface

De re aedificatoria (written between 1443 and 1452) is seen as the moment when architecture, in Europe that is, sets itself up as a discipline. In the preface, Leon Battista Alberti states:

> Before I go any farther, however, I should explain exactly whom I mean by an architect; for it is no carpenter (*tignarium fabrum*) that I would have you compare to the greatest exponents of other disciplines: the carpenter (*fabri*) is but an instrument (*instrumentum*) in the hands of the architect. Him I consider the architect, who by sure and wonderful reason and method, knows how to devise both through his own mind and energy, and to realize by construction, whatever can be most beautifully fitted out for the most noble needs of man, by the movement of weights and the joining and massing of bodies.[1]

I would like to read this passage in a counterintuitive manner, for it contains, I hold, an originary moment of an unexpected order. We should linger on the exclusionary clause.

> It is no carpenter (*tignarium fabrum*) that I would have you compare to the greatest exponents of other disciplines.

Those "other disciplines" were medicine, theology, and law, Alberti having been trained in law at the University of Bologna notable for its teaching of canon and civil law. To add a new discipline to these well-established ones was to be a tall order, however, since architecture at that time would have had still little to show for itself apart from some mostly unstudied Roman ruins, excerpts from Pliny's *Naturalis Historia*, a few medieval treatises on geometry, and the recently discovered manuscript of Vitruvius. But in wanting to place architecture in alignment with the better-established disciplines, Alberti also wanted to clarify who it is that sits at the table; it is to be the architect, not the *faber tignarius*.[2] The word "carpenter" in the translation is misleading since it derives from a Celtic word for carriage maker.[3] There is a big difference between a carriage maker and a *faber tignarius*, which means literally "maker of beams."[4]

The word carpenter is misleading for a second reason. From a modern economic point of view the leading wage earners in the building industry are the electricians and plumbers. But this was not the case in the past. Well into the twentieth century when it came to building a house the "carpenter" had more to do with the construction of a building than any other person employed by the architect. A testament to this is the eloquent description in the *Architectural Magazine* from 1834:

> Whether a building is to be erected of brick or stone, still it is the carpenter who forms all the patterns and guides for the bricklayer or the mason to work from. Nay, even if a cottage is to be built of mud, the first step is to procure boards adapted by the carpenter for forming moulds, by which this mud is brought into the required form; or, even if the mud is heaped up with forks, as in the cob walls of Devonshire and Wiltshire, the carpenter is required to supply what are called wooden bricks, to be built into the walls, for attaching, at a future period, the internal finishings. In the interior of a house, everything depends on the carpenter; and most things are, indeed, done by him. The floors, and the doors and windows, are almost entirely his work; and he forms mouldings for the cornices which are put up by the plasterer.[5]

The "carpenter" of the nineteenth century was not much different from the *faber* of the fifteenth. In fact, his duties might even have been not all that different from the days of ancient Rome. Cato the Elder writes:

> If you are contracting for the building of a new steading from the ground up, the contractor (*fabri*) should be responsible for the following: All walls as specified, of quarry-stone set in mortar, pillars of solid masonry, all necessary beams, sills, uprights, lintels, door-framing, supports, winter stables and summer feed racks for cattle, a horse stall, 2 quarters for servants, 3 meat-racks, a round table, 2 copper boilers, 10 coops, a fireplace, 1 main entrance and another at the option of the owner, windows, 10 two-foot lattices for the larger windows., etc.
>
> *De Agri Cultura*, paragraph 6, line 20

* * * *

So, when Alberti uses the word *faber* he is referring to the broader understanding of the word as "builder" or "contractor" as we would understand those words today.[6]

Alberti had good reason to be concerned about the definition of the architect. In those days, depending on the context, a *faber*-architect could have started their careers as a building administrator or even as an artist.[7]

Perhaps even more concerning was that the roster of these men in the early fifteenth century had begun to expand dramatically. Jacopo della Quercia (1372–1438), Antonio Federighi (*c.* 1420–83), Giacomo Cozzarelli (1453–1515), and Ventura Turapilli (*c.* 1460–1522), initially trained as sculptors, all came to lead ambitious building projects in Siena.[8] Furthermore, there were those who also began to even see themselves as intellectuals. Filarete, who started his career working for the sculptor Lorenzo Ghiberti to eventually work for the Duke of Milan in the 1450s, would, in fact, author a treatise on architecture of his own.[9] And the same holds true for Francesco di Giorgio (1439–1501), Sebastiano Serlio (1475–*c.* 1554), and Andrea Palladio (1508–80), all of whom worked themselves up through the ranks and eventually published treatises.

Even by the end of the sixteenth century, Federico Zuccaro, the first principal of the Accademia di San Luca in Rome, lamented that architecture had become "commonly professed"; he hoped that the Academia conceived to train and support "studious young boys, who wished to study the most noble professions of Design: Painting, Sculpture and Architecture," would rise to become the true experts, "proficient in letters and drawing, theory, and mechanics ... and all the requisite fields of knowledge needed for building design."[10]

Alberti, already anticipating these types of contestations, had made the line in the sand quite clear. For him the *faber* "is but an instrument (*instrumentum*) in the hands of the architect."

Instrumentum is both a prosthetic and the site of the disembodied Other. It is posited at the center of the architect's desire to complete itself, but is simultaneously excluded from the discipline's epistemological narratives since it is by definition voiceless. As an object, it is something that only a representation can represent.

✳ ✳ ✳ ✳

In separating the architect from the *faber* and in then excluding the upwardly mobile *faber* from the possibility of discourse-making, Alberti was certainly well aware that, in ancient Greek, *tektōn* (τέκτων) was a word directly associated with woodworking.[11] In fact, it was for him associated with the most basic activity of building. He used the word *tectum* to reference a shelter, or what we might more appropriately call a "roof over one's head," which, of course, links us to the occupation: *faber tignarius* (maker of beams).[12]

The word "carpenter" is not wrong as a translation. It is just incomplete. It, along with the words "contractor," and even what we today might call "maker" and "fabricator" are all latter-day avatars of *tektōn*.

So, from this basic trans-historical, trans-etymological point of view, Alberti's sentence that sees the architect, not the *faber*, as representing the discipline puts the very word "architecture," rooted, of course, in the etymological contraction of *archē* and *tektōn*, into stress.

The new, Albertian architect displaces and silences the *tektōn* in *archē-tektōn*. Better stated, the new *archē-tektōn* is an *archē(non)tektōn*. By maintaining the word "architecture" as if nothing had changed, the word conceals the *non* as a hidden esoteric figure within the framework of its meaning. *Archē(non)tektōn* is actually *archē(non)tektōn*, with a silent "non." From henceforth, the word architecture pronounces its hypocrisy, especially since it became the job of this new discipline to maintain appearances.

* * * *

The silent non in the word elevates the architect over the *tektōn* and is thus the source of an operation that one would have to label as theoretical, and not just because the figure of the architect announces itself as of a higher mental order, but because the architect disguises that elevation as if it were *not* a theoretical problem at all when in reality the new Albertian architect erases the socio-ontological structure of labor from architectural culture while still including it in its nomenclatural protocols.

There is no theory-of-the-theory that identifies this as a problem.

* * * *

Archē(non)tektōn is, of course, not a word. It is a grammar founded on the impossibility of its own possibility.[13] A grammar of autopoietic indeterminacy.[14]

* * * *

I will call this phenomenon simply "architecture" (with scare quotes) to differentiate it from architecture (without scare quotes) in its colloquial sense. The scare quotes are necessary to express the word's semantic slipperiness within its own disciplinary formations. I will always use the phrase "architecture (without scare quotes)" to avoid the easy tendency to read the word "architecture" universally as if it exists outside of its grammatological operations.

To not use the scare quotes, as is, of course, systemic in the literature, is to fall into the trap set out in the field's disciplinary pretentions and overdeterminations.

To not use the scare quotes leaves its universalisms and, by extension, its Euro-centrisms unquestioned.

To not use the scare quotes is to assume an asymptomatic indivisibility.

"Architecture" works to break open the pact that architecture (without scare quotes) makes with all who write about it.

* * * *

Archē(non)tektōn acknowledges the productive violence engendered by the splitting of *archē-tektōn* within the word architecture (without scare quotes). *Archē(non)tektōn* is a writing that returns from the "after" to the "before." It is the unconcealed, sealed up, and smoothed over by the discipline.

Prae-fatio is "a saying before-hand" and yet it is here written after—after centuries of writing on the subject of architecture—as an afterthought. As Derrida explains, "Every preface is in reverse. It presents itself the right way round, as is required, but in its construction, it proceeds in reverse; it is developed (processed), as one says of photography and its negatives, from its end or supposed purpose: a certain conception of the architectural 'project.'"[15]

Alberti's *archē(non)tektōn* is a pre-disciplinary imaginary that only later—"after"—would become something that we would associate with a discipline.

Alberti's *archē(non)tektōn* is the preface to "architecture."

* * * *

The central figure of negation within this grammatology gives to "architecture" a starting point. Nowhere from the Renaissance to the postmodern age were the other so-called arts from a *disciplinary* point of view defined as a "not ___." Mostly the arts were set out in categories and ranked. Alberti's *archē(non)tektōn* started a different type of game, as a figure internal to architecture's disciplinary structure.[16]

Once in play, the negations can easily shift and slide—*tektōn / non-tektōn* and *archē / non-archē*—and so on, shaping different destinies and opportunities producing any number of semiotic variants, divisions, avoidances, and, of course, negations not just between thought and labor, but also between soul and body, theory and practice, *mens et manus*, architecture and engineering, the academy and the office, the intentional versus the generic, and the human versus the machinic, all of which in their iterations and inter-catenations mark out the circulatory nature of modernity, and it is along these tracks that this short inquiry will navigate.

* * * *

What follows is not a contribution to the history of architecture but a contribution to the history of *archē(non)tektōn*. Nor is this a contribution to architectural theory, but a theoretical contribution to "architecture." Asking for a "theory of architecture" to straighten out the tangled web of misaligned meanings is to descend even further down the rabbit hole, as it assumes a transcendent cognitive subject in the here and now, one that pretends to place itself objectively and still critically in time and space, forgetting how much of an object it itself is. One should avoid what Gayatri Chakravorty Spivak has called a "clarity fetish."[17]

In exploring "architecture"s grammatological possibilities, I am not following the linguistic determinist pattern often deployed in these circumstances that searches for an inherent clarifying structure. Instead, I am using Derrida's idea of grammatology to study the way in which thoughts as recorded in writing affect the nature of knowledge. I am looking in particular to bring us closer to the *wound* that is at the heart of the etymological separation and contraction—a wound laid bare by Alberti and that, as I will show, has its prehistory in Greek philosophy.

I am also asking: When does a discipline become a discipline? On the surface, it is easy to recognize a discipline once it has been formed and in operation for some time. There are regimes of authority, texts, histories, academic departments, conferences, expertises and so forth. But in the case of architecture—in its European context—we are dealing with something quite special, and unique. For it is a discipline that is already theorized through its grammatological inscriptions in a way that forecloses certain types of conversations.

FIGURE 1.1.1 *Name of a construction company etched onto a steel plate on a street in New York, NY. Photo Mark Jarzombek.*

CHAPTER TWO

Arche-Tekton

Jacques Derrida, in his article "No (Point of) Madness—Maintaining Architecture" (1986), writes:

> The concept of architecture is itself an inhabited *constructum*, a legacy that understands us even before we try to think it. Certain invariants remain through all the mutations of architecture. Impassable, imperturbable, an axiomatic traverses the whole history of architecture. An axiomatic, that is to say, an organized whole of fundamental and always presupposed evaluations. This hierarchy has fixed itself in stone; henceforth, it informs the entirety of social space.[1]

Derrida makes it clear that this "axiomatic" is nothing less than "the dwelling [*habitation*], the law of the *oikos*."[2] *Oikos* is, of course, not habitation in the narrow sense, but, as famously discussed by Aristotle, a concept that saw the house, the household economy, and even the idea of constancy as part of a cultural formation all unto its own. The temple—as the house of a deity—embodies and models *oikos* in divine form.

> Despite appearances, this religious or political memory, this historicism, has not deserted architecture. Modern architecture retains nostalgia for it: it is its destiny to be a guardian.

That "modern architecture," as mentioned in the above quote, is the guardian of *oikos* is, for Derrida, not necessarily a bad thing. After all, what would be the alternative?

> Architecture must have a meaning, it must present this meaning, and hence signify. The signifying or symbolic value of this meaning must command the structure and syntax, the form and function of architecture. It must command it from the outside, according to a principle (*archē*), a grounding or foundation, a transcendence or finality (*telos*) whose locations are not themselves architectural.[3]

Let me dive a bit deeper into Derrida's claims since he argues that the *archē* in *archē*-tecture chains—and continues to chain—architecture to the world of ancient obligations.[4] Stated differently, because *archē* is imprinted into the word *archē*-tecture, "architecture" never loses sight of *oikos*, regardless of how distant. If *archē* is the bottle, *oikos* is the content. But when Derrida writes "Modern architecture retains nostalgia for it," some readers might have missed something cunning on his part. He slipped the adjective "modern" into the text after the last word in the previous sentence, "architecture." In between the Then of "architecture" and the Now of "modern architecture," something happened, quite literally in the gap between these two sentences. The word "modern" must have been added to imply a self-consciousness to "architecture," but about what? The culprits are not mentioned, but the usual ones are secularism, technology, rationalism, and consumerism, singularly or in some combination. No one knows exactly when the change took place either. The possibilities are the fifteenth century and the rise of secularism, the nineteenth century and the rise of industrialism, and the twentieth century and the rise of advanced capitalism. The best we get by way of explanation of how we moved from "architecture" to "modern architecture" is a sentence that casually states that Martin Heidegger "encourages us to think properly the real distress, poverty, and destitution of dwelling itself behind the housing crisis."[5]

Derrida implies that this so-called "modern architecture" is a space where *oikos*, pointing forward in time, and nostalgia, pointing backward, intersect. Loss and awareness become one and the same. In other words, "modern architecture," despite its various claims for a release from the metaphysical, cannot truly escape its ancient gravitational pull, which it can only sense as a remote and lingering desire. "Modern architecture" as used by Derrida is thus not a real historical formation; it is a semiotic indicator for the dislocation of Being made invisible within the configuration of its own Subject. This "modern" is now—apparently—baked into "architecture." There is no simple "architecture" any more, and yet it longs to get rid of its adjectival burden and return to architecture (without scare quotes). But it cannot. It is doomed to forever announce the scar of rupture: "modern architecture."

"Modern architecture" should, therefore, be rewritten where the adjective has been doubled and crossed through. "Modern architecture" is really "modern (~~modern~~) architecture" where the traumatic presence indicated by the word is both pronounced and erased. It is presented as a fact, as a given that needs no explanation, and yet is unexplainable. Though it is given a space "in history", no one is sure how it came to have that space. Its appearance is nothing short of magical—a sleight of hand.

I diagram Derrida's argument in the following way, where the point of divergence seems to be known, though its actual history is purely ideological, if not fictional. But once split, there is no turning back even if a recuperation of sorts is implied. Derrida is hesitant to instrumentalize deconstruction, and he seems happy to leave "modern architecture" gazing at its distant

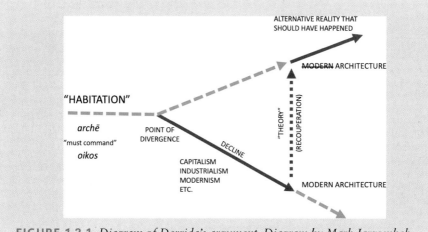

FIGURE 1.2.1 *Diagram of Derrida's argument. Diagram by Mark Jarzombek.*

obligations through the lens of its nostalgia. And yet, his text suggests that there is a possibility of resolution, perhaps to be undertaken by others.

* * * *

For Derrida, what survives within the tension between "architecture" and "modern architecture" is the estranged substance of "habitation." But there is a problem. "Habitation" is, to put it bluntly, a disciplinary cliché that brings us no further than what Vitruvius claimed [*Ten Books on Architecture*, Book 2, Chapter 1.7] and as repeated ad infinitum through the chain of disciplinary copying from Alberti onward. A dictionary from 1851 states: "Architecture: The art of forming dwellings, or buildings of any kind."[6] The consequence of this iterational disciplinary fetish toward "habitation" is that it ignores the bipolarity of the term architecture.

Derrida separates *archē* from *tektōn* to reattach it in its diminished "modern" form, but overlooks the problematic secondary position of *tektōn* and its roots not in habitation, but in woodworking and the making of beams, and, if we wanted to take its origins serious, with the making of ships, not houses.

My point is simple. Derrida's discussion of "habitation," though certainly well-meaning, overdetermines and overdramatizes the role of *archē*. Furthermore, it completely ignores the obvious fact that there is a second half to the word.

* * * *

It is not the *concept* of architecture (without scare quotes) that is an inhabited *constructum*, but the word itself.

This begs the question: When then did *archē-tektōn* become a *constructum*? When did it become an estranged theoretical proposition unto its own in Western discourse?

Plato's dialogue *Statesman* (*c.* 360 BCE) argues that a distinction needs to be made between a statesman, a sophist, and a philosopher. The participants are "Socrates" and a mysterious philosopher from Elea, a city on the western shore of the Peloponnese, who is referred to as "the Stranger." They discuss what mistakes to avoid and what paths are worth pursuing. Plato had good reason to want to define what it took to be a statesman, since he had little respect for the republican leadership of earlier generations. He felt that it was responsible for Athens's humiliating defeat to the Spartans in the Peloponnesian War (431–405 BCE) that had ended Athenian hegemony. He was looking for a clearer, more philosophically grounded form of leadership.

In one passage, the conversation comes around to the term *technē*.[7] It is a term that has little to do with what we today would call "technology" but more with what we would call "expertise" as it implied some form of relationship between learning, making and teaching. It refers to purposeful knowledge as opposed to knowledge in the abstract. A *technikos* would be an expert in something concrete.[8] One could be a *technikos* in the fields of music, rhetoric, and even, so Plato argues, in statesmanship where there, too, the king is expected to possess the relevant expert knowledge.

Plato describes two types of *technē*, one is productive and the other theoretical (*gnostic*), "calling the one practical, and the other intellectual."[9] As an example of the "practical," Plato mentions the carpenter or *tektonicos* (τεκτονικός). As an example of the "theoretical" he mentions the *archē-tektōn* (ἀρχι-τέκτων), the reason being that the latter places things in order, and so in that sense, Plato argues, is not unlike what a statesman does, though the latter works purely in the world of governance.

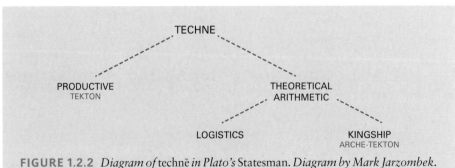

FIGURE 1.2.2 *Diagram of* technē *in Plato's* Statesman. *Diagram by Mark Jarzombek.*

Every architect [ἀρχι-τέκτων], too, is a ruler of workmen [ἐργαστικός], not a workman himself . . . As supplying knowledge, not manual labor . . . he may fairly be said to participate in intellectual science.[10]

Archē, for Plato, would never be tyrannical in form, and his most famous analogy, as described in *Laws*, is that of a ship captain or a thoughtful doctor, but there is no doubt that in the end it is meant to be obeyed. And so we see here the location in the history of Western theory of the troublesome—and tragic—split between *tektōn* and *arche-tektōn*. The difference becomes more fully theorized with Aristotle, where the architect is said to know the causes, whereas the craftsman works simply by habit.

For the same reason we consider that the *architéktonas* in every profession are more estimable and know more and are wiser than the artisans [*cheirotechnón*, meaning roughly "hand-working *tektōns*"], because they know the reasons of the things which are done; but we think that the artisans, like certain inanimate objects, do things, but without knowing what they are doing (as, for instance, fire burns); only whereas inanimate objects perform all their actions in virtue of a certain natural quality, artisans perform theirs through habit [ἔθω (éthō)]. Thus the *architektonas* are superior in wisdom, not because they can do things, but because they possess a theory [*logos*] and know the causes.[11]

The architect operates within an epistemological and expository framework, the carpenter does not. The architect receives his instructions from the logos and also delivers it back in good order. The craftsman works by means of an *éthō*, translated as habit, but meaning a type of knowledge produced only through making.

Already here it is clear that one speaks and the other is mute.

Arche is not just the power over the *instrumentum*, it fashions the *instrumentum* to its particular needs. And so, it is not in the dialectical mysteries of "habitation" that we should begin, but in Plato's distinction between those who give orders and those who take them, between those who give *themselves* a voice and those who are *not allowed* to have a voice and between those who cement this relationship in the form of "philosophy" and those who would never even be part of the conversation. The narcissism of the enterprise is concealed behind the ostensible pragmatism and efficiency of its operations.

* * * *

There is a twist. Greek philosophers had the habit of making distinctions as a way to map a theory of society, not to study society itself, the aim being to define and *defend* what we might call the political within the polity, where the political was always associated with the sensibilities of leadership and with the interests of the aristocratic, slave-holding class. That means that this distinction as it applies to architecture was in no way real. It is more wordplay than statement of fact. To translate *archē-tektōn* (ἀρχι-τέκτων) as architecture (without scare quotes) can be misleading. There were no schools of architecture in ancient Greece and every person who was identified as an *arche-tektōn* was certainly a person who had made his way up through the ranks because of some combination of personality, skill, and social connection. It is doubtful that Plato's or Aristotle's *archē-tektōn*—even if he was to some degree literate—had spent a lot of time in the libraries pouring over ancient codices about the building arts. What the distinction thus ignores is not only the intimate bonds between craftsman and architect, but that the skills of a *tektōn* were handed down father to son, regardless of how much "logos" was at stake.

✳ ✳ ✳ ✳

Let us compare Plato's point of view with that derived from the ancient Hindu text, the *Mānāsara* [Sanskrit: *māna* (measurement) and *sara* (essence)], from about the eighth century CE, that provides detailed guidelines on the building of temples, sculptures, houses, gardens, water tanks, and even towns.[12] It explains that there are four divine architects emanating from the four faces of Brahma: Visvakarman ("all maker") and the source of all prosperity; Maya, who created and maintains the physical universe; Tvashtar, the creator of forms and the crafter of living beings and wombs; and Manu, the first man. The text further elucidates that the sons of these architects each translated their father's essence into the human dimension: Sthapati ("master-builder") possesses knowledge that encompasses the sciences as well as metaphysics and theology; Sutra-grahin ("one who grasps the measuring cord") specializes in geometry; Vardhaki is known as the "increaser"; and Takshaka is the "cutter of timber." As regards the area of their activity, Sutra-grahin is known as a draughtsman, Vardhaki as the master of representation, and Taksaka as a carpenter. The text accords to Sthapati, the son Visvakarman, the rank of "director general" and "consulting architect."[13] He must be an expert in a wide range of fields, but also be meritorious, patient, dexterous, and modest.

There is clearly a command structure, since the taksaka-carpenter should follow the instructions of his three superiors, namely the chief architect, the geometrician, and the mason-painter, but at the same time he must be capable of doing his work independently. What we see here is a theory that emphasizes complex, interlocked relationships that together emanate from and reproduce the unity of Brahma.

Stated more simply, whereas *arche-tektōn* marks out a type of violence in the name of a well-ordered society, there is no such tension in the *Mānāsara*. The distinction between the four architects is rather around activities: leading, measuring, building, and carpentrying. Furthermore, the four have to work collaboratively toward a common goal. They are, after all, all part of Brahma.

The *Mānāsara* helps us recognize the artifice—if not the powerful, reductive banality—of Plato's division that is based solely on the principle of command and action, a principle that perhaps because of its simplicity worked its way through Western discourse to find itself reflected in the dualisms of theory/practice, mind/hand, and thinking/working, all the way to Derrida's catenation of so-called "musts." Architecture

must have a meaning . . .
must present this meaning . . .

Derrida is quite literally ventriloquizing the voice of Plato's *archē* that renders the *tektōn* invisible.

* * * *

Plato's differentiation and elevation of *arche-tektōn* over *tektōn* is not the origin of architecture (without scare quotes), but the place where the origin of absence can be marked out.

What started as a wordplay ended up becoming a disciplinary reality, a conceit that became real only in the long march toward modernity.

The history of architecture (without scare quotes)—as we understand it today—cannot be some rational or linear unfolding of the materiality that goes under the heading architecture, for clearly already here with Plato, that history has to include the "history" of the not-*archē* of the *tektōn*. That history has to include the "history" of the silencing of the *tektōn*.

It is in this split that we register the doomed beginning point of "architecture."

If one is to begin (or perhaps even end) the conversation about architecture's origins, it is not with *oikos*, but with "architecture" as the collateral damage of the attempt to theorize what it takes to make a good king.

If there is a "modern" to architecture it is born not in the presumed loss of some magical *oikos*, but in the slippery brutality of a wordplay.

* * * *

Architecture's schismatic modernity has to be understood—in its post-Platonic, European formation—as the inauguration of the subject through its separation.

FIGURE 1.2.3 *A building in Cambridge MA under construction, January 18, 2020. Builders unknown. (A temporary art installation?) Photo: Mark Jarzombek.*

CHAPTER THREE

Shell Games

In ancient Greece, the *tektōn*, with the axe and the level as its symbol, had honed their practice over the many centuries, fashioning palaces, ships, and, of course, wooden temples.[1] Their role in building temples changed, however, in the early sixth century BCE. In the preceding period, Greek warriors had begun to serve in the pharaoh's army as bodyguards and specialized fighting units, and while in Egypt, they saw the vast stone structures and huge columns imitating bundles of reeds and flowers. The Greeks brought the technologies and ideas back home. Within the span of a few generations, the changeover was complete and the old wooden temples either fell into disuse or were replaced. Given the vast number of temples, the changeover was astonishingly rapid.

When Pausanias, a Greek traveler and geographer visited the temple of Hera in Olympus around 170 CE, he notes that though everything was in stone, "in the rear chamber one of the two pillars is of oak."[2] It might well have been the last surviving wooden column in Greek architecture and I would venture to say it had probably become a shrine in its own right, a shrine to a lost world.

The transition meant that building sites in ancient Greece changed. Making a stone building required multiple layers of activity, staging, and oversight; it required a wide pallet of tools, instruments, and lifting equipment. It required metallurgists, plasterers, painters, laborers of various types, and even accountants. Cost estimates had become no small task and even Vitruvius makes it clear that financial management was one of the main tasks of the builder in charge.[3] A new word came into being, *architectōn*, used, as far as we know, for the first time by Herodotus in the mid-fifth century BCE in reference to the Samian chief builders, Rhoikos and Eupalinos, who were responsible for "the greatest works of all the Greeks."[4]

Archē carries with it the insignia of the building's managerial complexity. The Greeks of the fifth century BCE were not the first to discover this. The Egyptians and others had been familiar with it long before the Greeks.[5] The Greeks, however, gave it a name.

The addition of *archē* as a prefix onto the ancient word *tektōn* marks a moment when the primacy of the *tektōn* was disappearing. Woodworkers were no longer wanted; masons now ruled the roost.[6]

Archē came to be fixed "in stone" only after the *tektōn* had set out the design in wood. In other words, the fixing in stone postdates the fixing in wood.[7]

The *archē* in architecture is a post-*tektōn archē*.

The addition of *archē* as a prefix marks the "constructedness" of authority onto the building site, embedding it into the historicity of the word itself.

When Plato was using the word only two centuries later for his word games, he was well aware that it was a neologism—a modernity unto itself marking the distinction from simpler days. Just as the *tektōn* of old now had to adhere to the commands of its new *archē*, so the politics of old had to give way, so he hoped, to a new command structure—to a new way of building the state.

❋ ❋ ❋ ❋

A paradox emerged that the Greek philosophers ignored.

The Greeks were not interested in the materiality of stone *qua* stone, but wanted the stone to look like wood—or even flesh as in their sculptures. The columns and beams were all painted, even the beautiful statues of the people, animals, and gods that adorned the frieze and tympanum. There is thus more to *archē* than just governance and management skills as emphasized by Plato. The *archē* was the master of shapeshifting materiality. To state it simply, this new *archē* operated in multiple domains, but was also the master of illusion.

We make a mistake when we equate the *archē* that we find in "architect" with some singular, archaic voice or "principle."

It was neither archaic nor principled.

Archē is the magician that turned wood to stone—or is it stone to wood?

❋ ❋ ❋ ❋

In Plato's haste to describe the nature of kingship, he missed this important aspect of *arche-tektōn*. But this was not the case with post-Platonic Greek poets who were already using even the word *tektōn* to express linguistic trickery, such as fabricating lies or making something unreal look real or playing with the intricacies of the spoken word. Richard Sennett feels that this proves that "[i]f the artisan was celebrated in the age of Homer as a public man or woman, by classical times the craftsman's honor had dimmed."[8] I argue just the opposite: the expansion of *tektōn* into the orbit of *archē* was not some sort of loss, but a cultural formation that accepted situational ambiguity. It positioned architecture between magic and making. In fact, well into the Middle Ages, the word "craft" meant more than just skill; it implied specialized processes of learning that could be applied just as much in making things as in making love. It could even be seen as duplicitous as in the word "craftiness."

* * * *

Once again, Alberti comes into the story, for when he renegotiated the split, he also separated the *tektōn* from its potential for craftiness. When the faber becomes simply "an instrument in the hands of the architect," the architect forces labor to occupy dutifulness. There is no remainder to the equation.

Archē in that sense, in that *modern* sense, uses the *(non)* not just to command over the *tektōn*, as Plato had wanted, but to steal from it the capacity for craftiness, to become the sole signifier of both principle and shiftiness.

After Alberti, *archē* alone possesses the dialectical right to both command and deceive.

Bernie Maddoff, Architect of Largest Ponzi Scheme in History, is Dead at 82.

The New York Times, 2021[9]

Here there is a second beginning to the story of "architecture"—a craftiness on the part of Alberti, all its own.

* * * *

Derrida did not realize that architecture [*archē(non)tektōn*] plays a double game; it is only within the dialectic of agency and duplicitousness that we can find the potential for the beginning of a critique.[10]

The division that Derrida makes between "architecture" and things that are "not themselves architectural" is not an inside/outside problem, but an inside/inside problem.

* * * *

The dislocation of Being within the configuration of its own Subject happened not in spite of *archē*, but because of it.

The redeeming feature of *archē* is not its singular orientation toward "principle," but toward the parallel power of illusionism.

* * * *

If the *(non)* in *archē(non)tektōn* is accepted and not denied or dismissed as the haunted/haunting figure within, that does not itself yield any particular answers as to what it then signifies. The rift between the shifting Subject and its silenced, objectified Other has any number of blanks that can be filled in in any number of different ways, each of which can bring us close to what is "possible" in/within the tension between architecture/"architecture." They are not things that we might label as "the irrational" or "the subjective" if one were to follow the classic pathologies of conventional dualism. These blanks are, of course, not always invisible either, and often have names like the idiosyncratic, the unintelligible, the "artistic," the odd, the visionary and so forth. Though usually relegated to the footnotes of disciplinary history, they are not isolated from a legitimate place with the larger frame of "architecture." They are the oil in its machinery.

The blanks are not the opposite of disciplinarity. On the contrary, they give it its shape.

Occasionally, as in a renovation project in San Francisco from 2019, one sees the effort of the modern, dutiful (i.e., Platonic/Albertian) *tektōn* in its naked reality. These works of normative engineering—invisible in the body of architecture—are structures in more ways than one, since they produce a *structuring* not just of the architecture [as in its proportions or window placements, etc.], but also of the social realities associated with architecture, all the way down to the level of the building industry. "Structures" operate as metonymic devices, identifying some part of a complex social reality while at the same time explaining—directly or indirectly—the whole. And yet, though bound together inseparably, it is clear who speaks and who does not. It is not much different from Jules Hardouin-Mansart's dome of Les Invalides (1670s) except that here the location of the *tektōn* was completely hidden between the two domes that were held up by a rather inelegant assembly of sticks that would have pained the carpenters that constructed them.

* * * *

The history of "architecture" is, however, not the history of the dutiful *tektōn*, but of its tortured alignments with the *archē*. Tel Aviv Museum (2010) by Preston Scott Cohen is celebrated for its "subtly twisting geometric surfaces that connect the disparate angles between the galleries and the

FIGURE 1.3.1 *The Aronson Building, San Francisco, 1903, 2018. Photograph by Mark Jarzombek.*

FIGURE 1.3.2 *Dome of Les Invalides, Jules Hardouin-Mansart, 1670s, Paris. Jules Hardouin Mansart, cross-section, illustration from* Denkmaeler der Kunst *(Monuments of Art), by Wilhelm Luebke and Carl von Luetzow, 3rd edition, Stuttgart 1879, volume 2, steel engraving by H. Gugeler. INTERFOTO / Alamy Stock Photo.*

context while refracting natural light into the deepest recesses of the half-buried building."[11] At least that is the story. In reality (which is nothing to be ashamed of) it is more of a decorated box. As one can see from construction photos, the floor plates hold up a muscular steel frame onto which the triangular, concrete panels each weighing several tons are attached. The building's crystalline surface belays the massive weight of the facade. Here the *tektōn* is on the same order as a truss that holds up a ceiling. It is as if the messy assembly of sticks that were hidden in the dome of Les Invalides had spilled out of over the facade to define and enhance the building's anti-gravitational desire. The facade is a tour de force of illusion. The *tektōn* does the heavy lifting and even the form-making to the greater glory of *archē* who in this case can make concrete look like paper.

FIGURE 1.3.3 *Tel Aviv Museum of Art, Herta and Paul Amir Building, Tel Aviv: View of it under construction in 2010. Photograph by Mark Jarzombek.*

FIGURE 1.3.4 *Tel Aviv Museum of Art, Herta and Paul Amir Building, Tel Aviv,* *2010.* ‫טייכר צילום :ד"ר אבישי‬.

* * * *

Though much has been made of the exotic materials for the floors and walls of the Barcelona Pavilion (1929, 1986), there has been less focus on the roof, which is always the traditional haunt of the *faber tignarius*. It was held up by a grid of steel beams covered underneath and above with gypsum board and thinly plastered for uniformity to make it look like concrete. To increase the effect, Mies van der Rohe gradually thinned the beams toward the edges, like the brim of a hat, from about 75 centimeters to 24 so that the true thickness of the roof is invisible from the ground.[12] This refinement resulted in a seemingly weightless white surface more on the order of cardboard than even of concrete. Unlike the walls and floors which have clear material attributes, where the stone is stone and the metal is metal, the roof was and in fact remains enigmatic. One wonders what modernism might have looked like if Mies had made the roof its full thickness.

* * * *

In 1785, Étienne-Louis Boullée (1728–99) envisioned a grand design for a French National Library. It featured a long reading room with a vast, barrel-vaulted ceiling. The walls were stacked with books. The hall was more like a plaza than a reading room as there were no desks; visitors were free to wander about and converse in small groups. And indeed, it was a courtyard of a building that still exists today along Rue de Banque. In his treatise, Boullée explained that he was transforming this space "into an immense

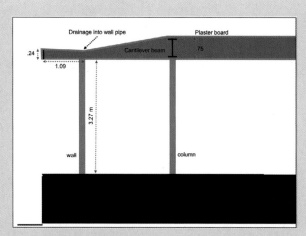

FIGURE 1.3.5 *Partial section of Barcelona Pavilion, drawing by author. Diagram by Mark Jarzombek.*

FIGURES 1.3.6–7 *Barcelona Pavilion, Ludwig Mies van der Rohe, 1929, 1986, Barcelona. Right: with roofline altered by author. Ralf Roletschek, photographer © 2021 Artists Rights Society (ARS), New York / VG Bild-Kunst, Bonn.*

basilica lighted from above . . . [with] attendants spread about so that they could pass the books" from tier to tier.

The library proposal is mostly discussed in terms of Enlightenment ideals and the rise of neoclassicism. Boullée himself argued that the most important thing in architecture was "the effect of mass" [*l'effet des masses*] and did not hide his fascination with geometry. Much of the scholarship has thus focused on the austerity of Boullée's stereometric forms. As Emil Kaufmann notes, "Extreme frugality of ornament contributes also to the impression of size" along with plain surfaces and effective lighting.[13]

But there are several moments that force us to pause. The vault, and indeed most of the building, is made of plaster. Boullée admits this in his text and shows this clearly in the section where we see the rather under-engineered, wooden trusses supporting the curved ceiling. Naturally, one can ascribe this to pragmatism. Most of the baroque vaults of the previous century were also plaster. But these were usually painted. Boullée's vault was not much different, except that the underside was meant to appear "structural" like Roman concrete, a material that was, of course, unknown at the time. Making the coffered vault out of stone would have been impossible, and not just because of the lack of such a vast amount of material, but also because it would have meant a complete redesign to manage the loads. The massive slit at the apex could not even have been done in stone (and not even in unreinforced concrete). In other words, this

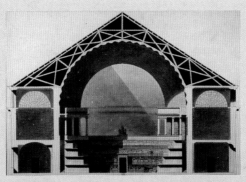

FIGURE 1.3.8 *Section: Design for the French National Library, Étienne-Louis Boullée, Drawing, 1785–8.* © *Bibliothèque Nationale de France.*

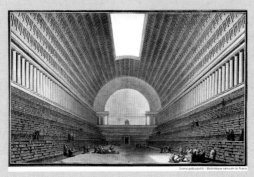

FIGURE 1.3.9 *Perspectival drawing: Design for the French National Library, Étienne-Louis Boullée, Drawing, 1785–8.* © *Bibliothèque Nationale de France.*

was never intended to replicate a stone building, but rather exploited the potential of plaster. And even then, how the vault would have been supported without unsightly compression bars is unknown. Nor would the space have been open to the elements, but rather protected by an upper glazed roof, not, of course, shown in the perspective view.

The visual aspect of the design speaks to the noble origin of civilization, and of the permanence and stability that enable civic engagement with learning. The contractor knows, however, that the roof is little more than a glorified shed that might last no more than a few winters.

* * * *

Junya Ishigami's Serpentine Pavilion 2019 was designed as a hollowed-out hillock of Cumbrian slate meant to feel, so the architect claimed, "primitive and ancient."[14] Ishigami did not want a real hill, but rather rested the slate on a metal mesh that in turn was supported by toothpick-like, white columns. It is a variation on Boullée's vault, except that the much-sought-after "effect of mass" is experienced from within the rafters rather than from outside. As it turned out, the 62 tons of slate needed more reinforcement columns than the architect wanted and the wind sweeping under the work meant that clear polycarbonate walls had to installed to prevent the

FIGURE 1.3.10 *Serpentine Pavilion, Junya Ishigami, London, 2019. Images George Rex, London, England.*

furniture from blowing away. According to the fabricator, Stage One, Ishigami was "the most conceptual architect we have ever worked with. It was a very strained process."[15] After all, the *tektōn*—as the representative of "stability"—has always had as its mission to protect the human, even if that goes against the ideas of the architect. Ishigami didn't hide his disappointment with the changes, but the issue is not how the architect and builders are of different worlds, but of the same. The fabricator not only haunts the system of expression but speaks for a past of betrayal and conflict.

At the Serpentine Pavilion, the disassociation between *tektōn* and *archē* is repaired as an awkward compromise where the tension is visible to all in the unsatisfying, but manageable, final result.

* * * *

With these somewhat arbitrary examples, we have a range of inversions: disguises that serve as the real, illusions that are served up as profound, seductions that are served up as normal, and chimeras that are served up as the natural, all of which are foundational to the dynamics of "architecture."

Archē(non)tektōn puts a gap between *archē* and *tektōn*, but then, as in a shell game, all too often makes it conveniently disappear.

"Architecture" lies in the productive space between *archē* and *tektōn*, in resisting the illusion of its seamlessness.

The question then arises as to where to locate these dissimulations in the disciplinary horizons.

* * * *

In 2006, Takeshi Hazama designed the Nana Harbor Diner in Naha City, on the Japanese island of Okinawa on the main road that links the airport to the city. (It has, regrettably, since been torn down for an office building.) Nana Harbor Diner plays on the difference between nature and the "natural" and between the man-made and the "man-made."' It is not a conventional tree house, but has a modern and rather absurdly typical concrete building that could be found by the dozens anywhere in the world, montaged into the branches. One can see the bottom of the "foundations" hovering overhead. It is almost as if the building was launched into the tree by a great tsunami. At the base of the tree there is a faux Buddhist shrine as if this were a sacred tree such as exist throughout Japan and indeed throughout Asia. The building is actually a steel frame structure that lifts up the reinforced concrete slabs of the restaurant's floor and ceiling. The skin of the tree is made of fiberglass and the vines are, of course, plastic. This syntactically complex building interlocks the serious and the profane, the sublime with a roadside attraction. How does one read this building?

Compare Nana Harbor Diner to the Statue of Liberty (1875) in New York harbor. There the *archē* and the *tektōn* adopt traditional roles, one

FIGURE 1.3.11 *Exterior: Nana Harbor Diner, Takeshi Hazama, Okinawa, 2006. Photograph by Mark Jarzombek.*

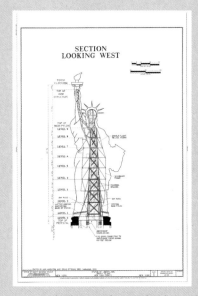

FIGURE 1.3.12 *Section: Statue of Liberty, Liberty Island, Manhattan, New York, 1875. American Engineering Record, National Park Service, Library of Congress, 1875.*

subservient to the other—the figural and the repressed—where only the former carries any narrative value. At the Diner, if our story began with the historical-fictive moment when Greek architects made a stone to look like wood and flesh—the "origin" of *archē-tektōn*—here we see one of several possible extrapolations that carry on that dialogue across time and geography. The steel framing is hidden, leaving the tree to look like it is doing all the work. The *archē* has miraculously survived the force of nature that placed it in the upper branches, but is no longer connected to the ground. It is quite literally a floating signifier at the mercy of the tree. And yet the tree is no less a simulation than the columns of the Parthenon bringing us into spaces of interpretation that are on the edge of theological. This building is certainly not architecture, and it is hardly ever mentioned as one of the great accomplishments of our age, but it is certainly "architecture." Like any Greek temple, the inversion between what is made and what is implied is a brilliant example of the potential of "architecture" to conceal and reveal its internal paradox.

At the other end of the spectrum—at the negative end—there is the Media Lab complex of the Massachusetts Institute of Technology (MIT) designed by Maki and Associates in 2009. The building contained six double-height spaces scattered through the interior. The atrium was a set of two interlocking voids that span five of the building's six levels. All of this required a complex load-bearing system with huge beams. When the building was completed, none of that was visible. Instead, the public feasted its eyes on a building remarkable in its appearance of elegance, transparency, and lightness. According to one reviewer, "The aluminum and glass curtain walls that

FIGURE 1.3.13 *MIT Media Lab, Maki and Associates, Cambridge, Massachusetts, 2010. Photograph by Sayamindu Dasgupta.*

FIGURE 1.3.14 *MIT Media Lab under construction, Cambridge, Massachusetts, 2008.* © *Bond Brothers, Inc.*

surround the steel-framed building extend the feeling of openness and transparency to the exterior and make the building appear like a luminous jewel at night."[16]

We see in the Media Lab Complex the traditional roles of *archē* and *tektōn*. It is the culmination of the Albertian disciplinary project and not much different from the Statue of Liberty, except that here we talk about it as architecture (without scare quotes) and miss the grammatology of violence that is necessary to its disciplinary proclamations of success. If the Media Lab Complex is a symptom of the repressed that is often called good architecture, Nana Harbor Diner celebrates the elastic sematic slippages between *archē* and *tektōn* to reveal their narrative interdependency.

PART TWO

CHAPTER ONE

Befores and Afters

Completion is a simple rule that has lasted the ages. A boat builder cannot make half a boat, a house builder half a house; the builder of a palace, only a part. Even so, completion requires a *culture* of completion. It is not just the architect who embodies "the must" of delivery, but the builder as well. In a paper from 1922 by F. E. Davidons, an architect from Chicago writes:

> Only as architects plan well can the contractor build well. A structure well built must be one which has been anticipated in imagination and then by blueprint—integration even down to every detail. It is then, and then only *with true fidelity* that this can all be reduced by the contractor to terms of beams, and bricks and concrete.[1]

* * * *

Alberti would be pleased. In a similar vein, from a dictionary from 1854 we read:

> It is within the province of the architect to examine and see that the materials used by the different artificers in the construction of the edifice be of good quality; that the workmen proceed in their several departments, according to the plan he has given to them; and when the work is completed, to measure and value the whole.[2]

And in an article from 1897:

> A building contract is an agreement in which an owner and a contractor are mutually and equally interested . . . The completion of the building is worth to the owner the price agreed upon for its erection, and its erection is worth the price agreed upon to the contractor.[3]

* * * *

The teleology of completion in the European context has deep-seated roots in the tradition of church founding. Any number of saints are depicted

FIGURE 2.1.1 San Agustín, *Baltasar del Águila, Oil on Panel, 1564. Museum of Fine Arts of Córdoba.*

holding a model of a church. It is more than a symbol of the institution that they hold dear, but a type of promissory contract that the real building will be delivered, and in reverse that the real building, even after its construction, models the instructional teleology of the Church.

* * * *

This teleology is not a simple one, like an acorn that becomes an oak tree. It is a metaphysical project that requires hundreds of different types of work and work processes, each with their own horizon of temporality and finish, which is why a building is of a cultural-theoretical order that no artwork could ever equal. Philosophers have talked about beginning and ends, but rarely about the metaphysics of completion, namely what it means to finish something through the complex stages of unfinished-ness. They rarely talk about what finished-ness signifies in the cultural-onto-epistemological realm.

In architecture, teleologies are associated not with where things begin or end, but on an anticipated end that transcends the realities of the building.

* * * *

Miriam Otte and Lidia Tirri from Berlin create photographs that show a "before" and "after" from the same spot of a building under construction. At stake is more than just a glimpse into the background of the building process, but proof of the obsession for clarity and finish by the architect, a finish so compelling that it is impossible, even sometimes for the architects, to realize what went into the making of a building.

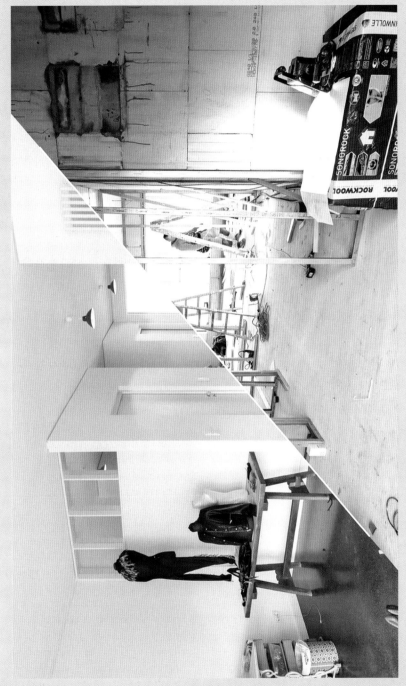

FIGURE 2.1.2 LU7—Project Berlin-Kreuzberg, Flake + Otto Archikten, 2018–19. © Lidia Tirri and Miriam Otte by Baudoku Berlin www. baudokuberlin.de.

The finished building—materialized and de-materialized at the same time—is more than just a moment in time, but an erasure of almost all that preceded it, an erasure not just of the materials and labor, but also of a vast array of histories. For the building to be legitimate in the field of architectural history, the history of its making must evaporate from view.[4]

* * * *

Alberti was the first to give the teleology of completion its theoretical armature. He made it clear that the architect operated under a particular set of guidelines, a double-fold ontology built around a cross-section of terminological pairings: *ratio et via* and *mente animoque.*

> Architectum ego hunc fore constituam, qui certa admirabilique ratione et via tum mente animoque diffinire tum . . .

> Him I consider the architect, who by sure and wonderful **reason and method**, knows how to devise both through his own **mind and energy** . . .

* * * *

First to *ratio et via.* Though translated as "reason and method," more is implied. *Via* means, of course, "road" but in this case when allied with *ratio* it means something like: the path used by reason to fulfill itself; a plan of action. *Ratio et via* does not necessary need an origin, but it does need a goal. It needs a clear place to get to. It has to be an easy, large-format goal—a building—and yet one that points to a goal well beyond the building since it has its origins in the predecessorial abstractions of *ratio.* *Ratio* also requires of itself an explanatory capacity. It is not just a method internal to the subject matter of expertise, but something that must be communicated and shared with a patron or client, or now with the public. *Ratio et via* is the site of the discipline's operative connection *to* the world, where *via* points to the active, teleological purpose of reason and expectation.

Because *ratio et via* is oriented to the promises of completion, it intertwines itself with the *faber* in an act of strategic reconciliation. *Mente animoque* ("mind and energy"), the second element in Alberti's pairing, moves at a different pace. *Animus,* associated with courage, purpose, or spirit, points to the active element of a masculine mind.[5] Vitruvius used it in the following sentence: *Philosophia vero perficit architectum animo magno et uti non sit adrogans* (1.I.7), which can be roughly translated as "Moral philosophy empowers the architect with an enlarged mind/spirit and to not use arrogance." Just as *via* sets in play *ratio*'s extroverted orientation, *animus* is an inward-looking energy to the more static *mente.* It overcomes resistances, political or economic, and even those of the *tektōn.*

Animoque (*animo*—the ablative form of *animus* + *que*: and with) serves as a supplement to *mente.* Imagine a motor and gasoline. From an operative point of view, the motor makes no sense without the gasoline. This supplement is not just added as reinforcement, but itself is the mark of an emptiness, in this the emptiness of reason that parallels the supposed thoughtless of the *tektōn* as mere *instrumentum*. Just as the architect's "body" needs the supplement of the de-ontologized fabricator, the architectural mind needs the supplement of "animation" in order to be properly effective.

✵ ✵ ✵ ✵ ✵

Mente animoque breaks down the deliberate processes of *ratio et via* and disconnects them from the moorings of conventionality. Not everyone is cut out for it, not everyone hungers for it, and not everyone survives its impact; it creates and destroys, builds up and tears down, and derives from this dynamic its superiority over that which claims only to deliver. It operates in an asymmetrical relationship to the categories of social functioning.

If *ratio et via* collapses the knowing subject into the known objective, *mente animoque* disrupts habits and functions.

If *ratio et via* orients itself toward pragmatism and is a generative force, *mente animoque* is transformational, the latter the more appropriate locus of originality.

Mente animoque requires an apprenticeship in the semiotics of expectations.

FIGURE 2.1.3 *Loggia of the palace of Agostino Chigi, Rome. Photograph by Mark Jarzombek.*

* * *

Vasari's description of the Palace of Agostino Chigi designed by Peruzzi is a perfect example of Alberti's *mente animoque*. It was

> executed with such beautiful grace that it seems not to have been built, but rather to have sprung into life; and with his own hand he decorated the exterior with most beautiful scenes in terretta. The hall, likewise, is adorned with rows of columns executed in perspective, which, with the depth of the intercolumniation, cause it to appear much larger. But what is the greatest marvel of all is a loggia that may be seen over the garden, painted by Baldassare with scenes . . . such that nothing more beautiful can be imagined; and . . . the ornamentation, drawn in perspective with colors, in imitation of stucco, is so natural and lifelike, that even to excellent craftsmen it appears to be in relief.[6]

Here the deceptiveness that is at the core of *archē* is fully embraced. The wall is flat and yet appears full of niches, pilasters, and windows.

* * *

One could, of course, draw a line from *mente animoque* to Howard Roark and the star architect phenomenon of today. But the issue here is not the history of genius or of the social construction of genius (about which much has been written), but rather how genius serves *in* its social construction to separate itself from the conventions of skill and occupation.

* * * *

Though the work associated with *mente animoque* was not an occupation, there was still no single term to describe it. Today we would use the phrase "creative work," but this is a thoroughly modern concept. The word "creativity" was used almost exclusively until the seventeenth century as a theological term. It is thought that the first person to use it in respect to endeavors that were human in nature was the Polish poet and theoretician of poetry, Maciej Kazimierz Sarbiewski (1595–1640), who wrote that a poet "creates anew (*de novo creat*) in the manner of God" (*instar Dei*). It would take another two centuries for the concept of creativity to become more secularized and applied to other arts.

Alberti and other Renaissance theoreticians were, of course, laying the groundwork for this type of modern subjectology. The philosopher Marsilio Ficino, for example, wrote that the artist "thinks up" (*excogitatio*) his images.

Later theorists would use the word *fantasia*.[7] It is not the same as intuition, though it might well begin as, or have the appearance of, intuition.

Today, the word "design" carries the load of its signification.

* * * *

Mente animoque opens the architect to a world of contingencies, uncertainties, and instabilities. It is the space of the *archē*'s emancipatory ambition. In the making of a temple, for example, Alberti praises the "brilliance and dexterity (*ingenia et manus*) of the artists" and links it directly to a positive reception of the building and to the "enthusiasm of the citizens."[8] Alberti allows the architect to savor up front just "how much applause, profit, favor, and fame" he will gain from the successful execution of his work.[9] But fame was far from secure and so Alberti warned the aspiring architect that if he "goes about anything ignorantly, unadvisedly or inconsiderately," he exposes himself to "disgrace" and "vituperation." In other words, the Albertian architect must possess both *ratio et via* and *mente animoque*, but in what proportion and in what way do they oppose and integrate? It is the mystery of this lamination that differentiates the architect from the *tektōn*. It is the mystery of this lamination that the discipline uses to demarcate its position in the cultural firmament.

* * * *

When it all comes together, there is no getting around the teleology of design as the premonition of completion. The *faber*'s efforts are foreclosed in its vice grip. The job has to be finished. A typical set of specifications even today will read like this:

> The Contractor will distinctly understand that the building or buildings described and shown is or are to be a perfect and finished job of its kind; and it is therefore supposed that he will use all diligence to inform himself fully as to its or their construction and finish and in no case to proceed with any part of the work without obtaining from the Architect, at his office, or otherwise, such directions, explanations or supplement or supplementary drawing as may be requisite for conveying to him a full and satisfactory understanding of the work.[10]

* * * *

The end result is a "design" usually spoken in one aesthetic voice. For this, architects often produce special plans to show what the project will look like. Their role is represented in the etching *Der Architect etc.* from the series *Der Mensch und sein Beruf* (*c.* 1840) by Karl Joseph Geiger that shows a busy construction site.[11] The finely dressed architect and his draftsman assistant are presenting a drawing to a bishop that shows the plan of a chapel to the Virgin Mary, the model of which is to the architect's right. The bishop is not looking at the workmen all around him nor even at the finely crafted Corinthian column, but intently at the design. The heads of the two men are leaning toward each other indicating, quite literally, a meeting of the minds, the perfect coincidence of *ratio et via* and *mente animoque*.

* * * *

FIGURE 2.1.4 Der Architect etc. *from the series* Der Mensch und sein Beruf, *c. 1840, by Karl Joseph Geiger. Wien Museum, Vienna.*

The cultural importance of the plan was cemented into disciplinary behavior in the form of pattern books beginning in the eighteenth century. For palaces, monasteries, fortifications, and other more major buildings, a comprehensive plan would not have been available to the general public. But in the eighteenth century onward, the vast majority of buildings for the rising bourgeoisie and junior nobility became a currency of conversation, with pattern books helping owners and builders come to easy agreement as to what was to be built, mostly based on budget, social standing, and available materials. William and John Halfpenny's *The Modern Builder's Assistant* (1757) has pages and pages of plans accompanied by a type of bullet-point list of the program: The Parlour: Hall and Staircase: Dining Room: Bed Room: Closet: Study and so forth.

    This commodification of the house, as a clearly legible plan and program (reinstitutionalized later in the work of Rem Koolhaas and others) along with an elevation drawn on white paper with no context, had a powerful effect on the profession. It institutionalized the idea of completion as such. The drawings were a type of visual-based contractuality. A complete building in representational form facilitated the choice of something desired by the client. The representations even assumed that these building had already

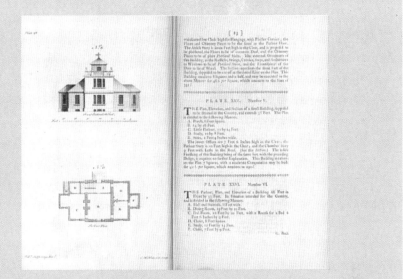

FIGURE 2.1.5 *Page from William and John Halfpenny,* The Modern Builder's Assistant, *1757: p. 23. © Getty Research Institute.*

been built and tested out. The representations collapsed the before, the present, and the future.

From the early nineteenth century on, completion became ever more loaded down with the weight of expectations. The three Adam brothers, of which James Adam (1732–94) and Robert Adam (1728–92) were the most widely known, were maybe the first to integrate the interior into the strategies of completion, supplying the clients with designs for ceilings, fixtures, fireplaces, carpets, walls, and furniture. In the previous era, clients would go on buying trips to London to purchase the furnishings; now all of that could be provided for by the architect who unified everything into an aesthetic package. By the end of the nineteenth century, such packages were the norm, and then, as time wore on, one had to add fixtures, wiring, cabinetry, knobs, sockets and the like, all the way down to hot-water heaters, air conditioners, PVC pipes, outdoor lighting, alarms and on and on.

The modern house involves a somewhat complex system of processes, and when one considers the many departments to be accommodated it is not surprising to find a large number of details entering into the construction and operation of even the smallest houses. Americans demand every device which makes for more convenient housekeeping, and that is one reason why the various details of plumbing, heating, ventilating, and mechanical cleaning have been developed to such a high state of efficiency. The American idea is to make each house as automatically complete as possible, and that is a very worthy ideal to strive for.[12]

* * * *

Today, few people can read plans.

> . . . in the hospital area, because doctors basically cannot read a plan—they will not admit that they cannot read a plan—and can never make their minds up until they see the thing being built.[13]

The problem is not just a question of literacy. Plans today have indeed become complicated. Their importance has thus been supplanted by a drawing called a rendering. It is more than just a pretty picture. Frank Forrest Frederick, a noted late-nineteenth-century watercolorist and teacher, advised:

> The architect must learn to generalize and to express much in a simple way; he must learn what to leave out, as well as what to put in, to suggest without fully stating; in fact, he must not try to draw every moulding, every pane of glass, every joint between bricks, every leaf on the tree . . . giving variety where simplicity is needed; but he must suggest all these by rendering his building in simple flat washes, with detail judiciously introduced where a little will suggest much.[14]

The rendering—mostly today produced using computer graphics—gives optical "proof" of what the building will look like. Once it has been approved by the client it becomes the expectation.[20] For large corporate projects it will be featured in a lobby or even in the boardroom and will be published in newspapers.[15]

What started out as a rendering soon became a corporate vision.[16]

FIGURE 2.1.6 *Architect's rendering of the new ESO Headquarters Extension (daytime), Garching, Germany. ESO/Auer+Weber (https://www.eso.org/public/images/eso1215a/).*

FIGURE 2.1.7 *A mock-up for a planned building along Riverway, Jamaica Plain, Boston, Massachusetts. Photograph by Mark Jarzombek.*

* * *

To make a rendering more real, before a major construction, the architect will have a small one-to-one mock-up of a piece of the facade built at ground level to impress the client and to show off the main elements and features of the design.[17] These strange architectural bits sometimes become permanent features of a street corner, fragments that are not fragments.

* * *

Despite the illusion of completion—and completion as illusion—as the core mission of architecture's disciplinarity, there are any number of starts and stops in the making of a building. The making of the Ise Shrine in Japan is an almost twenty-year process and involves dozens of elaborate rituals. Regular buildings are not so encumbered, but still can have a wide range of beginnings, such as foundation-laying ceremonies, a ceremony as ancient as architecture itself. Though they are still essential throughout South Asia and in the village world of Africa, they have almost disappeared in the West, where the ones that have gone down in history are for the grand and noble

FIGURE 2.1.8 Capitol Cornerstone Ceremony, *1793; Allyn Cox; Oil on canvas applied to the wall, 1973–4; Hall of Capitols, Washington DC. © Architect of the Capitol.*

edifices, mostly churches. One document relating the rebuilding of the Abbey of St. Denis under Abbot Suger from 1140 states:

> We descended with humility and devotion into the trench cut to lay the foundations of the edifice; the bishops themselves had mixed the mortar with holy water; after invoking the Holy Spirit in order that the happy commencement of the house of God should have a good end. They placed the first stones, singing psalms. The most holy king himself descended into the trench, placing the stone with his own hands; many other persons, abbots and monks laid also other stones; several of those present through love and respect for Christ, threw rings into the foundation singing *Lapides preciosi omnes muri tui* [All your walls are precious stones].[18]

* * *

The foundation stone ceremony for the Congress building in Washington DC took place on September 18, 1793. Activities began at 10:00 a.m. with the appearance of President Washington and his entourage on the south bank of the Potomac River. Crossing the river with the president was a company of volunteer artillery from Alexandria, Virginia. The procession joined Masonic lodges from Maryland and Virginia, and all marched two abreast, "with music playing, drums beating, colors flying, and spectators rejoicing," to the site of the Capitol about a mile and a half away. There the procession reformed and Washington, flanked by Joseph Clark (the Grand Master) and Dr. E. C. Dick (the master of the Virginia lodge), stood to the east of a "huge stone" while the others formed a circle west of it. A commemorative plate was handed to Washington, who stepped down into the foundation trench, laid the plate on the ground, and lowered the cornerstone onto it. With the president were Joseph Clark and three "worshipful masters" bearing the corn, wine, and oil used to consecrate the stone. Chanting accompanied Washington's ascent from the trench. Clark gave a speech punctuated by numerous volleys from the artillery. Following the formal exercises, a 500-pound ox was barbequed and those in attendance "generally partook, with every abundance of other recreation." A painting of this ceremony appears in the Cox Corridors of the US Capitol Building's House Wing.

In 1991, a search for the Capitol Cornerstone was conducted including use of a metal detector to locate the engraved plate—it was not found. It turns out that they were perhaps looking under the wrong corner.[19]

* * *

The foundation ceremony is a beginning/ending all unto its own, and perhaps in its antiquity and metaphysical significance the most important element in the architectural game of completion. Its absence in the general architectural culture of today is itself yet another ending, the ending of one type of architecture and the beginning of another.

* * * *

The Latin translation of Filarete's *Libro Architettonico* that was commissioned by the Hungarian king Matthias Corvinus between 1488 and 1489 has a beautiful opening page illustrated with a drawing that shows a construction site of the building.[20] Among the various people portrayed are the patron and architect. The patron, his back to the viewer, is talking to the architect who is pointing to the busy laborers behind him. Hands clasped in front of his chest

FIGURE 2.1.9 and 2.1.10 *Architecture,* Libro Architettonico, *Filarete, c. 1488–9.* © *Biblioteca Nazionale Marciana, Venice. On permission of Biblioteca Nazionale Marciana, Venice. Reproduction is strictly forbidden. Detail, below left.*

FIGURE 2.1.11 *Building Work (work being carried out on a building at a 16th-century construction site), 1558. © Rischgitz / Stringer, 51246516, Hulton Archive.*

in a pleading gesture, the patron seems to be asking, "When is it going to be finished?" The architect has his left foot resting on a completed column indicating a symbiotic relationship between the column, the hopefully soon-to-be-completed building, and the complete design as imagined in his head.

A drawing representing *Architectura* from 1558 shows a building site; the client with his expensive, fur-lined cape has his back to the viewer and is talking to the architect with the lead carpenter to his right. From the gesture of the client, it is clear that he is asking why things are not moving ahead. He is the impatient teleology, wondering when the *ratio et via* of his commission will come to an end. The architect gesturing nervously with his right hand to the boyish carpenter seems to be either putting the blame for the slow pace of things on the carpenter, or perhaps asking for his reassurance that the job will get done on time.

****

Architecture can only pronounce itself as an "after" to completion—and yet as a completion it also envisions itself as a "before." In between is the danger zone of incompletion.

There are any number of things that slow down the road to completion: lack of material, lack of funding, lack of labor, lack of time, or even perhaps too much time. And, of course, there is always the factor of weather and the perennial issue of wages. A German encyclopedia on architecture from 1840 already complained: "The work based on day wages goes very slowly because the worker . . . is only concerned to stretch out the work as long as possible in order to earn from [his] day wage."[21] In Sicily, there are places where buildings are left purposefully and visibly incomplete so as to avoid paying taxes.[22] And, of course, there were the ubiquitous complaints about the workmen themselves. The following is from the sixteenth century by Cardinal Wolsey of Christ Church, Oxford:

> The most cunning workmen were there prepared with ordinances to speedily do everything; nothing was therewith spared to assist in this assign purpose. One thing was a hindering it: because of the lack of good overseers the workfolk loitered the time [away] like false trifelers.[23]

Or a posting from 1899 in the journal *Carpenter*:

> William Craig, formerly of Union 170, Bridgeport O, is a slick fraud. He skipped that town leaving numerous creditors and indebted to several Union members. He is 5 feet 10 inches high, black hair and black eyes, and claims to be a stair builder, carver, artist and photographer.[24]

* * * *

The danger of incompletion from the point of view of *archē* is that its potential entropy surrounds the teleological imaginary like a dark cloud and can siphon off its energy in any number of possible directions. Typical words of advice sound like this:

> "Incomplete plans throw off the entire process," notes construction manager Robert Masucci. "If something is inconclusive or left out, a contractor will simply interpret what isn't there; the varied interpretations are what accounts for wide discrepancies in bidding." Carpenter and general contractor Peter Devine, of Peter Devine Remodeling and Design, agrees, adding, "People tend to complete their vision of a project at the end rather than at the beginning. Toward the end, they begin to see what it's really going to look like. Spending a few more dollars on the architect's papers before the job starts could save the homeowner thousands of dollars down the line.[25]

* * *

In some rare cases, political events give us insight into the life of a building. For twenty years, *Palacio Legislativo*, now the *Monumento a la Revolución*, designed by Henri Jean Émile Bénard, remained unfinished in central Mexico City. Construction was stopped during the Mexican Revolutionary War and was only completed in 1938. The photograph from 1912 by Guillermo Kahl captures its remarkable steely profile. Few grand buildings remain incomplete for such a length of time in the modern age leaving few opportunities for people to take in the sights, sounds, and even the meaning of a construction site.

Construction sites are now walled off often so that one cannot even see in. Perhaps to protect passersby from construction debris or perhaps to keep

FIGURE 2.1.12 *An incomplete building in Sicily (contractor/builder unknown by author). Photograph taken October 16, 2005. © incompiuto siciliano.*

FIGURE 2.1.13 *Photo of the Palacio Legislativo, now the Monumento a la Revolución, Mexico City, Guillermo Kahlo, 1912. © Revista Imagenes.*

materials from being stolen, the walls nonetheless seal off the site from the optic experience of the city. It is as if something private is going on, something that should not be seen, something mysterious. Access is often only acoustic, the grinding, hammering, or pounding. The "non" in the *archē(non)tektōn* is expressed as a hard physical separation of the *tektōn* from the life of the city. Here we see a site being prepared in Brooklyn, New York, by a painter, who might well also be—in my view at least—an artist. In fact, is this not a work of contemporary "architecture"?

****

FIGURE 2.1.14 *A construction site being prepared in Brooklyn, New York. Photograph by Mark Jarzombek.*

Topping-out ceremonies celebrate the moment the last beam is put into place. Though the term "topping out" seems to be from the early twentieth century, the tradition is certainly old and seems to have originated in Scandinavia and Germany and then spread to other parts of Europe and America and now can be seen in many parts to the world. In Germany, where the custom is known as *Richtfest*, the ceremony consists of fastening a small fir tree (or in some areas a wreath made from the branches of a fir tree) to the top of the newly completed frame. Dignitaries are invited to make speeches, or recite poems for the occasion, and food and drink are served to the assembled workers and visitors. As John V. Robinson relates, in 1774, while raising a meeting house in a town in New Hampshire, the supply of rum ran out "just as the workmen were about to put on the roof; so the men refused to work for half a day while a messenger was sent down to Newburyport for another half-barrel." The implication is that with the arrival of the rum, calm was restored and the job was completed.[26]

"Topping out" occurred the day the last course of bricks was laid in a house and was to celebrate the event. On the morning the "topping out" was to take place a flag was raised on the building. It was also a signal for the owner of the building to prepare a lunch and the customary drinkables, especially the drinkables, for all hands engaged on the building. The day Mr. Hall "topped out" his house on C Street . . . he not only furnished all the ale and porter necessary, but used up three baskets of fried chickens, cakes and other things. it was the talk of the town for year, especially among the mechanics.[27]

[N]o matter what symbol is used, the topping-off tradition remains an important symbol of teamwork, quality, craftsmanship and luck for the future. If Odin and his pals are still around, surely they are pleased with how a ceremony that originated to honor them has evolved in modern times.[28]

* * *

In late June 2007, the Illinois Holocaust Museum & Education Center near Chicago hosted a beam-signing ceremony at the construction site for holocaust survivors. They were invited to come to add their signatures to one of three beams, each to be permanently installed in the new building. The beams were designed to be visible to all who visit the new center and so provided a way for each survivor to literally "leave their mark" on the building.[29] "It was a very moving moment," according to the architect, Stanley Tigerman.[30]

* * * *

Howard Roark blowing up a building that he designed, but that was in his view badly botched by the intervention of others, stands as the ultimate portrayal of completion's ideological compulsions.

* * *

In the end, as David Chappell, an architect with a law degree, a PhD, and fifty years of experience in the construction industry, admits, no building is ever totally finished:

> Show me a building which you say is complete in every particular and I will always be able to find something slightly wrong or not done, whether it is something small like a missing screw or some unwanted scratches or something more substantial such as a piece of flashing missing.[31]

And then, of course, there are always legal issues:

> There is no good building without a good lawsuit.
>
> Hanno Wolfensberger, lawyer specializing
in architectural cases[32]

* * * *

When it is all done, there is good reason to celebrate. In 1753, Marc-Antoine Laugier, who authored the *Essai sur l'architecture*, describes the great sense of accomplishment and purpose that a building embodies:

> The sight of a building, perfect as a work of art, causes a delightful pleasure which is irresistible. It stirs in us noble and moving ideas and that sweet emotion and enchantment which works of art carrying the imprint of a superior mind arouse in us. A beautiful building speaks eloquently for its architect.[33]

He makes no mention, of course, of the builders except to say:

> When one speaks of the art of building, the chaotic mess of clumsy debris, immense piles of shapeless materials, a dreadful noise of hammers, perilous scaffolding, a fearful grinding of machines and an army of dirty and mud-covered workmen—all this comes to the mind of ordinary people, the unpleasant outer cover of an art whose intriguing mysteries, noticed by few people, excite the admiration of all those who penetrate them.[34]

The Romans marked the transition of a building as a site of labor's occupation to a building as occupiable by means of an *inauguratio*, where the priest, or augur, responsible for the design of a temple, entered and activated the sacred rites that made the temple alive with the presence of the deity. In our more prosaic world people host a housewarming party. Some hold christening ceremonies:

> Call a priest, minister or religious leader and invite him over to bless the room, or the house itself. For example, a Catholic priest may say the Lord's Prayer and sprinkle the room with holy water. A minister may use a Bible passage, such as "But as for me and my house, we will serve the Lord" (Joshua 24:15). Depending on the denomination, the religious leader will bless the room using the prayers or customs of that religion. If you want to make a celebration out of it, you can also invite some friends and family to gather during the occasion.[35]

At these moments, when wish becomes reality, architecture has no scare quotes. It exists in perfect alignment between interests, expectations, fantasy, and the ever-present reality principle. The multiple temporalities, representations, and imagined zones of completion collapse into one thing. Here is the opening of a speech give recently by a CEO:

> Ladies and Gentlemen, distinguished guests, colleagues, staff, and friends, Thank you for being here today for the inauguration ceremony of our brand-new building. This is a special moment for many of us. Dreams do

not come true very often. Today, some dreams did come true. As you know, IPMU, Institute for the Physics and Mathematics of the Universe, started about two and a half years ago. We literally started from scratch: no space, no staff, no building, no scientists; no nothing. Today, we have more than seventy full-time scientists, more than thirty staff. We exceeded the mark of a hundred members.

* * * *

Here a short excerpt from a speech at the ceremony held in 1892 that dedicated the building of the Boston Chamber of Commerce:[36]

> As the work has progressed, day by day, with clock-like precision, every stone fitting the niche where it was intended to be placed, so quietly has it been carried on, under the direction of that able master-builder, Mr. J. N. Durkee, we have often been reminded of the temple of old, "which was built of stone made ready before it was brought thither, so that there was neither hammer, nor axe, nor any tool of iron, heard in the house while it was building." We were not, however, obliged to call upon any foreign potentates for our timber, and our stone; in the workshops of our builders were fashioned the timbers of oak, and from the solid hills of our grand old commonwealth was quarried the stone from which is builded [*sic*] this temple of trade, that shall stand as a monument to the enterprise of the merchants of Boston.
>
> And now, Mr. President, on behalf of the Building Committee, I surrender these keys and the possession of these halls of trade. Guard well the trust; its responsibilities. (William O. Blaney, President of the Building Committee)[37]

* * * *

In 1873, Viollet-le-Duc wrote an astonishing book with his own illustrations, *Histoire d'une Maison*, about a successful young man who builds for himself a house, actually a small mansion. Viollet-le-Duc writes a beautiful description of the housewarming party:

> Paul was anxious to see everything and his cousin allowed him to wander at will over the house for an hour, as he himself was in conference with some workmen about various details ... "Well, little cousin, are you satisfied with your work; have things been done, in your absence, to please you?" "I wish very much that it was my work," replied Paul, "and I am sorry not to have been able to follow it to the end; for it seems to me, in seeing the completed house, that almost everything was done while I was gone. It is with buildings as with all human works. You the saying, '*Finis coronat opus*.' The finishing is the whole."

For the party itself, Viollet-le-Duc paints a charming and idealized picture of social contentment:

> The contractors and shop-masters who had worked upon the house were invited, and a dinner was to be provided for them in the garden . . . there was a ball in the evening, in the new park, for the country people, with ample refreshments; and the poor of the parish were to receive a distribution of food and clothing throughout the day.[38]

From the moment of completion on, when the structure is dependent on culture for its use, owners are left to their own devices.[39] Even Viollet-le-Duc, known for his preservation projects in France, in this book, does not warn the young man who commissioned the house about the heavy burden of ownership.

Wear and tear will soon reveal the thin illusions on which the building rested. Time will expose the gap between *archē* and *tektōn* in one way or another.

* * * *

The architect standing in front of his or her building as the exclamation point of completion is the moment the clock of time starts to tick.

* * * *

In 1900 Adolf Loos wrote a short sarcastic piece called "Poor Little Rich Man" that approached the problem of completion from a refreshingly different angle. It tells the story of a rich man who, wanting to be up to date with everything, hired an architect to remodel his home, which the architect did, down to every last detail. One day when the architect came by to visit, the rich man tells of how he got some presents:

FIGURE 2.1.15 *The architect David Chipperfield standing in front of the James Simon Gallery, Berlin, July 10, 2019. Photo: Christoph Soeder/dpa—Berlin/Berlin/ Germany. © AGE Stock Photo / Picture-Alliance.*

FIGURE 2.1.16 *The author re-enacting a pose from a 16th manuscript during a barn renovation. See: 2.1.10. From left to right: Wilson Wiemes (carpenter), Mark Jarzombek (proprietor), Aron, Feiring (carpenter/builder). Photo: Mark Jarzombek, June 14, 2022.*

"How dare you presume to receive presents! Didn't I draw everything up for you? Haven't I taken care of everything? You need nothing more. You are complete!" "But," the rich man replied "I should be allowed to buy things."

"No, you are not allowed, never ever!" . . .

"But what about when my grandchild brings me something from kindergarten as a gift?"

"You are not allowed to take it!" . . .

Thereupon a transformation took place within the rich man. The happy man felt suddenly deeply, deeply unhappy, and he saw his future life. No one would be allowed to grant him joy.

He had to pass by the shopping stores of the city, perfect, and complete. Nothing would be created for him ever again, none of his loved ones would be allowed to give him a painting. For him there could be no more painters, no artists, no craftsmen again. He was shut out of future life and its strivings, its developments, and its desires. He felt: Now is the time to learn to walk about with one's own corpse. Indeed! He is finished! He is complete![40]

CHAPTER TWO

Dialectics of (In)completion

When the building is complete but before the clients arrive, it is ready to be photographed. This type of documentation started in the early twentieth century when architects sent in photos as "Proof of Completion" to city building departments.[1] The photo creates a congruity between it and the originary conception, almost as if the process in between was irrelevant. It is a moment of magical quietude between the befores and afters that were and the befores and afters that are yet to come. The sounds of hammers and chisels have not yet been replaced by the sounds of habitation of the days to come. It is the moment of the *architectural* photograph with future occupancy hinted at not by people, but by a chair or table—as already practiced by the turn of the twentieth century and then with Mies as at his Villa Tugendhat (1928) as the exemplar used by almost every architect and real estate agent.

Though artworks are photographed relentlessly, a photograph of a recently finished painting is not presented to the art world as a moment of particular relevance. In architecture, the photograph of a just completed

FIGURE 2.2.1 *Dining Room, Country Cottage, Max Schemel, near Bremen, H. Licht Architect,* c. 1890.

FIGURE 2.2.2 *Tugendhat House, Brno, Czech Republic. View of study and living room. 1928–30. Silver-gelatin print, 6 1/8 × 9 1/8" (15.6 × 23.2 cm). Mies van der Rohe Archive. Digital Image © The Museum of Modern Art / Licensed by SCALA / Art Resource, NY.*

FIGURE 2.2.3 *Interior, Mike Osean, Real Estate Agent, Newport, Rhode Island, 2019.*

building is *the* photographic moment of completion. It, not the building, is the teleological end that speaks to the discipline.

The photograph documents the place/time where the ends and ideas overlap (or at least should overlap). It is the place where the beginning in the mind of the architect seems to have come to fruition. It is the literal "end" of the *ratio et via*, as if we are seeing directly into the mind of the architect, an intimate subjectivity. The photo is also an object made for the eyes of the discipline, for the discipline in which the architect is situated and in which the architect expects to be situated in its ongoing historical self-observations. The photo is staged to prove not just completion, but the completion of the idea of completion moving into the realm of publication and discourse, and ultimately into the objectivities of History.

The architectural photograph is made as if by the discipline itself, anonymous and yet possessive. It is the signifier of architecture's contractual obligation to perform up to expectations. It is the signifier of the *tektōn*'s displacement.

* * * *

Prior to the late nineteenth century, interiors of buildings were not frequently portrayed in professional literature. Mostly images focused on important architectural elements like fireplaces, columns, or entrances. It was only in the latter part of the century that interiors of ready-to-use domestic spaces started to become just as important as the exterior perspective.

The architectural photograph constructs completion not in the contractual middle ground between patron and builder, but in the post-contractual delivery of a pre-contractual idea. It symbolizes the "before" that happened in the metaphysical darkness of the architect's mind.

But there is a twist. The modern, architectural photograph will always have furniture in it, for the building is really complete only after the furniture movers have arrived.

Latin-based languages make the distinction between *Meuble* in German, for example, that means "furniture," and *Immobilien* that means "buildings." The word hinges on the dualism of movable and immovable. The architectural photograph brings the two together. Neither is complete without the other. The *Immobilien* only become "architecture" with its *Meuble* locked into place.

> [It is] generally understood among builders that the owner by moving into or occupying the building constructed under the contract, implies an acceptance of the work.[2]

The furniture is the modern embodiment of the culture of completion.

The furniture is the proof of mission accomplished. It marks the transition from "architecture" to architecture (without scare quotes) and then back to "architecture"—since it is less architecture than a real estate commodity.

The furniture speaks of the industrialization and commodification of comfort, but it is also the semiotic proof that the social—ostensibly—was taken seriously.

The furniture unlocks the register of architecture's claim on meaning.

* * * *

The architectural photograph is the first "after" to completion, for just as there is a completion before the building is built, there is a completion *beyond* completion that is in the non-disciplinary space of the "after."

This opening toward the teleological-beyond comes to be expressed in different ways, but inevitably as the naturalization of discipline's desire to perform theoretically where there is a completion of a very different order than that related to deliverability. It is the completion of the discipline as defined through its writers, theorists, intellectuals, and historians. Architecture (without scare quotes) organizes these agents into neat categories. "Architecture" (with scare quotes) works in the messy interfaces.

* * * *

It is in the space between the anticipated/realized complete, and the anticipated/unrealized incomplete where the discipline operates, pushing out the discourses of theory and history in the direction of the incomplete, and discourses about practice in the direction of completion.

One can speak of the dialectics of (in)completion. This is not a Hegelian-styled dialectic of complete, incomplete, and resolution. Here the "complete" and the "incomplete" are not stationary. Each is a necessary condition of the other at any moment in time.

* * * *

In some cases, architecture's *terminus ad quem* becomes utopian, but in all cases, it projects forward from the moment of the already complete building that is not yet even started, even for nineteenth-century historicists. Yes, a neo-Gothic building has a strong origin point, but it is not the origin as such for Augustus Pugin, designer of London's Palace of Westminster (1840–76), that was important, but rather its implications forward as an instrument of social modulation that anticipates some form of a better world, in this case, more Christian and more medieval-like. In 1836, Pugin published *Contrasts* in which he argued for the revival of the medieval Gothic style, and also a return to the faith and the social structures of the Middle Ages. Each plate is a "now" and a "then" of the same scene, the former portraying moral decay and the latter a state of contentment. In the former, buildings are falling apart, in the latter they are well-built and properly used.

This "now" and "then" is really a "not-really-then"/"not-yet-now" as clearly expressed in a drawing in the second volume of Pugin's *Examples of Gothic Architecture* (1836) that depicts a medieval architect at work in his study. Dressed as a monk and holding a compass, the man sits in an appropriately medieval environment. But the books behind him are not from the twelfth century. They are Pugin's own works, as are the drawings propped up for display. The collapse of past, present, and anticipated hegemonical future makes the drawing hard to interpret. It does not hide the

Frontispiece to Augustus Pugin, *Examples of Gothic architecture*, v. 2, 1836. Designed by A. W. N. Pugin.

FIGURE 2.2.4 *Frontispiece,* Examples of Gothic Architecture, *Augustus Pugin, 1836.*

fact that it is staged, and yet it is staged not to enact some form of bland neo-medievalism, but to compress the past into the future through the body of Pugin's own work—and even through the body of Pugin himself, a socio-ontological completion and the true guarantor of the work.

To call Pugin a "historicist" because he liked the Middle Ages is to miss the point. He embodied a dyschronometric presentism.[3] A "before" that can now be seen as legitimate because it is encased in the theatrics of the "after."

In such situations, the architect, the building's completion, and its teleological imaginary are in alignment, and yet the teleology remains active only because it is incomplete and incompletable. This is the eternal promise of "architecture."

❋ ❋ ❋

Teleology as the cover story for the dialectics of (in)completion has one switch and it is either on or off. Its only metric is the scale of its operation, whether real or imagined, whether fully utopian or seemingly eminently practical. It applies just as much to the design of the Houses of Parliament by Pugin as to the design of a garden shed. Either way, things that do not contribute to the "end" are simply shut out, removed from the equation, just as the "non" is removed from *archē(non)tektōn*. Its mission-centrism forces aesthetics to comply as well. An example is the following quote by Frank Lloyd Wright:

> Everything has a related articulation in relation to the whole and all belongs together: looks well together because all together are speaking the same language. If one part of your building spoke Choctaw, another French, another English and another some sort of gibberish, you would have what you mostly have now—not a very beautiful result.[4]

This call for linguistic, aesthetic—and, by implication, racial—purity has been more or less the mantra since the days of the Renaissance, carried forward by classicism, industrialization, engineering, modernization, all the way to advanced capitalism. Computation has added its bit. That history traces well with the history of the discipline, with the history of "innovation" and with the history of building practices. The result is a type of *archē* narcissism.

> I think I am interested in consistency in its most general sense. Probably this is a reaction to the architectural culture where we were educated, which was more interested in questions of fragmentation, disjunction, juxtaposition, etc. I believe that to devise arguments of consistency has become a critical contemporary question, on a political, social, and cultural level ... And geometry plays a primary role in establishing consistency across spatial domains at every scale.
>
> Alejandro Zaera-Polo[5]

****

An architecture marketing firm writes:

> One of the biggest challenges to gaining brand awareness is a lack of brand consistency.[6]

****

The Beaux-Arts system mastered this operation, bringing the language of completion and design uniformity into alignment with nationalist aesthetics, governmental professionalism, civic ambition, and the colonial gaze. One architectural textbook from the late nineteenth century writes:

> A well designed building is one where the whole mass, considered as a solid block, is of pleasing proportions and outline; the arrangement of its openings and wall spaces, and its high lights and deep shadows, are well studied; while the ornamentation of its details is sufficient to attract the eye to the beauties of its proportions, but not so excessive as to distract the observation from the composition of the whole.[7]

Unlike pattern-book buildings that were meant to make "architecture" replicable and transportable, these buildings were one-offs. Each was a universe unto itself with powerful protective and exclusionary enforcements. Each was some version of ethnic purity, a mini-nation—a microcosm for the citizen-within.

These buildings did not need to worry about context. They were monuments to the master narratives of nation and institution. There was, therefore, no need to draw the context in the plan, since whatever context there was, was meant to soak in the building's grand narrative.

From that point of view there is no difference between a design for a building to house the academies by Marie-Joseph Peyre (1756) and the Rolex Learning Center in Lausanne, Switzerland designed by SANAA in 2010. Both are simply bookends of two centuries of the naturalized teleological assumptions about what the architect delivers: not a furnished building, but a territory of socio-cognitive transcendence. The Rolex Learning Center is in no way unique. It stands in for almost every building designed today.

*　*　*　*

Unlike in contemporary art where the artist has long since given up the idea that art speaks for some great knowable mission, welcoming even the instability of meaning, architecture in its contemporary setting has embraced the presumed knowability of its mission, firming up its disciplinary purpose by giving "wholes" their meaning, even if these "wholes" are tactical and

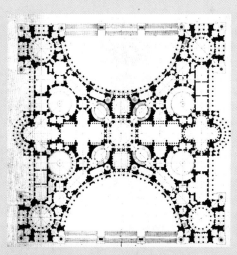

FIGURE 2.2.5 Bâtiment qui contiendroit les Académies *(Building that would house the Academies), Marie-Joseph Peyre, Plan. 1756.*

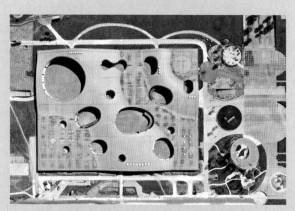

FIGURE 2.2.6 *Rolex Learning Center, SANAA, Lausanne, 2010. Photograph by Bernard Vogel.*

FIGURE 2.2.7 *Deloitte Building, Christchurch, New Zealand. Photograph by Michal Klajban.*

illusionary.

What is posited by the architect is, however, not the whole, but the wholeness of the whole since it carries with it the semiotic indicator of the Idea. Photographically this "wholeness" lies in the middle ground of external shots of buildings. Just as the interior photograph with furniture points to a delivery and contractuality, these photos point to an irrevocable thereness.

Too far away, the building blends into the context. Too close, we will tend to personalize the experience. This wholeness of the whole requires of the viewer an ostensibly objectivizing position that transcends the "I" into some form of "We"—as in "we" of the planners, "we" the owners, or "we" the citizens, etc. This wholeness speaks to architecture's ostensibly irrefutable commitment to a knowable, larger purposefulness, even if that knowable is unknowable, a heuristic that conceals its instrumentalizing violence.

The wholeness of the whole defines a space where alienation is not possible—at least within the framework of its offering. Alienation is someone else's problem. The wholeness of the whole instead operates as quasi-ontological contract, producing an objectified subject without that the subject might even be aware of it. Everywhere one goes in the building, the architect has preceded in thought and in execution. The building can be experienced only in a position of acceptance, its teleology hovering safely over the subject as a cultural and historical determinant. The wholeness of the whole positioned in the thin representionality of the photograph is the attempted enforcement of architecture (without scare quotes).

* * * *

A building implies an object of some sort, but there can be no clear determination of what is meant by an architectural "object" since that meaning and its history are only given as already worked over by forces that have been silenced precisely in order for that architectural "object" to meet its teleological requirements.

* * * *

In recent decades, the dialectics of (in)completion has come away from the conventions of plan and rendering to something called "program." At a more technical level a program

> is a communicable statement of intent. It is a prescription for a desired set of events influenced by local constraints, and it states a set of desired conditions and the methods for achieving those conditions . . . The program is also a formal communication between designer and client in order to determine that the client's needs and values are clearly stated and understood. It provides a method for decision making and a rationale for future decisions. It encourages greater client participation, as well as user feedback.[8]

For Rem Koolhaas, program—in some of his work—has a more decisive role. Unlike the contracts that define the wide range of realities in the making of a building—contracts between architecture, builder, suppliers, service providers, etc., some written but most oral—the "program" as the architects understand it is a contract of a special type. It is not between the architect and client, the result of some private arrangement, but between architect and society (which should be spelled more correctly: "society"), not unlike what we saw in Halfpenny's book from the eighteenth century. It represents the syntax of social organization and control that is deployed in a building. "Program" pronounces its superiority over the much messier realities of the real contracts that are, of course, invisible to the public. At the Seattle Library (2002), for example, the design team studied the brief of the library and simplified it down into a series of basic elements that, when stacked, defined the building itself.[9] According to Koolhaas:

> Hidden in it [the diagram] is a more simple reading of which elements of a particular kind of building can be stable, and which have to remain volatile. This is simply an end product, a retroactive illustration of what, in a more private sense, is a way of thinking.[10]

* * * *

There is more to it than that. The underlying ideology of Koolhaas's idea of "program" dates back to the Enlightenment. In 1690, John Locke, in *An Essay Concerning Human Understanding*, wrote:

> Justice, and keeping of contracts, is that which most men seem to agree in . . . That men should keep their compacts is certainly a great and undeniable rule in morality.[11]
> And thus every man, by consenting with others to make one body politic under one government, puts himself under an obligation, to every one of that society, to submit to the determination of the majority, and to be concluded by it; or else this original compact, whereby he with others incorporates into one society, would signify nothing, and be no compact, if he be left free, and under no other ties than he was in before in the state of nature.[12]

"Program" as understood by the Koolhaas is a type of originary, philosophically scaled contract. In older times, the architect used precedents (as in Palladianism) or history (as in classicism or neo-Gothic) to negotiate and simplify the divide between architect and social imaginary. "Program" is more open to contemporary secular and democratizing forces. Whereas those earlier teleologies were grounded in an aristocratical culture of books and learning, this new one is grounded in the bourgeois culture of law and governmentality. In that sense, it sees itself as anti-elitist and eminently pragmatic.

That does not mean that it is any less potent in its ideological ambitions. It pretends to be freely and fairly negotiated, and ultimately an honest and transparent mapping of reality. A structure unto itself, it speaks to the metaphysics of its own immanence, and yet in its play with the signifiers of governmentality it speaks just as eloquently to its immanent obsolescence.

"Program" is what locks the building in place in its own conditions and

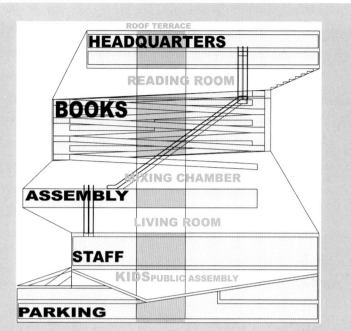

FIGURE 2.2.8 *Diagram, Seattle Library, OMA, 2004. Image courtesy of OMA.*

times. It is not—as with Pugin—the architect who vouches for completion by means of his predecessorial ontology—but the building as artifact that is complete, with the architect being little more than the insightful negotiator, the facilitator—the ostensibly disembodied representative of *ratio et via*.

The building speaks to the teleology of completion in an incomplete world. It ties society to itself (*ratio et via*) in a world of loose ends.

* * * *

The Seattle Museum has the same promissory clause as deployed by Pugin, though in reverse. Koolhaas did not need to spell out the "now" and the "then": it is unmistakable. The building completes the image of a New World over and against a state of Nature. For Locke, the state of Nature was not associated with war and chaos as it was for Thomas Hobbes, but rather a condition where Nature served as the lawmaker not humans. For that reason, civil society with its contracts in hand stands in opposition to the state of Nature. Furthermore, the need for civil society comes in part from the perpetual existence of the state of Nature, represented in society, for example, by children who have not yet matured into adulthood.

The library is a physical demonstration of that contractuality, servicing the still incomplete world around it. It is a test case for a more developed and expanded enterprise of capitalist nationalism of which this building is only a small, utopian representative, demonstrating nonetheless the tactical power of the teleological project. If only all the world could be as "transparent" as this building, it seems to say.

* * * *

Program is the foundation ceremony for the secular age. Though it is not encased in mystical assumptions about architecture's presumed origins, it carries metaphysical assumptions about the nature of society and its orderliness nonetheless. It is not an actual event, but the semiotics of an event, the event of modernity itself.

* * * *

In this case there is a program within the program. For the architects divided the functions according to the "stable" ones, which did not imply movement in themselves; and the "volatile" ones that were mainly spaces where any kind of exchange and movement could happen.[13] The "volatile" functions were then spread across the section of the building.[14] The "stable" program elements are from bottom to top: the Parking Garage, the Staff Area, the Meeting Area, the Book Spiral, and the Administrative Headquarters. The "volatile" elements are: the Children's Section, the Living Room, the Mixing Chamber, and the Reading Room. It is perhaps not surprising given the latent paternalism of architecture that things associated with the institution are defined as "stable" whereas things associated with social life are seen as "volatile." One suspects here a latent colonial attitude as well.

The "library-as-institution" is the architecture within the architecture. In this, the Seattle library serves as nothing less than the model of Man—by which I mean a Man of a particular type. The administration is on the top floor whereas parking and its association with the messy city is in the basement. This classic elevation of mind over matter reflects itself down the line. The Mixing Chamber in the middle serves as "the stomach." Kids and staff are of a lower order and so near the bottom. This ideal Man from the Age of Enlightenment, well organized and purposeful, has placed the volatile children at the lower registers of consciousness, as Locke would have wanted.

The library contains two "architectures." One is oriented to the building's presumed social obligations, and the other to the hidden institutionality of reason and masculinity.

Is the library an example of architecture or of "architecture"? Does it operate in a way that demonstrates the value of thoughtfulness and research as exemplified by an academic and disciplinary alliance with the powers that be—a descendent of Plato's *archē-tektōn*—and reinforced by Locke's paternalist colonialism, or does it operate in the slippery, overdetermining disguises of *archē*?

As in all contracts, one should perhaps read the fine print.

FIGURE 2.2.9 SITE: BEST Showroom: Inside/Outside Building, Milwaukee, Wisconsin, 1984. © I-Beam Architecture and Design.

* * * *

One of the few firms that managed to turn the dialectics of (in)completion into a representational project was SITE (Sculpture in the Environment) headed by James Wines with their Inside/Outside Building in Milwaukee (1984).[15] SITE designed several showrooms for BEST Products, all of which were highly experimental and were seen as architectural commentaries on consumerism. It was a courageous client that could understand the architectural and salesmanship value of such an approach. The Inside/Outside Building, the last of the series of Best showrooms, stands out since it featured an "unfinished" front of concrete blocks that allowed the shopper to see not just the showrooms within, but also the structural steel elements, the heating ducts, and even the flimsy metal wall studs, all of which was in essence staged in front of the building. A great deal of attention was taken to make the exposed part be as close to a "construction site" as possible. Even the masonry ties that were spot welded to the steel posts were left on. The hung ceiling below the ducts, however, instead of acoustic tile, had to be simulated in sheet metal. The whole thing as well as the products that are on display—some of which were half inside and half outside—were painted an off-white color.

Though often seen as a ruin, it most certainly was not. According to Wines the idea was that of a cutaway drawing such as is sometimes used in technical or architectural documents to show the inner workings of an object or building. "SITE has simply translated this graphic commonplace into a physical reality."[16] Transforming a cutaway drawing of a projected building into a construction drawing thoroughly disrupts any attempt to locate this building within the conventional linear understanding of completion. One can imagine the building as a form of teleology interrupted—as a building that was design with a backward motion, explaining itself and exhibiting itself at the same time. As perhaps could be expected, this remarkable building lasted only a few years before being rebuilt along more conventional lines.

* * * *

The teleologies of architecture slip and slide between the indeterminacies of the complete and the determinacies of the incomplete.

The teleologies of architecture are not fixed in stone, but in the power of their operative illusions.

CHAPTER THREE

Post-Teleology

Once the building is handed over to its occupants and positioned by the architect into its disciplinary formation it enters a strange theoretical space, that of post-teleology (assuming I am permitted to use a word like that), a disciplinary zone remarkably devoid of theoretical qualifiers. It is like a long dotted line within the dialectics of (in)completion.

A history of architecture only touches the surface of the problem, and that strange discipline called "theory" does its best to avoid it altogether.

* * * *

Ninety-nine percent of the books on architectural history are about finished buildings, not about how buildings survive past their expiration date. Bold

FIGURE 2.3.1 Architectural Ruins, a Vision, *Joseph Michael Gandy, Watercolor on Paper, 1798.* © *Sir John Soane's Museum, London.*

is the architect who even shows us what the building will look like in a future. In 1798, John Soane, who had just completed the Bank of England in London, hired Joseph Michael Gandy to make a painting of it as if it was a Roman ruin. Small figures of men with pickaxes work around a fire pillaging marble from the site to be burned into lime. Ironically there was little marble, as the building was mostly made of brick and plaster, so the image shows not just the predicted death of the teleology of classicism, but also the already dead nature of its imitation.

* * * *

With an "end" that is not an end, where then does reflective judgment come into play?

* * * *

In today's more powerful economy, we demolish buildings when they are no longer needed. In most years, the United States throws away about 600 million tons of construction debris, which is more than twice the amount of generated municipal solid waste.[1] But well through the nineteenth century most buildings, even palaces and castles, would have been in some form of disrepair. A walk into the countryside would inevitably bring one past some form of ruined structure, like The Old Chapel at High Burton (not far from Manchester), where a chapel was being used as a hayloft. Jacob Isaacksz van Ruisdael in the mid-seventeenth century painted *The Little Bridge* that shows a dilapidated timber-frame building, the back of which is almost fully eaten away. A nineteenth-century visitor to Versailles would have also seen more a ruin than a palace. Barrington Court, in southwest England, the

FIGURE 2.3.2 The Little Bridge, *Jacob Isaacksz van Ruisdael (Netherlands, b.1628–9, d.1682), 1650–5. Etching, 19.5 × 28 cm. Art Gallery of New South Wales. Bequest of Tom Roberts, 1931. Photo: AGNSW. 62.1998.*

backdrop of many movies and visited these days by 120,000 people a year, was at the turn of the century almost derelict, with a tenant farmer living in one wing and his chickens and livestock in another. Even the famed Hōryūji temple in Japan, rebuilt, repaired, and reassembled several times, had by the nineteenth century fallen into almost complete oblivion; cows and horses roamed the premises.[2] No wonder that the general lexicon related to modern conservation, restoration, and adaptation of heritage buildings emerged in the nineteenth century.[3]

* * *

Though a traveler through New England might still see an abandoned barn or a traveler through the rust belt might pass an old steel mill, the acceptance today of architectural dereliction is mostly frowned upon.

* * * *

Even though *all* built architecture is in the domain of post-teleology, we have become ever more sensitive to the everyday needs of buildings. Vast subdisciplinary worlds have emerged of repairmen, janitors, cleaning people, window washers, handymen, and roofers, all the way back up the ladder to carpenters and contractors. In fact, it is quite likely that a vast majority of contractor work today does not involve starting a building, so much as maintaining it.

* * * *

Unlike the teleological system of completion which is more or less circular, moving from imagined completion to the just-completed, where everything reinforces the efficiencies of delivery, the post-teleological world—dependent

FIGURE 2.3.3 *Abandoned barn north of Boston, Massachusetts (contractors/ builders unknown by author). Photograph by Mark Jarzombek.*

FIGURE 2.3.4 *Street advertisements for various contracting services, New York City. Photograph by Mark Jarzombek.*

on the vicissitudes of finances, weather, material degradation, natural events, politics, cultural habits, and changes in technology—is opportunistically organized. On the one hand, the management of a high-end skyscraper can run out of money and the building be demolished; on the other, a cheap, temporary building can wind up lasting for many decades.

✳✳✳✳

Compared to what architects know about what goes into making a building (which can be less than one might think), what architects know about post-teleological efforts is practically nothing. Alberti in the tenth book of *De re aedificatoria* goes over some of the rudiments in an age when the architect lived closer to consequence:

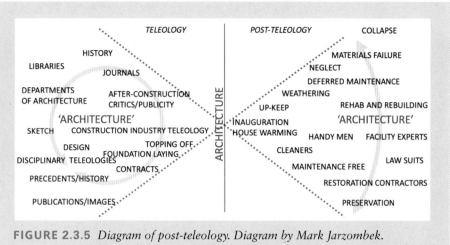

FIGURE 2.3.5 *Diagram of post-teleology. Diagram by Mark Jarzombek.*

I now come to walls. Walls are liable to the following faults: they may crack, they may fall apart, their bones may be broken, or they may lean away from the vertical. Each one of these faults may have a different cause, and also a different remedy. Some of the causes are obvious, but others are more obscure, and it is not always clear enough what needs to be done, until the damage appears. Other faults are not concealed at all, though men convince themselves in their idleness that they are not as damaging to the work as in fact they are.[4]

He also warns that "buildings should be free of pests," and that "plastering and gypsum thicken the air and makes it harmful to the lungs and brain." And so on. But worst of all is a society that abandons its obligations:

God help me! [*Me superi!*] I sometimes cannot stomach it when I see with what negligence, or to put it more crudely, by what avarice they allow the ruin of things that because of their great nobility the barbarians, the raging enemy have spared; or those which all-conquering, all-ruining time might easily have allowed to stand for ever.[5]

* * * *

Filarete, writing *Libro Architettonico* in 1464, a few decades after Alberti, was even more explicit. Indeed, as a practically oriented architect, many of his commissions were basically repair jobs. Unlike Alberti, he developed a clear theory. He saw buildings as living entities that need to be fed, and that, like all living things, have a certain life span:

You can say that a building does not sicken and die like a man. I say to you that a building does just that, for it sickens when it does not eat, that is, when it is not maintained and begins to fall off little by little exactly as man [does] when he goes without food, and finally falls dead. This is exactly what the building does. If it has a doctor when it becomes ill, that is, the master who mends and cures it, it [will] stand a long time in good state. This is obvious. I can attest to this, for the court of the Signoria of Milan was ill from lack of food and half dead, when at great expense I restored it to health. Without this protection it would soon have been finished. You need to maintain it continually and to guard it from corruption and too much fatigue, because, as man becomes thin and ill from too much fatigue, so does the building. Through corruption, the body of the building rots like that of man. Through excess it is ruined and dies like man, just as is said above. This I would not deny. I do not believe that you have ever seen a building with walls so large or so thick that it did not weaken in a short time if it was not maintained.[6]

* * * *

Filarete's theory of tectonic animism did not survive the ages. Even Alberti's foray, though more technical in nature, found few subsequent elaborations. Once treatises on architecture began to focus on beauty and style, the emphasis was solely on the teleology of delivery. The fact that Alberti's discussion appears in the last chapter is already an indication of the minor place that the post-teleological was to have in subsequent architectural theory. As the ideology of completion came to dominate architectural discourse, issues of maintenance began to disappear. Today one would be hard-pressed to locate the issue anywhere, except in books that architects and theorists do not read, like *The Well-Built House* (1988) by Jim Locke, a contractor:

> Sills are among the first things to rot in a house, and should be protected. The conditions for rot are a combination of dampness and oxygen; all that's needed is a light covering of autumn leaves.[7]

What architect would ever read something like *Comprehensive Facility Operation & Maintenance Manual*?

* * *

The question is not about pragmatics and common sense, rather: How does one integrate the topics of moisture and air, for example, into the theoretical concerns?

Anyone searching for information about mold in buildings will be overwhelmed by the sheer volume of sources.

A recent Google check turned up more than 40 million sites that deal with mold ... A dry building not only prevents mold outbreaks, but also creates a more pleasant, healthier environment. And dry buildings are more

FIGURE 2.3.6 *Indoor mold on the head jamb of the inner window in multistory building, Russia, 2018. Photograph by Alexander Davronov.*

durable, and will have fewer maintenance problems—so controlling moisture is truly a win-win for builders, owners, and occupants.[8]

* * * *

We humans do not need to change out the duct work; we do not need periodic skin grafts, nor the application of toxic chemicals to keep out vermin. Above all, we do not need to avoid water. Just as the human body survives because of water, the architectural body survives because it is water adverse.

* * * *

Mold once had theological dimensions. In the Book of Leviticus, we have one of the most astonishing and fulsome attempts to deal with mold prior to the modern age. It is worth quoting in full:

> The Lord said to Moses and Aaron, "When you enter the land of Canaan, which I am giving you as your possession, and I put a spreading mold in a house in that land, the owner of the house must go and tell the priest, 'I have seen something that looks like a defiling mold in my house.' The priest is to order the house to be emptied before he goes in to examine the mold, so that nothing in the house will be pronounced unclean. After this the priest is to go in and inspect the house. He is to examine the mold on the walls, and if it has greenish or reddish depressions that appear to be deeper than the surface of the wall, the priest shall go out the doorway of the

house and close it up for seven days. On the seventh day the priest shall return to inspect the house. If the mold has spread on the walls, he is to order that the contaminated stones be torn out and thrown into an unclean place outside the town. He must have all the inside walls of the house scraped and the material that is scraped off dumped into an unclean place outside the town. Then they are to take other stones to replace these and take new clay and plaster the house. If the defiling mold reappears in the house after the stones have been torn out and the house scraped and plastered, the priest is to go and examine it and, if the mold has spread in the house, it is a persistent defiling mold; the house is unclean. It must be torn down—its stones, timbers and all the plaster—and taken out of the town to an unclean place. Anyone who goes into the house while it is closed up will be unclean till evening. Anyone who sleeps or eats in the house must wash their clothes. But if the priest comes to examine it and the mold has not spread after the house has been plastered, he shall pronounce the house clean, because the defiling mold is gone. To purify the house he is to take two birds and some cedar wood, scarlet yarn and hyssop. He shall kill one of the birds over fresh water in a clay pot. Then he is to take the cedar wood, the hyssop, the scarlet yarn and the live bird, dip them into the blood of the dead bird and the fresh water, and sprinkle the house seven times. He shall purify the house with the bird's blood, the fresh water, the live bird, the cedar wood, the hyssop and the scarlet yarn. Then he is to release the live bird in the open fields outside the town. In this way he will make atonement for the house, and it will be clean."

Thus spoke the Lord.

We might consider ourselves fortunate these days that maintenance people do not arrive in the morning with bird cages, cedar wood, scarlet yarn and hyssop (a type of mint).

Architecture does not protect humans from the environment, as it is so often claimed. Architecture protects itself from (divine-induced) moisture. This is the first principle of its post-teleology.

* * * *

Architecture (without scare quotes) ends when maintenance begins. When maintenance begins, "architecture" finds its new home.

The principal job of the architect of the Congress, as appointed by the President of the United States,

> is supervising the army of maintenance men and caretakers around the Capitol and various other buildings.[9]

* * * *

The post-teleological revolves not just around the question of weathering, but even, according to one website that deals with maintenance:

FIGURE 2.3.7 *Man on ladder cleaning house gutter from leaves and dirt, c. 2018. Photograph by ronstik. Getty Images / iStockphoto.*

FIGURE 2.3.8 *Black & Decker advertisement, 1950s. Neil Baylis / Alamy Stock Photo.*

1 Observe Your House

Observing is not figuring out. It is not analysis. Observing is a wonderment. It is open and receptive. It is true learning. Once you can observe potential problems around your home, then what? You can learn where to look and for what . . .

2 Control Dust. Dust has the potential to be a serious health hazard . . .

3 Keep Floors Vacuumed . . .

4 Check the Exterior . . .

5 Check Windows and Walls . . . etc.[10]

Whereas women are usually shown in the interior, men are usually shown on the exterior.

FIGURE 2.3.9 Cleaning a Gerrit Rietveld Building, *Job Koelewijn, Amsterdam, 1992. Thanks to E. v. d. Boom. © Job Koelewijn.*

****

On March 16, 1992, Cornelia, Jane, Greetje, and Weimpje Koelewijn Vermeer, the mother and aunts of artist Job Koelewijn, cleaned a pavilion designed by the Gerrit Rietveld Academie in Amsterdam wearing their traditional costumes of Spakenburg, Koelewijn's place of birth. With his spring-cleaning performance, Koelewijn washed away his time at the academy to make a fresh start in his new profession as an artist. The performance was also a tribute to Rietveld and his sober and functional architecture as well to the Dutch culture of neatness and cleanliness.

The book that was produced to document this event included a pair of yellow rubber gloves and two yellow cleaning pads. With these items, one can "perform" a cleaning, I presume, in one's own house or at some grand edifice nearby. I tried it at MIT, where I teach, dusting the walls with the cleaning staff. No one seemed to notice. But maybe we should all chip in.

****

After all, MIT has admitted:

> Over the years, MIT's deferred maintenance backlog has grown steadily and includes updates to obsolete systems, changes required by codes or regulations, user-driven changes (when the use of a building has changed),

FIGURE 2.3.10 The Ethics of Dust, *Westminster Hall, London, 2016. Commissioned and produced by Artangel. Photograph by Marcus J. Leith.* © *Jorge Otero-Pailos.*

and the repair or replacement of building systems including roofs, mechanical equipment, utilities, major building components, plazas, walkways, landscaping, and roadways.[11]

****

Jorge Otero-Pailos uses a technique developed recently by a company in Belgium where a liquid applied to the wall absorbs the grime and soot and then hardens into a latex.[12] When the latex is then peeled off, it reveals the accumulated layers of dirt, leaving the wall unaffected. It is "an environmental history because the dust comes from the air," allowing us to see the interaction between building and atmosphere over time. Using this technique, Otero-Pailos was commissioned to clean the walls of the Palace of Westminster in London. The result, *The Ethics of Dust* (2016), was a 50-meter-long cast of Westminster Hall's east wall contained hundreds of years of surface pollution and dust held captive in translucent latex. The sheets were suspended from the roof in front of the cleaned wall, and backlit to reveal the ghostly presence of the dirt captured in the resin. The sheets run the length of the thousand-year-old space. The wall itself is not restored. The chipped bricks and missing mortar remain, only it is now all clean. In that sense, its age value is left intact, but its visual age is a new one. A new before and a new after. The title is taken from an essay by John Ruskin, the great late-nineteenth-century theorist who differentiated between destruction and preservation.

The piece—though an artwork in its own right—had an unusual post-telological life. Since a number of museums asked to exhibit it, it was decided, in consideration of the public art fund that produced the work, to cut it up and distribute it to museums in each of the nations of the United Kingdom.[13]

* * * *

Facility management has been recognized as an academic discipline only since the 1990s. Initial research in the field took place in universities in the UK, the Netherlands, and the Nordic countries. The British Institute of Facilities Management (BIFM) was founded in 1993. As one representative in the field noted:

> As with any maintenance position, a facility manager should understand there is no light at the end of the tunnel. You build the light and carry it with you.[14]

According to one member of the maintenance guild:

> The apartment industry is a culture that people don't understand. Being a maintenance tech is a thankless job that deserves respect. We may not be perfect. But most of us care and get the job done.

In movies, the maintenance man is often portrayed as stupid, insincere, and unreliable. Perhaps that has something to do with the fact that enrollment in apprenticeship programs has declined 40 percent between 2003 and 2013.[15]

> The worldwide facilities management outsourcing market is expected to grow from $972 billion in 2012 to $1.314 billion in 2018. The growth is evident across all markets, from North America and Europe to Latin America and Asia Pacific with a general tendency to more and more integrated services, focusing on strategic initiatives within longer-term contracts.[16]

* * * *

Alison Elizabeth Taylor uses thin wood veneers to create collaged, *trompe l'oeil* images. Her work constitutes a modern update of the ancient craft of marquetry or inlaid wood intarsia. Some of her pieces evoke the battered plywood sheets left on construction sites around New York City. One of her pieces, "Tap Left On" (2008), represents a corner of a house that had been damaged by a water leak. We see the studs and corroded edges of plywood. It is not a photo or a painting, but meticulously made out of wood veneer, a completion representing the post-completion world of post-teleology.

* * * *

FIGURE 2.3.11 *"Tap Left On," Alison Elizabeth Taylor, 2010, wood veneer, shellac (71 × 75 × 48 inches).* © *Alison Elizabeth Taylor.*

The field known as "post-occupancy" has only risen to a field of inquiry in the last twenty or so years—after how many centuries of architecture?

* * * *

Instead of teaching humans how to maintain the house, we now want maintenance-free houses. Lumber is treated with chemicals to resist rot, paints and shingles are made to be ever more durable. PVC pipes are specially designed to be mold-resistant. The new neocolonial house of my neighbor has a plastic skin imitating wood that the owner will never need to paint or even wash. Arkitema Architects have gone one better in their so-called Innovative Maintenance-Free House, designed with the goal of lasting 150 years, with minimum maintenance for the first fifty. The house was, of course, prefabricated, but most astonishing, the whole house is enclosed in sheets of glass, on the sloping roof and on the vertical facades, protecting the wood components against rain. The house was also lifted half a meter or so off the ground on stilts of concrete to ventilate from below. The gap creates a natural chimney effect, sucking in air at the bottom and letting it out at the top of the roof. No complicated mechanical ventilation system is needed—natural

FIGURE 2.3.12 *Maintenance-Free House, Denmark, Arkitema Architects, 2014.*
© Arkitema Architects. Photograph by Niels Nygaard.

forces are at work, or so it is promised.[17] Here the dialectics of occupation is writ large. Should such things become normative, it would be the death not just of the *tektōn*, but of the *tektōn* imaginary.

* * * *

The history of "architecture" includes the history of prosthetics, devices installed here and there to prolong the life of a building. An arch in Venice is supported by an elegantly constructed subarch of wooden beams, or elsewhere of metal rods. In another place a stainless steel Y-clamp holds the door fame securely to the wall. And in yet another place a scaffolding holds a wooden framework that in turn supports a corroding brick wall. In all cases, the maker's name has not gone down into the annals of history.

Gionata Rizzi works to recover historic buildings using various conservation and restoration techniques.[18] He is particularly interested in small-scale problems that do not require foreign experts. For such situations he developed a type of prosthesis for roof beams that would otherwise need to be replaced—like a splint that is inserted into the damaged end and in this way extends the life span of the house.

* * * *

"There are two churches that you have to visit when you go to Rome: Santa Marian in Restauro and St. Maria Chiuso." (Joke by architectural historian Henry Millon.)[19]

I admit that the joke made more sense back in the 1980s when he told it than today. Today, after several decades of restoration efforts, the churches of Rome are in better shape than back then.

* * * *

FIGURE 2.3.13 *Prosthesis for a beam, Gionata Rizzi, 2021. Photograph by Mark Jarzombek.*

FIGURE 2.3.14 *Detail of wall support, Venice (contractors/builders unknown by author). Photograph by Mark Jarzombek.*

FIGURE 2.3.15 *Arch, Venice (contractor/ builder unknown by author). Photograph by Mark Jarzombek.*

FIGURE 2.3.16 *Detail of door support, Venice (contractors/builders unknown by author). Photograph by Mark Jarzombek.*

The exterior of the White House in Washington DC will never be changed as long as there is a United States. Its teleology is frozen in time and space. Since the 1980s, the preservation industry has sought to maximize these examples, to go past completion into the realm of the metaphysics of permanence. The Monastery of Melk in Australia was built in the eighteenth century. It does not look like it, of course, since it was recently restored to look like it was built yesterday. This is hardly unique, but has become so widespread in fact that we hardly even notice how extensive the world of the timeless is.

* * * *

Because the preservation industry focuses on special buildings, it constitutes only a tiny part in the spectrum of post-teleological practices, and the one that since the nineteenth century has developed its own field of disciplinary theory, one that has become increasingly thick and complex, and like all disciplines has become the object of its own epistemologies.[20]

Alois Riegl, an Austrian art historian in "The Modern Cult of Monuments" (1903), laid the foundation of any attempt to move into the post-telological.[21] He identified several ways that monuments survive the ages. They are:

Age-value, structures are allowed to decay because of our visual appreciation of age. Here we refrain from preservation. This is very rare today.

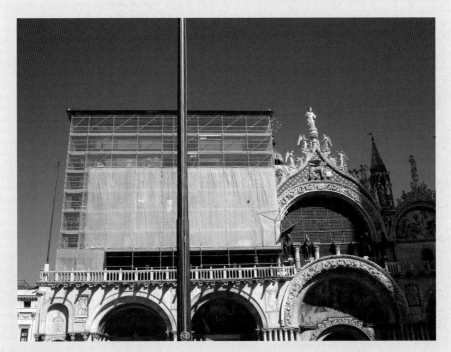

FIGURE 2.3.17 *Italian church under restoration (contractors/builders unknown by author). Photograph by Joanbanjo.*

Historical-value, structures are preserved to represent a precise moment in history usually in relationship to their original state. Here we talk of preventative conservation. This is very common today.

Intentional commemorative-value, structures that are preserved as new to honor a particular moment in time or a particular person. This is relatively rare; one can think, for example, of the White House.

All this is quite outdated. We can add:

Obsolescence Value:[22] *Purposeful Obsolescence Value: Purposeful Ruin Value: Purposeful Destruction Value: Purposeful Reconstruction Value: Purposeful Failed Reconstruction Value: Purposeful Fake Reconstruction Value:* etc.

❋ ❋ ❋ ❋

Purposefully Misdirected Reconstruction: When the great ritual mound of Newgrange (*c.* 3200 BCE) in Ireland was rebuilt in the 1970s, the restorers

FIGURE 2.3.18 *Church building under restoration, near Barcelona (contractors/builders unknown by author). Photograph by Mark Jarzombek.*

imaged a vertical wall of stones on its front which they built out of reinforced concrete. It is so implausible that one can only show pictures of the structure in a textbook on modern architecture.

For the recent restoration of the Parthenon, the architects had the computer scan the surfaces of the broken bits and then were able to perfectly match the old bits to the newly constructed bits, using even the same quarry. How do we interpret this prosthetic enhancement? Is the stone now ontologically satisfied, or are we simply showing off the tools of computation? Is the stone renewed, the trauma of its destruction now a thing of the past, or is the stone now permanently redamaged? Though we know that the stone was originally painted, the restorers will not paint the stone. In that sense, we are restoring not the Parthenon, but the nineteenth-century, white, neoclassical version of it, the version with no magic, no *archē*.

The building is now restored to the moment when it was finished from the point of view of the masons, but before it was finished from the point of view of its divine inhabitation. In our secular world, we have no problem with the building being a monument to the cleverness of computation, a monument to national pride, or even a monument to the tourism industry, but God forbid, a pagan temple! We "restore" the building—not the temple. There is no talk of restoring the altar which was right next to it and which was removed stone by stone by the Christians in the fifth century CE.

* * * *

Increasingly, there are architects who are at home in the world of adaptive reuse, another space of activity within the post-teleological. It has now become a large part of the architectural profession's normative activity. Yet there are few architects who accept the incomplete as such. Among those is de Vylder Vinck Taillieu, who is one of the few who actually has established a post-teleological practice. His work is in "correction mode—like how to get along with what went wrong." House Sanderswal, for example, evokes the motif of ruins in the form of a dilapidated structure abandoned between a house and a brick wall. The structure includes a bare-bones frame for a roof which is only partially covered by corrugated metal sheets, and a barren brick facade which seems to stand alone as one enters the building. In Switzerland, he took a parking garage that was in danger of collapse, but repaired it with conventional contractor struts creating "a symphony of posts."[23]

* * * *

An installation entitled "There is no more place in this place" of Cinthia Marcelle (2019, San Francisco Museum of Modern Art) featured a hung ceiling that was coming apart. It looked like a ceiling in an abandoned office building, and indeed few visitors that I noticed even looked at it, not sure perhaps whether it was an artwork or some deferred maintenance on the part of the museum. The cleverness of the installation was supreme, its message of ambiguity hiding in

FIGURE 2.3.19 *House Sanderswal, De Vylder Vinck Tallieu, Belgium, 2015. © architecten de vylder vinck taillieu. Photograph by Filip Dujardin.*

plain sight. What we see is the cumulative collapse of both *archē* and *tektōn*, in their cross-negational logic: the false-work of the *archē* falling apart, on the one hand, and the *tektōn* hapless in the face of institutional negligence, on the other. And yet perhaps we are also seeing the precarious persistence of the *tektōn* outliving the ambitions of the *archē* shadowing itself forth into the space of a future without offices. The project represents the "decline and fall" of architecture as we know it—existing at the extreme remote edges of acknowledgment. As a "whatever," it posits no particular hope, but rather a repetition of the same.

* * * *

Among artists who work on soon-to-be-dismantled buildings is the Dutch artist Marjan Teeuwen. She often starts the demolition herself, using the available material to in essence paint with the debris. In her work, the constructive power of the building goes hand in hand with the power of devastation and decay. Floors are tilted or fall perpendicularly downwards; walls are partially or completely smashed out. Stacks of debris are then crammed into awkward shapes. The artist operates in dialogue with what is left over of the building, most of which already belongs to the world of the *tektōn*, the architectural meaning and intentionality have long since become a thing of the building's past. Is the debris awaiting the delivery truck? Is it being sorted and analyzed? Does it have some unknown value? Or is it the result of an attempt to clean the floor for some activity? We see the last possible moment of silence—replicating the originary silence after construction—but this time before the boom and crash of the wrecking ball. For one last time, the building is, as Filarete might say, "fed."—but this time knowing that it is the last meal.

FIGURE 2.3.20 *Mark Jarzombek inside the Cinthia Marcelle installation, San Francisco Museum of Modern Art, 2019. Photograph by Mark Jarzombek.*

FIGURE 2.3.21 *Destroyed House in Gaza.* © *Marjan Teeuwen, Courtesy Bruce Silverstein Gallery.*

＊ ＊ ＊ ＊

In 2013, the firm NLÉ, founded by Kunlé Adeyemi, designed a Makoko Floating School for the water community of Makoko in Lagos, Nigeria. It consisted of a 10-meter-high A-frame resting on a 10m x 10m base that was deemed "an ideal shape for a floating object on water due to its relatively low center of gravity." The architects saw it as an innovative approach that addressed the community's social and physical needs in view of the impact of climate change and a rapidly urbanizing African context. The structure was celebrated with numerous awards as proudly listed on the architect's website. Unfortunately, not soon after the school was delivered, this "ideal shape" collapsed into a pile of useless rubble following a rainstorm. Apparently, a structure that was stable on calm water served as a sail in the wind.

According to the architect, the collapse was "due to deterioration resulting from a lack of proper maintenance and collective management." In other words, it was the fault, if not of nature, then of the community. Had its owners been more responsible, so the architects implied, things would have turned out differently.

Needless to say, this type of disengagement with the community where the architect simply walks away from a project plays out the darker side of the grammatology of *archē(non)tektōn*. Disassociation grounds itself on the imperialism of the *archē*, and on the hard line of teleological obligation.

＊ ＊ ＊ ＊

The pathological dualisms of creativity and work, mind and hand, designer and laborer that so dull and paralyze our understanding of architecture was brilliantly deconstructed in 2003, in a Diller + Scofidio installation that could be experienced on the fourth floor of the New York's Whitney Museum

FIGURE 2.3.22 *Makoko Floating School, Lagos, NLÉ, 2013. Image by NLÉ.*

FIGURE 2.3.23 *Makoko Floating School, Lagos, after its collapse, 2016. Photograph by Allyn Aglaïa.*

of American Art. Entitled *Mural*, it comprised a network of white walls along which travelled a drill on a movable track. Guided by a computer, the robot randomly selected points on the wall. Accompanied by sound effects, the drill would then pierce the wall leaving half-inch holes. As the exhibition continued, the walls became increasingly perforated. Eventually, holes on both sides of walls would align, opening small views through the gallery. The operation lasted an interminable three months.

The title of the piece is a play on the Latin word for "wall" (*murus*) and on the relationship between wall and a tradition of painting on walls. It also evoked the architectural nature of wall as a fortification, as something that protects. Here the wall was eaten away bit by bit so that its ancient cultural material evocations were metamorphosed into an aesthetic suitable to the computationalized, post-Industrial world.

The wall is, of course, a drywall, invented in the 1930s or so as a labor-saving device that replaced the old lath and plaster. The carpenters' unions protested their use. "Upstart Drywall" appeared on huge billboards in Los Angeles telling people "Knock on the wall. Demand genuine lath and plaster."[24] Interior walls needed three layers of plaster and the process of application and drying took weeks. But it was a losing battle and plastering soon became a dead craft. It went the way of typesetting in the 1970s.

The modern wall of today, the normative location of the modernized and absented *tektōn*, is revealed to be shallow, permeable, and vulnerable. It is attacked, however, not by some brute force, but by a tool that belongs seemingly to its own orbit of consciousness. Though a "hand tool" it is in the "hands" of the robot, the symbol par excellence of the Albertian *instrumentum*. This deliberateness evokes the methodologies of *ratio et via*, and indeed it was guided by a computer that the architects call an "intelligent navigator." But the *ratio et via* is here inverted, making something that is not "complete" but slowly, bit by bit, removing completion from its metaphysical security, a death by a thousand drill holes. And yet, as Diller commented, "the confused drill occasionally slipped."[25] Furthermore, as the drill did its work, the plaster dust rained down to the ground. Dust to dust. And once the dust started getting into the air-conditioning system, the architects had to add a plexiglass box below the drill.

Though the drill is occupied by its obsessive, yet mysteriously dutiful activities, its labor reengineers the classic equation of mind–hand into an *instrumentum* of a new type, as it is not passive, but seeking a messy revenge on behalf of displaced laborers, prolonging the torture of the wall for all to see. In the end, the sheetrock eventually stood defeated by the drill's insistent savagery, exhibiting the painful and public process of destruction.

The architects salvaged part of the wall and cut it into 2' x 2' pieces, keeping one piece and giving away the rest as souvenirs to friends. Several years later, New York's Museum of Modern Art (MoMA) acquired a piece

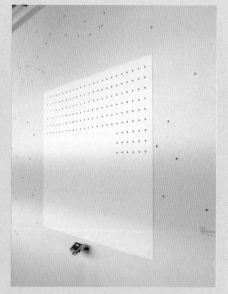

FIGURE 2.3.24 *Sheetrock advertisement, 1923. Courtesy of Historic New England.*

FIGURE 2.3.25 Mural, *Diller + Scofidio, Whitney Museum of American Art, New York, 2003. © Elizabeth Diller.*

FIGURE 2.3.26 Mural, Diller + Scofidio, Whitney Museum of American Art, New York, 2004. © Elizabeth Diller.

for its permanent collection, an architectural fragment, but a fragment of what exactly? Or maybe not a fragment at all. Here the post-teleological comes not in the form of the civilian's encounter with the unfamiliar body of the building, but the architect's encounter with its own desire to defamiliarize the normative in its own operations.

FIGURE 2.3.27 *The back of a truck advertising maintenance work. Photo: Mark Jarzombek, 2022.*

PART THREE

CHAPTER ONE

The Curse of Socrates

Filarete, or more properly Antonio di Pietro Aver(u)lino (*c.*1400–*c.*1469), began his training under the noted sculptor Lorenzo Ghiberti, moving to Milan in the 1450s to rise through the ranks to become court architect of the Sforza, designing a range of buildings including the Ospedale Maggiore (*c.* 1456). Unlike Alberti, a member of a noble family, Filarete was an upwardly mobile contractor. His *Libro Architettonico*, completed in 1464, stands as a powerful contrast to Alberti's treatise which was finished just a decade earlier. Its reception, however, was, shall one say, brutal. In his famous *The Lives of the Most Excellent Painters, Sculptors, and Architects* (1568), Giorgio Vasari wrote:

> Although there is something of the good to be found in it, it is nevertheless mostly ridiculous, and perhaps the most stupid book [*è nondimeno per lo più ridicola e tanto sciocca*] that was ever written . . . [He was] meddling with something that he did not understand.[1]

What irked Vasari was not Filaret's drive for upward- mobility. After all, Vasari was born of relative humble origins himself and rode the wave of ambition with great success. It was rather the approach that Filarete adopted in writing his text. Filarete states outright that if any of his readers were "more skilled and learned in letters [they] will read the above-named authors," by which he means Vitruvius and Alberti.[2] Filarete narrated his *Libro Architecttonico* through the first-person singular account, a bold move indeed.[3] Furthermore, his book is not a treatise, though that is how it is often called today, but a narrative meant to be read aloud, maybe at dinner.

> To this degree turn your ears to this. If you do so, I think that it will please you and it will not be at all tedious for me to talk. While enjoying it, you will derive some utility from it.[4]

He also imagines himself, shockingly, on rather familiar terms with the ruler.

The next morning early, I went to the work and put all the masters and laborers to their assigned task. I divided them into eight groups, each with the abovementioned orders and means, explained to them what they had to do, and reminded the overseers of their office. At this point my lord came and on seeing everyone attending to his work he was pleased. He said, "Let us go see those gates."[5]

* * * *

To fully contextualize the nature of Vasari's put-down of Filarete, and, of course, Alberti's attempt to distance the architect from the *faber*, we have to go back all the way to Socrates. Socrates may be seen as one of the founders of the Western intellectual tradition, as its first moral philosopher, and as a martyr to free thinking, but do not sing his praise in front of the *tektōn*.[6] For the *tektōn*, his name is mud. Greek philosophy was written for and reflected the viewpoint of the nobility. Craftsmen and builders were, of course, occasionally honored.[7] The *Homeric Hymns* make it clear that it was the creation of crafts that separated the primitive from the civilized. The word that is often used is *erga* which means more than "crafts" but "works" as "works of engineering" and implies the social cohesion necessary for such efforts.[8] It would not be wrong to argue that the ancient work of the *tektōn* was governed by the ethos of *erga*:

> Sing, clear-voiced Muse, of Hephaestus famed for inventions [*klutomētis* = renowned skill]. With bright-eyed Athena he taught men glorious crafts [*erga*] throughout the world,—men who before used to dwell in caves in the mountains like wild beasts. But now that they have learned crafts through Hephaestus the famed worker [*klutotechnēs*], easily they live a peaceful life in their own houses the whole year round.[9]

But some five hundred years after the age of Homer, values had changed—considerably.[10] Herodotus, more or less a contemporary with Socrates, already noticed the shift in tone; he argued that his countrymen had learned to look down upon craftsmen as a result of their contact with "barbarians" who held only the warrior class in esteem:

> Now whether the Hellenes have learnt this also from the Egyptians, I am not able to say for certain, since I see that the Thracians also and Scythians and Persians and Lydians and almost all the Barbarians esteem those of their citizens who learn the arts, and the descendants of them, as less honorable than the rest; while those who have got free from all practice of manual arts are accounted noble, and especially those who are devoted to war: however that may be, the Hellenes have all learnt this, and especially the Lacedemonians; but the Corinthians least of all cast slight upon those who practice handicrafts.[11]

ii.167

Separating the citizen from the craftsmen was a relatively widespread phenomenon, found throughout Asia, but the Greek philosophers inscribed it into the bones of their speculation. In the *Republic* (495e) when Socrates discusses the manual crafts, he uses the word *banausos*, which means "of an artisan" and which generally referred to potters, stonemasons, carpenters, professional singers, artists, and musicians. In all cases, *banausos* implied a lowly activity and was even used as a term of invective by Aristotle, meaning "cramped in body" (*Politics* 1341a7) and "vulgar in taste" (1337b7).

Craftwork was lowly because it was mostly the work of slaves, the ranks of which had been thickened during Athens's successful military campaigns. These men soon displaced the more homegrown laborers. Even if they were no longer slaves, having worked their way out of it in one way or another, they were still not citizens and could be taken as slaves as soon as they were no longer able to play a tax.[12] But for the likes of Socrates it was not the association with the slave class that made craft so lowly; it was because a man who worked all day would have no time to adequately socialize and so could not possibly develop a free nature. It was inconceivable to any Greek citizen—where citizenship required so much time, effort, and cost in the context of one's standing in society—that those who struggled for the necessities of life could be good citizens. Xenophon, an Athenian military leader, philosopher, and student of Socrates, wrote:

> Lack of leisure to join in the concerns of friends and of the city is another condition of those that are called mechanical; those who practice them are reputed to be bad friends as well as bad defenders of their fatherlands.[13]

The generation of Socrates seems to have ignored the obvious fact that it was their slaves and the *banausoi* who, in doing all the hard work, created the very idea of leisure that was, for the Greeks at least, necessary for philosophical speculation. It was no different for the Romans who, even though they had a more advanced market and industrial economy than the Greeks, maintained the position unchanged.[14] Plutarch wrote:

> For it does not of necessity follow that, if the work delights you with its grace, the one who wrought it is worthy of your esteem.[15]

And Cicero would write in no uncertain terms:

> Unbecoming to a gentleman, too, and vulgar are the means of livelihood of all hired workmen whom we pay for mere manual labor, not for artistic skill; for in their case the very wage they receive is a pledge of their slavery . . . And all mechanics are engaged in vulgar trades; for no workshop can have anything liberal about it . . . But the professions in which either a higher degree of intelligence is required or from which no small benefit

to society is derived—medicine and architecture, for example, and teaching—these are proper for those whose social position they become.

De officiis I.42

He writes somewhat facetiously that it was

of more consequence to the Athenians, that their houses should be securely roofed, than to have their city graced with a most beautiful statue of Minerva: and yet, notwithstanding this, I would much rather have been a Pheidias, than the most skillful joiner [*fabrum tignarium*] in Athens.

Brutus 73.257

This was, of course, the exact same *faber tignarius* that Alberti did not want at the table.

* * * *

In the Middle Ages, philosophers distinguished between *artes liberales*, the seven liberal arts that were appropriate for a free man (the Latin *liber* means "free") and the *artes illiberales* or *artes mechanicae* that were pursued for economic purposes and involved vocational and practical arts. The *artes mechanicae* (that included weavers, blacksmiths, farmers, hunters, navigators, soldiers, or doctors) were not necessarily viewed prejudicially, given the importance of these crafts in monastic environments.[16] Nonetheless, the distinction remains a real one in the regime of theory-making.

* * * *

Peggy Deamer, in mulling over a comment she heard once that architecture "isn't a career but is a calling!", asks the question: "How could architecture have become so completely deaf to the labor discourse that it could so unselfconsciously subscribe to the honor of labor exploitations?"[17] Good question. A hint of an answer might come from a thirteenth-century drawing showing the construction of a church with a priest, a king, and the architect on one side of a wall, and builders busily at work on the other. It is almost a literal depiction not just of the class division, but also of the creativity–occupation dualism implied in *archē(non)tektōn*: the curse of Socrates in visual form.

* * *

Alberti, who came from a noble family, would certainly have seen no reason to question this point of view. Alberti's masterstroke was to link the presumptive discipline of architecture with the conventions of aristocratic elitism using the emerging culture of humanism as the bonding agent. He would have been appreciative of Vasari's put-down of Filarete and, I am sure, of Vasari's praise for him:

FIGURE 3.1.1 *A 13th-century drawing showing the construction of a church. Possibly drawn by Matthew of Paris.* © *Culture Club / Getty Images.*

This man, born in Florence of the most noble family of the Alberti, Leon Batista Alberti, who, having studied the Latin tongue, and having given attention to architecture, to perspective, and to painting, left behind him books written in such a manner, that, since not one of our modern craftsmen has been able to expound these matters in writing, although very many of them in his own country have excelled him in working, it is generally believed; such is the influence of his writings over the pens and speech of the learned; that he was superior to all those who were actually superior to him in work … Leon Batista was a person of most honest and laudable ways, the friend of men of talent, and very open and courteous to all; and he lived honorably and like a gentleman—which he was—through the whole course of his life.

Alberti's *archē* is not just different from the *tektōn* because he commands the *tektōn*, as Plato had it, but because he is of a different cultural animal. Not only does Alberti's *archē* know the proper modes of behavior, he will also know Latin and maybe some Greek and be familiar with the world of codices and manuscripts and their collated wisdoms. This was to remain a feature of the architect's definition well into the nineteenth century. The *Architectural Magazine* from 1834 notes:

Before, however, any architect attempts to design even within the ordinary sphere of invention, he ought to have made himself acquainted, as far as practicable, from books and other sources, with all that has been done by his predecessors, in all ages and countries. The more richly he stores his mind with the ideas of others, the more likely will he be to bring forth new ideas of his own; for a new idea can be nothing more than a new combination of ideas which had previously existed. By making himself thoroughly master of all the ideas of others, the architect becomes, not only capable of inventing with facility for all ordinary purposes, but of inventing in what may be called a cultivated style of art, as compared with that crude style of invention sometimes seen in the productions of untutored genius.[18]

The demand that the architect be learned was a particularly tall order back in the fifteenth century, when only a few had access to the libraries of princes and elite merchants. Few knew how to perform all the necessary social graces with trained ease.

* * * *

European philosophy, in general well into the modern age, assumes that only the free Self not weighed down by economic obligations is worthy of—and possibly capable of—true philosophic speculation; only the free Self is open-ended enough to merit a debate about human destiny and purpose; only the free Self can embrace the welcoming tortures of metaphysical release. The *banausos*, foreclosed from such weighty deliberations, was at the outset collateral damage to the theory of thought, with its lowly position baked into the core of European disciplinary consciousness.[19]

Even Immanuel Kant, moving in many respects into the more complex modern world, did not substantially change that fundamental equation. In the *Critique of Judgment* (1790), he distinguished between two different types of work. One is the work of the genius, whose efforts are valued cumulatively, adding up to what he called an *opus*. The other work is mechanical and rote and adds up to, well, nothing. Kant used the Latin word *opus* to convey the higher civilizational status of the idea of work over the vernacular, *Arbeit*. Nowhere in Kant does he bother to address what then to do with the *Arbeiter* or worker:

> Art is distinguished from Nature, as doing (*facere*) is distinguished from acting or working generally (*agere*), and as the product or result of the former is distinguished as work (*opus*) from the working (*effectus*) of the latter.

To this, he adds:

> Art also differs from handicraft; the first is called free, the other may be called mercenary ... the second is regarded as if it could only be compulsorily imposed upon one as work (*Arbeit*), i.e. as occupation which is unpleasant (*beschwerlich*: a trouble) in itself, and which is only attractive on account of its effect (e.g. the wage).[20]

Whereas *opus* brings society closer to the apprehension of its inner naturalness, *Arbeit*, for Kant, does not. At best it is governed by the proverbial

ART	HANDICRAFT	NATURE
DOING/FREE	MERCENARY	ACTING
OPUS	WAGE	EFFECT
GENIUS	(WORKER)	(ANIMALS)

FIGURE 3.1.2 *Diagram of Immanuel Kant's organization of the arts. Diagram by Mark Jarzombek.*

"rules of skill" that keep those who perform *Arbeit*—the worker—from ever being in a position to contemplate truth.

Developed at the birth of the Industrial Revolution, the implications of Kant's thesis were profound, in a negative way, of course. What creative person would aspire to handicraft, "an occupation which is unpleasant (a trouble) in itself."

In all the literature on Kant, as far as I can tell, not one person has had any trouble with Kant's idea of *Arbeit* and the cruel legacy of Socrates.

The benefit went solely to those on the *opus* side of the equation. In the early nineteenth century, it was already fashionable for musicians to write using opus numbers, as did Beethoven; artists, too, all the way down the line to Le Corbusier's *Oeuvre Complète*. Artists also came to be featured in retrospectives from the early nineteenth century onward.[21] The language of *Louis I. Kahn: In the Realm of Architecture*, that was held in 1992 at MoMA, is right out of Kant. The catalogue claimed that the exhibition

> shows a range of work from the architect's formative years in Philadelphia to his international contribution to the design of religious and governmental institutions, centers of learning and research, and other public spaces. The installation also illuminates the developing philosophical underpinnings of Kahn's architecture.[22]

* * * *

A textbook on architecture from the end of the nineteenth century makes it clear that

> *construction* alone is not *architecture*, for it may be found among the most uncivilized people; only when it is governed by systematic laws of proportion, which are based upon a refined conception of what is most suitable for the purpose, can construction be classed as a fine art. It is for this reason we find no architectural advancement in a nation until its condition betokens culture. wealth, and prosperity.[23]

italics in original

FIGURE 3.1.3 *Construction workers on a building site in Mexico.* © *Tomas Castelazo, www.tomascastelazo.com.*

* * * *

Le Corbusier, who admired works of engineering, did not give up on the illusion that the arts—as a non-occupation—can be neatly separated and the former elevated over construction. Here in *Towards a New Architecture*, Corbusier might appear to be a "modern," but from a theoretical point of view he is fully Albertian:

> Architecture is a thing of art, a phenomenon of the emotions, lying outside questions of construction and beyond them. The purpose of construction is to *make* things hold together; of architecture to move us.[24]
>
> my emphasis

> You *employ* stone, wood and concrete, and with these materials you build houses and palaces. That is construction. Ingenuity is at work. But suddenly you touch my heart, you do me good, I am happy and I say: "This is beautiful." That is architecture. *Art enters in* . . . By the use of raw materials and starting from conditions more or less utilitarian, you have established certain relationships which have aroused my emotions. This is Architecture.[25]
>
> my emphasis

If we eliminate from our hearts and minds all *dead* concepts in regard to the house, and look at the question from a critical and objective point of view, we shall arrive at the "House Machine," the mass-production house, healthy (and morally so too) and beautiful in the same way that the working tools and instruments which accompany our existence are beautiful. Beautiful also with all the *animation* that the artist's sensibility can add to severe and pure functioning elements [*Belle aussi de l'animation que le sens de l'artiste peut apporter à ces stricts et purs organes*].[26]

my emphasis

In this, Le Corbusier was not far even from John Ruskin who, though a critic of the modern age, also elevated the *archē*:

The rule is simple: Always look for *invention* first, and after that, for such *execution* as will help the invention, and as the inventor is capable of without painful effort, and no more. Above all, demand no refinement of execution where there is no thought, for that is *slaves' work*, unredeemed.[27]

my emphasis

Approaches like this are tone deaf to the core problem, which is that *archē* is blind to its disciplinary self-infatuations.

* * * *

Clement Greenberg put all of this into an extremist formation in his famous article from 1939 where he distinguished between the avant-garde and kitsch, the former holding the strings to the future of art and its relevance to society, the latter a product of industrial capitalism's alliance with the aesthetically immature. Kitsch, for Greenberg, is where bourgeois bad taste and the working class find their fated commonality. It is equivalent to society's "dead load."

* * * *

Louis Kahn wrote:

I don't believe in pipes in living rooms. I hate them. I believe they should be in their place like children. I want to remain ignorant of how the mechanics really work. I'm impatient with the restrictions of mechanical and construction engineers and with details about how every little thing works. But its *place* I think I know. I want to express that which is worth expressing, that which has grown to be a distinct characteristic.[28]

Kahn's emphasis

Naturally, the architect cannot be expected to know everything on the technical side. The issue here revolves around the language that reiterates the traditional class distinction, in this case grounded in a good dose of paternalism. The *tektōn* for Khan, like a child, has to know it place.

* * * *

FIGURE 3.1.4 New Babylon, *Constant Niewenhuys, 1963 (ink on paper). Lithografieën in kleur: New Babylon, rechtsonder gesigneerd "Constant." Collection Het Nieuwe Instituut, ABAM1211+.*

In the 1960s, Constant Niewenhuys, inspired by the book *Homo Ludens* (1938) by Johan Huizinga, made drawings and models of cities and spaces in which man, liberated from manual labor, can dedicate himself fully to the development of creative ideas. The project was called New Babylon. Land was to be collectively owned and labor fully automated. People lived a nomadic lifestyle and focused on creative play. There was no need for art because its residents were to be creative in their daily life. In New Babylon, the bourgeois shackles of work, family life, and civic responsibility were be discarded. Individuals would wander from one leisure environment to another in search of new sensations. Beholden to no one, they would sleep, eat, recreate, and procreate where and when he wanted.[29] In Constant's own words:

> New Babylon offers only minimal conditions for a behaviour that should remain as free as possible. Every limitation of movement, of the creation of mood and atmosphere should be inhibited. Everything should remain possible, everything should be able to happen. The environment is created by the activities of life not the other way around.[30]

It is a bizarre—if not fearsome—prospect, something that only a hedonistic misogynist would like. Someone still has to collect the garbage. Maybe

Constant should have read William Golding's *Lord of the Flies* (1954). The issue here, however, is not the masculine fantasy of libidinal release, but the more prosaic question of the structures that Niewenhuys drew to represent his city: an ad hoc network of rods, cables, and platforms that grow out of the hefty poles that rise from the ground. Though everything is presumably made by automated assembly, it is not clear who makes and delivers the steel, the rope, or the winches. Who translates the "activities of life" into the actual structure? There is no *tektōn* in the strict sense and yet if we assume that some form of fabrication is necessary, there will be a class of people dedicated to the expertise of construction who will be skilled at representing the playfulness with their limited kit of parts. It is unlikely that everyone in this city can procure, lift, and fasten heavy beams and cables in a state of almost absolute freedom. Though appearing radical, New Babylon preserves, if not actually utopianizes, the old Albertian–aristocratic separation of creativity from fabrication. New Babylon is not radical at all except as the subliminal thesis of European philosophy.

****

At the recent exhibition *Space, Time, Existence* in Venice, architects from the US and Europe all showed buildings that were finished objects populated by a few well-dressed scale figures. Nothing was shown under construction. It is as if buildings just "appear." Western architects simply ignore the act of construction in their representational strategies, or only represent it if it involves some sort of "innovation."

Those few projects that showed buildings under construction were all sited in Africa, Southeast Asia, or China, and were often associated with ethnic production. An example was the insightful submission by Huanzhong University of Science and Technology which documents the building of a house by the Lahu people.[31] Even though the village world in parts of China is still considerably more robust than in the urbanized north, the absence anywhere in the exhibition of the relationship of architecture to the construction—apart from its "ethnic" variant—was remarkable. Yet another trace of the lingering curse of Socrates.

****

Still today, though much maligned, ignored, and disrespected, the *faber*/contractor/builder is not just "beyond" that which is signified by architecture (without scare quotes), but a "beyond" that can be signified by its absence.

Books about architecture are NA: Architecture [N: Fine Arts].

Books on construction are TH [T: Technology].

Every time I check out a book, I am enacting the Albertian *non.*

Every time I check out a book, I am enacting the Socratic distinction between the thinker and the *banausos*.

The guilt of never having renounced Socratic elitism haunts architecture (without scare quotes) to this day. The guilt extends to the institution of philosophy that placed Socrates on an exalted pedestal. Just imagine, if Socrates had valued the workman. The discipline of architecture and indeed of Western civilization might well have had a different cast.

****

The *banausos* is the blind spot in the theory of *oikos*, and yet it is the nerve bundle that transmits the image of the architect to the world.

****

Jacques Lacan wrote: "The more the signifier signifies nothing, the more indestructible it is . . . there must have been something there that had not materialized, at a certain moment, in the field of the signifier, that had been *verworfen* [thrown away], thereby making the object of a *Verwerfung* [rejection] reappear in the real."[32]

If we read against the grain of modern subjectology and its congratulatory elevation of mind over body, life over death, art over matter, play over work, and creativity over dullness, we gradually thicken the semiotic registers that define the complex disguises of the "not" in its old aristocratizing haunts.

What is at play is not just a categorical distinctions in the service of the elite, but a fated—and in some ways tragic—connection inscribed into disciplinary self-legitimation.

****

Zaha Hadid on worker deaths in Qatar:

> I have nothing to do with the workers. I think that's an issue the government—if there's a problem—should pick up. Hopefully, these things will be resolved . . . It's not my duty as an architect.[33]

****

In 1999, Greg Lynn wrote a book called *Animate Form*.[34] He explains that animation promises to move the discipline past "the ethics of statics" (9), comparing it to the advancement of calculus over standard mathematics. Form, he writes, "can be shaped by the collaboration between the envelope and the active context in which it is situated" (10), and even though he is talking here about the hull of a ship, he is providing us a good example of the post-Albertian worldview—of *mente animoque*. Lynn's argument that architecture is pervaded by an "ethics of statics" is convenient in the grand rhetorical play of Western metaphysics that has to continually demonstrate its antipathy to the conventions of *tektōn*.

But I detect in some of his project a brilliant twist. He writes that "through experimentation with non-architectural regimes, architects may discover how

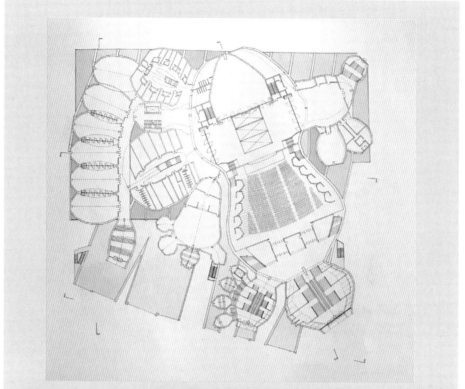

FIGURE 3.1.5 *Project for the Cardiff Bay Opera House competition, Greg Lyynn, 1996. © Greg Lynn.*

to engage time and motion in design" (18). By the phrase "non-architectural regimes," he means the computer and its animational capacity. Though it is the proverbial "instrument," Lynn writes that we should, in fact, see the computer "as a pet," since like a pet the "computer has already been domesticated and pedigreed, yet it does not behave with human intelligence" (19–20).

As an exemplar of how this gets translated into design, he shows a variety of projects including his entry for the Cardiff Bay Opera House competition (1996). Though the forms derive from ovals—an oblique reference to Borromini—the building looks like a large bug that has been dissected and its inner organs splayed out. The interior, however, was designed as pragmatically as possible with straight walls and mostly 90-degree angles. It is the locus of the standard occupationality of the builder.

The issue is not the outer form of the building, which steals the show, but this constructed dualism of inside and outside. Unlike Niewenhuys's project that celebrates creativity's self-entitling narcissism—Albertian monoculture at its extreme—this project sets up a contestation. If the "non-architecture"—

the architecture of the computer, the instrument associated with a newly emerging discipline—helped design the outside, then the inside is resolutely architecture—i.e., architecture without scare quotes—made, it seems, by a local contractor who wanted to get the job done as quickly as possible. It is the locus of the non-discipline.

It is in the tension between inside and outside that the building rises to the level of "architecture" leaving the investigator in a vertiginous space. Where to find its stabilizing narrative? The interior is the site of *tektōn*, the site where the building arts "do their thing" as they have since time immemorial (like perhaps the trusses in a vault), leaving the outside as the "non-architecture"-architecture, as Lynn seems to distantly imply (not in words but deeds). What makes this project thus succeed is that it exposes, tolerates, accepts, or even relies on the tension between *archē* and *tektōn*. Though the latter is in its traditional, subservient mode, hidden within the expressive powers of the external form, it is not simply "structure," but given the place of honor in determining program. The interior, the non-architecture that answers to the "non-architectural regimes" of the exterior gives the building its core structurality. The curse of Socrates is not removed from the equation, but rather inscribed in the body of the building as a play of signifiers. *Archē* and *tektōn* are mutually determinate in their proximate irreconcilability.

CHAPTER TWO

Occupationality

The carpenter's door is always unhinged.[1] *(Arab proverb)*

❊ ❊ ❊ ❊

Alberti's casting of the *faber* as an *instrumentum* was more than a reactionary protest against the upward mobility of the contractor. Alberti was implying that being at home in the discipline of architecture—ontologically—was distinct from an occupation. Architecture is a *non*-occupation *within the orbit of occupation*. What do I mean by that?

❊ ❊ ❊

In the building industries, occupationality (if I may use that awkward word) as the core to identity and subject position is hardly ever addressed by theorists and philosophers, and this despite the tons of ink spent on the issues of labor, work, and profession in the last one hundred and fifty years.[2]

The issue of occupationality does not have deep resonances in academe because it is assumed to be adequately defined by words like "skill" or, worse yet, "apprenticeship." The US Bureau of Labor and Statistics simply notes this about carpenters on its website:

Carpenters typically learn on the job and through apprenticeships.[3]

But in the building trades, apprenticeship is only a small part of the story.

❊ ❊ ❊ ❊

Alberti, though well aware of the importance of skill, made no effort to theorize it. His mind was focused elsewhere. It was only once we enter the modern age that skill becomes the topic of discourse. Though the distinction between skilled and unskilled appeared in the nineteenth century in the wake of industrialization, the difference hinged mostly on wage earnings and on workers learning how to use and manipulate labor-saving machinery, tasks that were "skilled" largely in their requirement for precise, often

FIGURE 3.2.1 *Carpenter's tools used by William Martin Knudsen in the building of the Minnesota State Capitol, St. Paul, c. 1900. © Minnesota Historical Society.*

repetitive movements.[4] The distinction does not match well in the building trades, where skill often means something different. A skilled carpenter, one author explained in 1878, should be a "thorough workman with his hands and a trained, educated mechanic with his head," the latter because of his need to thoroughly understand the weights and calculations of beams, and yet the carpenter in adding this all up "requires cunning, craft, skill and dexterity."[5] In an article from 1917 in *The Carpenter*, we read:

> Avoid all unnecessary conversation during working hours, except on subjects in connection with the work. Chewing tobacco is not objectionable, as it keeps the jaws active and the lips silent while the brain and hands are busy. Smoking out of doors helps, but a great deal depends upon rules and regulations; some mechanics can work and smoke, some can't. A little good judgment and common sense will guide any of us in this matter.[6]

In the same article:

> To be deliberate and accurate in the execution of all work, be it ever so simple, to be economical in laying sheathing, roofing, flooring and such like, using up all short pieces and overlengths when possible, and working steadily and rapidly. The present systems of working demand more rapid movement on the part of mechanics, especially carpenters and joiners, but it is a mistake to sacrifice quality of workmanship to haste, and it is only by maintaining a high standard of skill that a good fair rate of wages can be asked for, deserved and earned. In wet or damp weather, to keep bright all steel tools, which must be kept free from rust so as to continue of use, by rubbing them with grease or oil to prevent corrosion.[7]

* * *

In all of this, skill is more than just an individual attribute, nor can it be boiled down to a question of expertise.[8] It is a way that understands the world by bringing together a complex set of mostly invisible histories, associations, genealogies, obligations, and communalities directly into the conversation about getting things done. It even extends beyond the building site as it engages kin relations, friendships, and debts of various kinds, many of which are not monetary but paid in labor—as anyone knows who has gone through even a kitchen remodeling. The *tektōn* also always has a critical eye looking over its shoulder that it embraces as part of its ideology of delivery. In *Running a Successful Construction Company* (2002), we read:

> For the most part, successful builders—at least at the level of the small-to medium-volume companies that dominate our industry—have placed concrete and framed walls. They have hung and cased door, and flashed windows. Because they have put in years on the job site themselves, they can quickly recognize the moves of a skilled carpenter or of an uncertain one. They can hire and fire tradespeople effectively. They can reject work likely to fail and convincingly promote good craftsmanship.[9]

* * *

These numerous layers of histories and epistemologies—some overt, some covert—were key to the *tektōn*'s longevity and purpose since ancient times. In fact, if a *faber* from the period of the Roman Empire were to be put on a building site of a house today it would not take him too long to feel at home. The noises, comradery, the coming and going of suppliers and overseers, and even many of the tools would be familiar to his understanding of the world.

This powerful sense of collective came to resonate in Christian theology in the figure of the carpenter. After all, Joseph, the father of Jesus, was a carpenter who led the way as an exemplar of diligence and moral life.[10] According to Charles William Pearson, an Anglican missionary to Africa at the turn of the century, from his book on *Jesus: The Carpenter Prophet*:

> The carpenter is one of the earliest and most essential figures of civilized society. His occupation is honorable and useful. By his agency the dark cave in which man crouched like a beast is transformed into the house in which the moral virtues may develop and the home be created.[11]

We hear something of that position in the purposefully provocative words of Pierre Bélanger, a landscape architect and urban planner (2020):

Architecture, without Architects. Builders, contractors, constructors, craftworkers, artisans, are much more trustworthy.[12]

* * * *

Despite our retro-modernist desire to value "craft" and the "hand" in the building trades, the complex metaphysics of occupationality is not focused on the particulars of a trade; it is always a form of *inter*-occupationality. Building even a small house involves an astonishing interblending and intermingling of people: surveyors, foundation experts, masons, electricians, plumbers, bricklayers, carpenters, fine-work carpentry, concrete finishers, nailers, diggers, electricians, painters and paperhangers, plasterers, laborers, tile setters, pipe fitters, drywall installers, insulation installers, flooring specialists, carpet installers, sheet-metal workers, structural and reinforcing ironworkers, roofers, glaziers, acoustic tile installers, telephone installers, cabinet makers, kitchen installers, millwork carpenters, duct installers, marble and granite setters, temperature control installers, concrete curb and sidewalk installers, blacktop installers, landscapers, and rock blasters, not to mention truck drivers and deliverers, etc. Then, of course, there are the people who work in the contractor's office, and the city inspector's office.[13]

Plutarch's description of the building of the Parthenon in Athens is prescient:

> The materials were stone, brass, ivory, gold, ebony, cypresswood; and the arts or trades that wrought and fashioned them were smiths and carpenters, moulders, founders, and braziers, stone-cutters, dyers, goldsmiths, ivory-workers, painters, embroiderers, turners; those again that conveyed them to the town for use, merchants and mariners and ship-masters by sea, and by land, cartwrights, cattle-breeders, waggoners, rope-makers, flax-workers, shoe makers and leather-dressers, road-makers, miners. And every trade in the same nature, as a captain in any army has his particular company of soldiers under him, had its own hired company of journeymen and laborers belonging to it banded together as in array, *to be as it were the instrument and the body for the performance of the service.*[14]

my emphasis

* * * *

Unlike in the world of industrial labor, where laborers exchange work for wages, the making of a building requires a network of trades of different types and contractual arrangements which tend to be more informal than formal. In many cases even today such arrangements are oral. While the tendency in recent decades has been to clean this up and bring everything into the orbit of written contracts, one of the ironies in construction law is that even a contract containing a "no oral modification" provision can be orally modified in some circumstances.[15]

* * * *

Labor in the building trades operates in an environment that is known for demanding bosses, thin margins of profit, unreliable deliveries, difficult weather conditions and on and on, as would be true just as much during the Roman Empire as today. Its instinct, however, is gravitational and self-regulatory. The Associated General Contractors of America, founded in 1918, states that it is "an organization of qualified construction contractors and industry related companies dedicated to skill, integrity and responsibility."[16]

We can perhaps think in terms of Occupation-Entangled Ontology if by the word occupation we do not limit the discussion to *an* occupation, but see a broad network of relations, one that does not trim the messy edges into something that can be neatly called "labor."

* * * *

The Enlightenment theorizations missed this completely!

The *Encyclopédie, ou dictionnaire raisonné des sciences, des arts et des métiers* (Encyclopedia, or a Systematic Dictionary of the Sciences, Arts, and Crafts, 1751–72) edited by Denis Diderot and, until 1759, co-edited by Jean le Rond d'Alembert, is duly famous for celebrating manual labor by giving detailed, well-researched descriptions of the work, the workplace, and the tools. Though the authors of the *Encyclopédie* were eager to champion labor as dignified, there can be no doubt that by cleaning up the workshops and portraying the workers as serene in their activity, they were also expressing the commodification of labor as a form of social morality. Furthermore,

FIGURE 3.2.2 *Masonry: Illustration. Plate 276. Masonry.* Encyclopédie. *Edited by Denis Diderot (1713–84) and Jean Le Rond d'Alembert (1717–83).* © *Lannas / Alamy Stock Photo.*

though we see dozens of intricate descriptions of workshops, there is no description of a building site. Under "Masonry" we see men working on a stone building, operating asynchronously. Elsewhere, there is also a drawing of workers making a slate roof and another where workers are setting out the tiles for a floor. The discussion of carpentry shows men preparing beams, but here, too, it is impossible to get any sense of the powerful integrative realities that are at play in making a building. Johann Beckmann's *Anleitung zur Technologie* (1777) is another example.[17] Though he describes the almost one hundred types of skills necessary for specific tasks, he does not see skill very broadly as he is focused on the linear processes that transform a natural item [*rohe Matierialien*] into a man-made product—from extraction to seller [*Kaufmann*]. This does not map well into the building trades, which as a result do not figure highly in the list, apart from his descriptions of the manufacturing of bricks, lime, and glass. So, just as with the *Encyclopédie*, despite the incredible insights that are provided into workshop techniques, we learn absolutely nothing about the making of a house.

****

A much more insightful image was made by the mid-seventeenth-century Bolognese artist Francesco Curti. In his portrayal of a construction site, we see masons ("muratori"), a stonecutter ("tagliapietre"), and a laborer ("manouale") among others. The architect, holding a sheet identifying him, is flanked by the surveyor with his measuring rod. Behind them is the carpenter ("falegname") and in front is the painter ("imbianchitore").

****

By the nineteenth century, the word "trades" had become common, as in *The Book of Trades* (1807) or Edward Hazen's *Panorama of the Professions*

FIGURE 3.2.3 Trades Practiced in Bologna, *Etching (*Virtù et arti essercitate in Bologna, *Plate 6), Francisco Curti, Italy,* c. 1603–70. © *Los Angeles County Museum of Art (LACMA), M.69.7.1g / public domain.www.lacma.org.*

and Trades (1838), both printed at Philadelphia. But, somewhat astonishingly, the concept of "building trades" as a unified disciplinary field separate unto itself emerged only at the end of the nineteenth century, as in *Home Study for the Building Trades* (1898).[18] In the nineteenth century, groups—though they worked together on construction sites—were separated by task and ethnicity. German speakers formed one trade group, English speakers another, carpenters another, bricklayers yet another and so on. But by the end of the century building trades councils began to be set up in many larger cities to help sort out the rapidly changing nature of construction as larger buildings shifted from masonry to steel. Basic questions involved who should install accessories. Carpenters who had always done so? Sheet-metal workers who manufactured them? Iron workers? and so on.[19] The building trades councils sought to enforce jurisdictional rules by calling sympathy strikes, to offset the contractors who continually sought to play one group against the other. This new concept was also clearly tied to the growth of labor unions. In 1897, a group of building trades unions from the Midwest met in St. Louis to form a national organization. The new group was known as the National Building Trades Council.[20]

Unlike the capitalist-oriented understanding of skill as relating to the solitary individual, turn-of-the-century trade unions vigorously promoted skilled labor as a communitarian project. One mission statement listed its goals as

1: to discourage piece work,
2: to encourage an apprentice system and a higher standard of skill.
3: to cultivate feelings of friendship among the men of the craft.[21]

* * *

The "building trades" was the predecessor of what we today call the "construction industry," a concept that in turn only became common by the 1940s and that reflected the emerging corporatization of the building trade economy.

* * *

Occasionally, the voice of occupationality comes with a sharper tongue, as here by a representative of the New York carpenters' union in 1915:

A man who never shouldered a beam or laid it from foundation wall to foundation wall, a man who never wielded a pick or used a shovel, a man who never scooped coal into a white hot retort and had the flames shoot spitefully back at him, drying the perspiration ere it found vent through half-baked pores, a man who never wielded an ax, nor adz, nor maul, a man who never laid a brick or riveted a beam to a girder, a man who never mixed a pail of mortar or calloused his hand pushing a wheelbarrow—find such a man and you will see him rub his soft palms together and discourse learnedly upon the needs, and rights, and wrongs, and liberties, and restrictions that should be granted, withheld or imposed upon labor.[22]

* * *

Though "occupationality" is a code word for the *tektōn*'s collective consciousness, an attempt to understand it, to describe its merits, its economic realities, and even philosophical and metaphysical implications is difficult. It is yet another example of the lingering legacy of the silent ~~non~~.[23]

Charles Christiansen, in the 1990s, was the first scholar to make an explicit connection between an occupation and an individual's personal and social identity. He suggested that "participation in an occupation is the primary means to communicate one's identity, concluding that when we build our identities through occupations, we provide ourselves with the contexts necessary for creating meaningful lives, and life meaning helps us to be well."[24] Much of the conversation, however, still revolves around the issue of how to make sure that workers develop healthy awareness of themselves. It is the point of view of the surveillance mechanisms of an "enlightened" capitalist system. A recent article states that "establishing a strong, self-chosen, positive, and flexible occupational identity appears to be an important contributor to occupational success, social adaptation, and psychological well-being."[25]

* * * *

Though Richard Sennett does occasionally mention the word "vocation" in his book, *The Craftsman* (2008), the word "occupation" is not brought up once.

* * * *

FIGURE 3.2.4 *Electrician at work, c. 2018. Ken Altmann Electric.*

The relative absence of sociological studies on this issue—even among Marxists who tend to focus on the abstractions of labor than the socio-ontology of occupationality—means that when we turn our gaze to history, we can only discuss occupations when they are already "occupied" by specific craftspeople, carpenters, bricklayers, plasterers and the like, with history focusing in on one or the other.[26]

Because the task of modern philosophy has been so focused on the proverbial individual, it falls flat in situations where the subject cannot be separate from its entangled relationship with a range of people, from family to colleagues, bosses and mentors; with a wide range of economic systems, from the industrial to the informal; with global fluctuations in the price of materials, and to changing weather conditions; and even with tools and work clothes.

> When you're on a trim job, dress like a trim carpenter, clean and neat.
>
> 1991[27]

> Twice last year (1957) the mighty U.S. Treasury Department won court rulings, in cases against a painter and a carpenter, that work clothes are not deductible.[28]

* * * *

For a poignant short story about a plasterer who brings his college-bound son with him to help out on a job, read Steven Allaback, "The Plasterer," *Four Quarters*, XXIII/2 (Winter 1974) pp. 3–12.

* * * *

The *tektōn* is very much aware of its sublimation into the system of occupation and delivery that is set out for it. In the Preface to *The Illustrated Carpenter and Builder* from 1880, we read that a genuine mechanic

> is a thinking, planning, ingenious man, who has mastered not only the use of tools, but the laws which govern the forces he commands. He is a student of the subtle laws of Nature, and learns from her how to add beauty and utility.[29]

In 1986, a carpenter wrote:

> It's a special world, a peculiar world–one whose rhythms and cycles have rarely been recorded.[30]

In its embrace of the Social–as the embodiment of responsibility–the *tekton* counteracts and suppresses the mechanisms of its exploitation and oppression at the heart of architecture's disciplinary project. It is what gives the *tekton* its gravitas and purpose. Occasionally, but rarely, we hear something like the following, from a union carpenter in Massachusetts, Walter Stevenson (1930):

FIGURE 3.2.5 *Barn Raising. Construction workers, Massachusetts, late 19th century. Courtesy of Historic New England.*

As I pass up and down [my city's] streets I see in many places the work my own hands have wrought on her buildings and I feel that in a sense I am a part of our city. My strength and whatever skill I possess are woven into her material fabric that will remain when I am gone, for Labor is Life taking a permanent form.[31]

* * *

In 1986, Mark Erlich, an advocate for the carpenters' union in Massachusetts, wrote:

Craft pride has always been at the core, expressed in a variety of ways—in the turn-of-the-century carpenters with white coveralls over their white shirts and ties, in the ample toolboxes overflowing with finely honed saws and chisels and esoteric tools that are included "just in case," and in the ultimate compliment of being considered a "good mechanic" by one's peers.[32]

An article written in 1916 by the editors of *American Carpentry and Builder* admonishes:

A builder can only be impressed with the importance of proper wood finishing when he is also impressed with the importance of giving his customers a good job in every respect, such a job as will satisfy his customer, not only at first but permanently, and give the builder a reputation which will bring more orders from the same customer and from others upon the bases of quality.[33]

In the first volume of *The Builder* from 1842, there is a sermon by an unnamed preacher that articulates the classic conventions of fraternity among the crafts, a fraternity that, just as it sees itself as part of a larger mission, also accepts its status as instrument:

Pardon us good brothers of our building fraternity, and you who do us the favor to lend an ear to our counsellings . . . Should your approving suffrages incite a continuance of our vocation, it will be our ambition to discuss the relative duties of the stations you respectively fill—master, apprentice, or workman; father, brother, son or husband; neighbor or friend; and to do as we have done, namely to improve each and all, and is doing so, promote, in some degree, the cause of human happiness.[34]

* * * *

Jim Locke, a contractor working in western Massachusetts, wrote in *The Well-Built House* (1988):

You want to build a house, and I want to build a certain *kind* of house. Not necessarily a colonial or a contemporary, but a solid and enduring building that fits you and looks good . . . When you undertake to cover up a piece of the planet with something you build, you are duty bound to build it well.[35]

* * *

Architectural history rarely records instances where the laborers were anything other than just the usual, invisible *instrumenta* of the architect.[36] An exception was the Soviet Pavilion at the Paris World's Fair of 1925, designed by Konstantin Stepanovich Melnikov.[37] It was composed of two glazed triangular volumes bisected diagonally by a wide staircase. Above the stairway, a series of bold diagonals crossed the staircase like swords above the processional. From along the stairway on the outside one could look through the glass and view all the exhibitions inside the building. It was a remarkable building and rightfully situated within the context of Soviet experimental architecture. The Soviet government told the Front Populaire in Paris that they wanted to help unemployment in France by engaging French carpenters. While constantly striking on other pavilions in 1937, the workers spared the Soviets in gratitude.[38]

FIGURE 3.2.6 *Soviet Pavilion in Paris under construction, March 1925.* © *Melnikov House archive, State Museum of Konstantin and Viktor Melnikov. Inv. 581/25, neg. 2.*

* * * *

LiUNA, a Construction Union for Craft Laborers in Michigan, consisting of seven local unions with over 13,000 members writes: "We are united by contracts that guarantee fair wages, high quality training, safe jobsites, and good benefits."[39] The New York State Laborers' Union mantra is "Building Communities . . . Building New York State."[40]

In 2006, the British construction workers' union UCATT (now merged into UNITE) commissioned a statue near the Tower of London that is called The Building Worker. Each year local construction workers rally there to commemorate those who have died on the job. The inscription reads: "For the thousands of building workers who have lost their lives at work, we commemorate you. For the thousands of building workers who are today building and rebuilding towns and cities across the United Kingdom we celebrate you."[41]

* * * *

One should not overlook the power of the protectiveness in the building trades that has traditionally excluded minorities and women. A census of people in the building trades from 1895 begins:

FIGURE 3.2.7 The Building Worker, *Alan Wilson, London, 2006. Photograph by Glyn Baker.*

> Of those engaged in building—architects, builders, masons, bricklayers, carpenters and the rest—the census counts 129,432 ... There are practically no women employed in these trades.[42]

The situation is only marginally better today. The first national trades women's conference was held only in 1983 in San Francisco with 500 attending. In 1997, the International Brotherhood of Electrical Workers became the first building trade union to sponsor a woman's conference. Some other unions followed suit.

> What it Means to be a Female in the Construction Industry? ... The focus of Women in Construction (WIC) Week, which began March 1, is to highlight the hardworking women of the construction industry—a typically male-dominated field.[43]

One of the few accounts of a woman in the construction industry is Susan Eisenberg's *We'll Call You If We Need You: Experiences of Women Working in Construction* (Ithaca, NY: Cornell University Press, 1998).[44] One should also read *Hammering Through, Resisting Racial Prejudice, Systemic Biases, and Discriminating Setbacks in the Construction Industry in the USA* by Sylveste Augustus (2020). An excerpt:

FIGURE 3.2.8 *Contruction Workers in Duala, Cameroon. Photograph by Minette Lontsie.*

In addition to the personal discomfort, I had to deal very quickly with the reality of working at exceptionally high platforms. This came into full effect when the seasoned, middle-aged carpenters with whom I was assigned requested that I place one 40 lbs. scaffolds buck at the edge of the platform, otherwise referred to as the deck. Because the area was around the perimeter of the atrium, the surface below that edge was nearly a hundred feet. This task involved lifting and walking with the heavy metal frame and precisely placing the two ends on top of the lower frame. It went from four stories above to three stories below ground, and any error could send the scaffold close to a hundred feet below. For the very first time in my life I felt like a gymnast walking a tightrope. It seemed like I took about ten minutes to walk approximately 10 feet. The last thing I thought about was turning around; I had to get it done. So, after a staggering, long walk, I placed the heavy scaffold buck into the interlocking portions of the scaffolding that extended from the several layers of scaffolding. That was obviously an initiation task which I rightly performed, although at a snail pace.[45]

***

In 2018, Brittany Pochick was the first female carpenter to represent New Jersey in a national skills competition. She explained in an interview:

The first time I ever went into a Home Depot, I loved the smell of wood, and I like working with my hands and building things. I guess I have a little engineering in me.[46]

"Zambian woman carpenter inspiring others to venture into fields dominated by men," reads a recent headline.[47]

Carpenter Maria Klemperer-Johnson is used to being the only woman on the construction site—but, thanks in part to her own work, that is beginning to change. She's leading a class of eight women in the construction of a tiny house in upstate New York, and hopes that the growing number of similar classes around the country will lead to greater gender equality in the construction sector.[48]

* * *

The issue of race in the construction industry is also an enduring one. An early discussion can be found in the article, "Negro Workers in Skilled Crafts and Construction," written by Charles S. Johnson and published in *Opportunity: Journal of Negro Life* in 1933. *Opportunity* was a black-owned journal run out of New York between 1923 and 1935 and that was founded by Johnson. He was an American sociologist who later, in 1946, became the first black president of the historically black Fisk University. In

FIGURE 3.2.9 *Portrait of an African American bricklayer (between 1860 and 1870). Platt, A. C. (Alvord C.), 1828–84, photographer. Library of Congress, Prints and Photographs Division, The William Gladstone Collection of African American Photographs [reproduction number, LC-DIG-ppmsca-11288].*

this and other articles, he paints a distressing picture of decline. He points out that, in the building trades among African Americans, "there were bricklayers, plasterers, whitewashers, painters, and glazers, caulkers, and blacksmiths." This was "a result of both custom and special training under the institution of slavery." But things changed in the 1880s, so he notes. Foreign immigration in the North tightened the labor market; African Americans sought out industrial work; labor unions excluded African Americans and thus did not give them access to higher-wage jobs. He also pointed out that in southern cities there were deliberate efforts "to replace Negro carpenters, and bricklayers as well, with white workers and contractors . . . In Jackson, Mississippi . . . Negro carpenters and plasterers are being kept out of much of the work they once virtually controlled."[49]

> In many localities there are license requirements for plumbers and electricians. Often Negroes are not permitted to qualify for such work and are automatically eliminated from employment. Since these regulations are in accordance with municipal laws and administration, there is nothing the Public Works Administration can do to change them.[50]

* * * *

> One of the fastest nailers I worked with came from a sharecropper's family down in South Georgia right near the Florida line. Born before the civil rights movement, he never had a chance to go to school and learn to read and write. When he switched jobs, I used to take him to the new site because he couldn't read the street signs to know where to go. But, please, believe me, he could nail![51]

John Michael Vlach, in *The Afro-American Tradition in Decorative Arts* and *By the Work of Their Hands*, reveals how a field of different makers, builders, and craftspeople kept central tenets of "African culture" in their making practices in the United States. By studying formal resemblances between African-American and African communities, Vlach found cultural linkages maintained across the Black Atlantic.[52]

The Black Carpenter's Guide (2016) by Desmond Collins was written with the black, African-American, carpenter in mind. There are many books out there about construction but none that talk about the issues that confront the black carpenters.

* * * *

At issue here is not how to write a cultural biography of labor on the building site, but of the multiple absences of various types within architecture's disciplinary formations.

Why did skill only become conceptualized in the 1890s, when it was essential to the building trades for thousands of years? Why has its deep-seated sense of communality not been incorporated into philosophical thinking? Why has its subtext of racial and gendered exclusions not been addressed in architectural theory until recently?

How do we address the displaced representationality of the non-represented?

Mabel Wilson broke new ground with *Negro Building: Black Americans in the World of Fairs and Museums* (Berkeley: University of California Press, 2012), as did Charles Davis II with *Building Character: The Racial Politics of Modern Architectural Style* (Pittsburgh: University of Pittsburgh, 2019).

* * * *

It is a rare instance where labor leaves its actual trace in architecture. So, when we see a pour line in a concrete wall (the place where one concrete pour ends and then after some time another then begins), we are seeing not a bad pour, but perhaps a lunch break.

The Bruder Klaus Chapel by Swiss architect Peter Zumthor (2007) is one of the few instances where the concrete pour lines were turned into an aesthetic. First, 112 tree trunks were erected as a tower, then layers of concrete were poured and rammed into the pour below it at around 50cm thick. When the concrete had set, the wooden frame was set on fire, leaving behind a hollowed blackened cavity and charred walls. The concrete that comprises the envelope of the Chapel was poured at a rate of 50cm per day for twenty-four days that were spread out over the course of nearly a year since it was mostly built by local farmers.[53]

* * * *

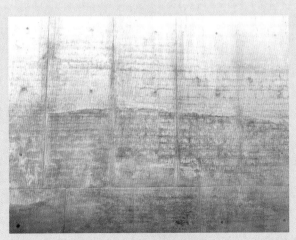

FIGURE 3.2.10 *A visible concrete pour line in a building in Berlin. Photograph by Mark Jarzombek.*

FIGURE 3.2.11 *The Bruder Klaus Chapel, Euskirchen, Germany, 2007. Peter Zumthor (Architect); Hermann-Josef and Trudel Scheidtweiler (Developers).*

FIGURE 3.2.12 *Detail of the Bruder Klaus Chapel, Euskirchen, Germany, 2008. Peter Zumthor (Architect); Hermann-Josef and Trudel Scheidtweiler (Developers).*

Pavillon Le Corbusier (also known as the Heidi Weber House) was began in 1964, a year before Le Corbusier died, and is famous for any number of reasons. But one feature is rarely commented on. The hexagonally capped bolts that fasten the steel flanges to each other are meticulously tightened so that an apex of the head of the vertical bolts (those facing into the facade) point upwards; those of the vertical parts (where the bolts are parallel to the facade) point outwards; those on horizontal parts point downwards. (The head of the bolt can be differentiated from the nut as it is slightly longer in dimension.) This might have been something Le Corbusier wanted, but there is no evidence of that. Instead, it is more than likely that builders took it themselves as a demonstration piece of their meticulousness. Here the *tektōn* shows the meaning of pride.

FIGURE 3.2.13 *Detail of Pavillon Le Corbusier (Heidi Weber House), Zurich, 1967. Photograph by Frederik Kaufmann.*

FIGURE 3.2.14 Beam Drop, *Chris Burden, Netherlands, 2009. Photograph by Funkyxian.*

* * * *

Chris Burden is known for his installation piece, *Beam Drop* (1985), for Art Park in New York. It was recreated at Inhotim, a foundation promoting contemporary art in Brazil in 2008 and again in the Netherlands in 2009. It consisted of seventy-one steel beams dropped into a pool of wet concrete from a crane, hovering some 40 meters above the site. The result was a random pattern of beams jutting out of the ground. Burden saw as his references the gesturalism of Abstract Expressionism, especially the paintings of Jackson Pollock. It is an impressive piece, bold not just in its production, but also in its realization.

Compare it with the building of the foundations for a new building in Boston, Massachusetts, where beams were driven into the muddy soil and unified through layers of concrete. Burden's project speaks directly to the art world. The latter speaks only to the world of "architecture." It is dutiful, not personological. It accepts its normative role as something invisible, both to the real world and to history, and in this it is the classic location of *tektōn*. The beams clustered vertically into the pit speak of friction, the force

FIGURE 3.2.15 *Construction site in Cambridge, Massachusetts, 2022. Contractor: John Moriarty & Associates. Photograph by Mark Jarzombek.*

necessary to fight against the weight that they will soon have to bear. They are not arbitrarily and elegantly dropped, but pounded into the soil, brutally yet carefully so that they remain vertical, to bond building and earth. They are mashed together for the single purpose of removing water from the soil so that the *archē* can rise effortlessly above it.

Beam Drop has translated the industrial into an aesthetic made familiar to us through Enlightenment theory of the liberated Self. It is the steely equivalent of a painting that might be called Nudes on a Beach. The foundation piece has no corresponding disciplinary location, theoretical valence, or even aesthetic position except in occupational imaginaries at the far corners of engineering.

CHAPTER THREE

Faber Ingenium

In 2016, a report called *Social Mobility and Construction: Building Routes to Opportunity* showed how, among UK industries, construction ranked near the top for social and economic mobility. While other industries, such as manufacturing, have shed skilled workers, the construction industry maintained a third of all employment in this occupation group. These skilled trades not only provided social status and solid earnings but also provided many with an opportunity and a platform for progression within their career, from the trades through to management and professional roles.[1]

The desire for upward mobility was and remains one of the key dynamics flowing through the world of occupationality, one that Alberti, of course, failed to even acknowledge and that even today is difficult to bring into theoretical and historical focus. The building trades were—and remain—notoriously open to the vicissitudes of change, and the work takes a cumulative toll on the body. Unlike goldsmiths and silversmiths who could work out of a shop, builders had no such luxury and inevitably had to live away from their family while on a building site. Furthermore, skill was itself a trap since a mason could not become a carpenter and vice versa. Nonetheless, as the centuries progressed, different types of opportunities began to present themselves to lead to or get recognition.

In fifteenth-century Italy, one of the important venues of mobility was Humanism, which took a form that Lionel March called "conspicuous erudition," in which patrons and scholars displayed their breadth of classical learning in their libraries and art commissions.[2] Understanding the requirements of conspicuous erudition was a must for upwardly mobile architects, and one way to develop that understanding was to first become a painter. After all, Alberti wrote that the activity of painting "contributes to the most honorable delights of the soul and to the dignified beauty of things."[3] Alberti was speaking as a member of the nobility, defending his own dalliance with painting. The view of the architect and would-be architect of that time would have been more complex. Knowing that painting had become valued by the elites, more so than architecture itself, helped them use it as a portal to get past the exclusionary, cultural space that separated the *faber*, physically and ontologically, from the world of the aristocrats. Already Serlio pointed out that Bramante, Raphael, and Peruzzi were painters before they became architects.

It was not just the making and delivering of a painting that was important along with the particular set of skills associated with perspective, it was also the interaction across class lines, an interaction that allowed the *faber* the opportunity to learn the manners necessary to explain and present their work. Painting was a code word for the processes by which a future *archē* could separate himself from the lowly occupationality of the *tektōn*. From that perspective, Humanism was more than just the attempt to reconstruct the ancient Roman intellectual sphere. Vasari, particularly sensitive to what it meant to be part of polite society, would give the Sienese painter Ambrogio high marks in the "conspicuous erudition" category:

> [H]e was not only intimate with men of learning and of taste, but he was also employed, to his great honor and advantage, in the government of his Republic. The ways of Ambrogio were in all respects worthy of praise, and rather those of a gentleman and a philosopher than of a craftsman; and what most demonstrates the wisdom of men, he had ever a mind disposed to be content with that which the world and time brought, wherefore he supported with a mind temperate and calm the good and the evil that came to him from fortune . . . every man should make himself no less beloved with his ways than with the excellence of his art.[4]

Peruzzi, though born of modest means, also possessed the proper demeanor of a man who could participate in cultured society:

> Baldassare Peruzzi, a painter and architect of Siena, of whom we can say with certainty that the modesty and goodness which were revealed in him were no mean offshoots of that supreme serenity for which the minds of all who are born in this world are ever sighing, and that the works which he left to us are most honorable fruits of that true excellence.[5]

* * * *

Francesco di Giorgio Martini (1439–1502), the son of a poultry dealer, and who found himself in the studio of the noted painter Lorenzo di Pietro, would go on to write his *Trattato di architettura* at the court of Federico da Montefeltro in Urbino around 1480. Despite his ascent, his concern with the processes of building design and construction remained quite practical and so found resonance with practicing architects. Reproduced in hundreds of manuscript copies, his *Trattato* was a standard reference manual in late-fifteenth-century Italy.[6] The great strength of the *Trattato* lay in its drawings. On nearly every folio, lucid images are paired with the text, illustrating each of the tract's core concepts. As Elizabeth M. Merrill points out, the unschooled architect could gain as much from the figures as he could from the commentary.[7]

****

To help smooth over the rough corners, some builders began to change their name. Filarete's real name, for example, was Antonio di Pietro Averlino. To win over the Duke of Milan, he must clearly have been a man with charisma and intelligence. Somewhere along the way, he adopted the fancy-sounding moniker "Filarete," which is Greek for "lover of virtue," even though he could speak neither Greek nor Latin.[8]

It was for that very same reason that Maria Ludwig Michael Mies, the son of a stonemason, and with a last name that means "lousy," changed his name, at the urging of one of his well-healed clients, to the more aristocratic sounding Mies van der Rohe so that he could more easily associate with members of the wealthy class.

****

For the builder, access to the culture of Humanism came also in the form of copying Roman ruins which had a distinct advantage for Italian contractors. Most buildings in Italy at that time were brick or stone rubble. Roofs were of wood and where there were vaults, they were of brick, which is even true for Palladio's buildings, meaning that though stonemasons were at the traditional upper register of social mobility, masons needed little in the way of complex drawings for vaultings. The only advanced stonework that was needed came in the form of lintels, window frames, doors, and columns—all of which could be fashioned in a shop—meaning that masons needed good detail drawings, and since Roman-era lintels and door moldings were all lying around in the weeds, there was little trouble in providing these to enterprising contractors. One of the first to tap into this in a more systematic way was Sebastiano Serlio (1475–c. 1554). He began his career in the workshop of Baldassare Peruzzi and was eventually invited to France to advise on the construction and decoration of the Château of Fontainebleau where a team of Italian designers and craftsmen were assembled. His treatise *Tutte l'opere d'architettura et prospetiva* (All the Works of Architecture and Perspective), published in stages beginning in 1537, was written in Italian and featured easy-to-understand drawings that catered explicitly to the needs of builders and craftsmen.[9] Though he did not provide measurements with his details, they were drawn in a straightforward and simple manner. Jacobo Strada, a goldsmith and courtier, living at the time in Austria as a court-sponsored antiquarian, published Sebastiano Serlio's seventh book of architecture in 1577 in Frankfurt-am-Main and sent a copy to the king, writing:

> In short, Serlio with this text of his makes it possible for an average architect (who nevertheless has the benefit of excellent judgement) to construct buildings worthy of admiration, since he cuts a straight path to the abstruse secrets of architecture which until now have lain hidden in the books of Vitruvius, obscured and almost unintelligible.[10]

Palladio (1508–80) was another upwardly mobile master builder. His real name was Andrea di Pietro della Gondola and his father was a miller. At the age of 13 he began as an apprentice for a stonecutter, but only at the age of 30, when the humanist poet and scholar Gian Giorgio Trissino commissioned him to rebuild his residence, did Andrea begin to see a different world. It was Trissino, a scholar of ancient Roman architecture, who introduced his mason to the writings of Vitruvius and who even supported and accompanied Palladio on his trips to Rome to see and study the classical monuments firsthand. It is quite possible that Trissino was even Palladio's ghostwriter when it came to the parts that mention Vitruvius. And it was Trissino who gave to his talented mason a new fancy-sounding name that means "Wise One" with its allusion to the Greek goddess of wisdom Pallas Athene and to a character in one of Trissino's plays. Unlike Alberti, Palladio, in his treatise *I quattro libri dell'architettura* (1570), made it clear that he was speaking as a *faber*:

> I shall avoid the superfluidity of words, and simply give those directions that seem to me most necessary, and shall make use of those terms which at this time are most commonly in use among artificers.[11]

And he was as good as his word: Book One opens with Palladio wandering an imaginary building site, and like any good contractor he explains to the patron some of the basics, making comments like the following:

> Those therefore who are about to build, ought to be informed from men thoroughly acquainted with the nature of timber, that they may know which is fit for such and such uses, and which not.

> There are three sorts of sand commonly found; pit, river and sea sand. The best of these is pit sand, and is either black, white, red, or ash-colored.

> The metals commonly employed in buildings are iron, lead, and copper.[12]

His tone is easy, with him addressing the patron very directly:

> Therefore, having made choice of the most skillful artists that can be had, by whose advice the work may more judiciously be carried on, you must then provide a sufficient quantity of timber, stone, sand, lime, and metals.

Compare that with the tone of Alberti which is oriented to some abstract disciplinary authority:

> Having procured the materials mentioned above—that is, timber, stone, lime, and sand—it remains now to deal with the method and manner of construction.[13]

※ ※ ※ ※

And since the language of Humanism, architecturally speaking, grounded itself, apart from the proportioning of plans, in the syntax of details, one is not surprised that if one does not count Palladio's representations of his own buildings, his treatises have about fifty elegantly rendered drawings dedicated to details compared to forty-five to elevations and thirty to plans. His details were also fully dimensioned.

* * * *

The distinction between the writings of Alberti and those of most of the subsequent builder/architects like Filarete, Serlio, Palladio and others is often missed, as none of the latter group are really writing treatises in the classical sense. Palladio explains that one of the reasons for writing was so that a builder

> may learn, by little and little, to lay aside the strange abuses, the barbarous inventions, the superfluous expense and (what is of greater consequence) avoid the various and continual ruins that have been seen in many fabricks.[14]

Serlio also makes it clear that the reason for writing was not to enhance the legitimacy of the discipline as a whole, but to improve the level of the workmanship. He hoped that workmen who read the book will no longer be counted

> amongst the number of stone-spoilers, who bear the name of workmen and scarce know how to make an answer what a point, line, plane, or body is, and much less can tell what harmony or what correspondences mean, but following after their own mind or other blind conductors that have led to work without rule or reason, they make bad work, which is the cause of much uncut or uneven workmanship which is found in many places.[15]

Once properly educated, they will, so he adds, "laugh and smile at their own former simplicities."

This is the sentiment of the dutiful master builder on the disciplinary stage, concerned less with the finer points of what can be gleaned from codices than with the finer points of occupational success.

* * * *

Not every builder in fifteenth-century Italy had the ambition, talent, or opportunity to become a painter. Not every builder could play the personality games of Humanism and not every builder had the good fortune of having a client who could coach them of proper behavior or fund extravagant works. That does not mean, however, that the *tektōn* was without its own disciplinary potential. In fact, momentum was on its side since the world of the *tektōn* had been shaped—*long before perspective*—by the art of geometry. But it was only with the rise of French economy and the construction of palaces and fortifications, where odd-shaped volumes were needed for staircases, vaults, firing holes and so forth, that stereometry became a fully fleshed-out discipline in the modern sense. Unlike the treatises of Palladio and Serlio where the contribution to geometry was quite minimal, the *Premier tome de l'architecture* of Philibert de l'Orme (1514–70), the son of a master mason who rose to become surveyor of the royal works under King Henri II (1547–59), included two chapters (Books III and IV) that were dedicated to stereometrically vaulted structures, rib vaults, and spiral staircases, all illustrated with beautiful drawings.[16] Like Palladio, de l'Orme shied away from authoring the type of elaborate treatises that some of his contemporizes produced:

> To be frank, if I wanted to explain everything in detail, I would need to undertake great work and excessive writing. And even if I wrote everything that I can think, there are many things in stonecutting practice that are not easy to explain, without showing with a finger how they must be done, either for tracing the stones, either for putting them in their proper place.[17]

* * * *

In England, as in Italy, there was little emphasis on vaults. Most of the roofs of even better buildings were made from wood. That was perhaps one of the reasons the English tended to gravitate more toward Palladio than to French models. Joseph Moxon's *Mechanick Exercises*, appearing as a series of pamphlets beginning in 1678, did not even treat advanced stonework; its subtitle was the "Arts of Smithing, Joinery, Carpentry, Turning, Bricklayery." Hans Blum's *Quinque Columnarum* (1550), which saw twenty-four editions, basically met the needs of craftsmen who had to adapt the new classical style to wood. Needless to say, neoclassicism in the United States was almost solely in the domain of the carpenters. The 1843 Old Whaling Church on Martha's Vineyard, which mimics an ancient temple front with six massive tapered, Doric columns, was built by skilled shipwrights during their winter layovers.

* * * *

To advance through the ranks, a talented *faber* could master the language of Humanist-oriented facades and details. Where applicable, he could also develop his stereometry skills. A more unrecognized zone of opportunity came from mathematics. Alberti had already claimed: "The Arts which are useful, and indeed absolutely necessary to the Architect, are Painting and Mathematics" (Book X). But in practical terms mathematics was not integrated into the building arts until well into the seventeenth and eighteenth centuries. In 1743, when Giovanni Poleni was requested to investigate the condition of the Vatican dome, he wrote, with some amazement: "Buonarroti non sapeva di Mathematica, e poi sempre seppe architettare la Cupola" (Michelangelo was unfamiliar with mathematics and could still build the dome).[18]

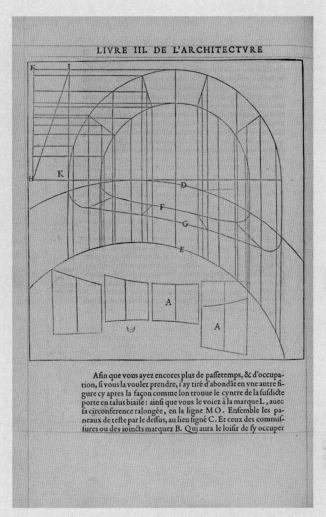

LIVRE III. DE L'ARCHITECTVRE

Afin que vous ayez encores plus de paffetemps, & d'occupation, fi vous la voulez prendre, i'ay tiré d'abondāt en vne autre figure cy apres la façon comme lon trouue le cyntre de la fufdicte
porte en talus biaife: ainfi que vous le voiez à la marqueL , auec
fa circonference ralongée, en la ligne M O. Enfemble les pa-
neaux de tefte par le deffus, au lieu figné C. Et ceux des commif-
fures ou des ioincts marquez B. Quj aura le loifir de fy occuper

FIGURE 3.3.1 *Skew arch opening in an inclined curved wall, Philibert de L'Orme,* Premier tome de l'architecture *(Paris, 1567) fol. 79v.*

****

Before the advent of mathematics, if problems came up, builders could rely on the help of angels. One of the earliest complete representations of the carpenter's life was the book *Iesu Christi Dei Domini, Salvatoris Nr̄i Infantia* (The Youth of Christ, *c.* 1600) that treats the life of Joseph, who was, of course, a carpenter, showing the young Jesus as an apprentice. The frontispiece shows a vast assemblage of tools including Maria's spinning

FIGURE 3.3.2 *Frontispiece*, Iesu Christi Dei Domini, Salvatoris Nr̄i Infantia, c. *1600.* © *Artokoloro / Alamy Stock Photo.*

FIGURE 3.3.3 *Baby Jesus helping his father Joseph*, Iesu Christi Dei Domini, Salvatoris Nr̄i Infantia, c. *1600.* © *BTEU / RKMLGE / Alamy Stock Photo.*

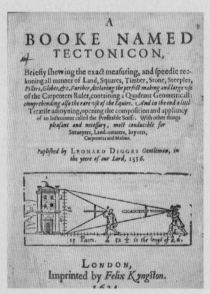

FIGURE 3.3.4 *Frontispiece*, Tectonicon, *Leonard Digges, 1634. Columbia University Libraries.*

wheel and lute. It is almost like something one might find in a modern-day farmer's museum. The plates portray Jesus at his task with the tools and scenes all very correctly detailed. One shows Joseph almost finishing a house. On the right, a workbench can be seen with tools: two planes, an axe, a rule and brace. Maria is winding thread spools. The young Jesus is drilling holes in the frame. One angel is helping him making a dowel. Meanwhile, another angel, helping Joseph, is busy hammering away at a joist.

It is clear from these images that apart from the angels, a building site was still heir to the technology of imperial Rome. The builder did not need to make cumbersome calculations, purchase and read handbooks to brush up on details, or compete with other highly skilled people for the eye and pocketbooks of fickle clients. That slowly changed and by the seventeenth century we see the emergence of a cultural space of operation that required mathematics. One of the earliest books to move in the new direction was *Tectonicon* by Leonard Digges (1520–59), a self-educated "man of leisure."[19] He was writing not for some learned member of the discipline, but for the ambitious builder. The laws of geometry were not the main issue, but a rather more basic one: how to count. Its first line reads:

> As there are fewe Craftsmen which have all the kinds of Arithmetike readily: so I doe suppose none so ignorant, but that they noe [know] or may easily perceive the simple signification of these Characters or figures, 1.2.3.4.5.6.7.8.9.10.

Mathematics was to remain the essential starting point for most trade pocketbooks well into the twentieth century. The title plate of *Tectonicon*

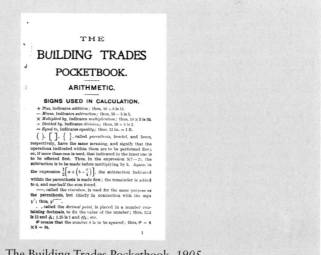

FIGURE 3.3.5 *Page 1,* The Building Trades Pocketbook, *1905.*

makes clear that the mathematics of this sort played an important part in land surveying, which was quickly becoming a key aspect of the builder's profession:[20]

> A boke named Tectonicon briefely shewynge the exacte measurynge, and speady reckenynge all maner lande, squared tymber, stone, steaples, pyllers, globes. [et]c. Further, declaringe the perfecte makinge and large vse of the carpenters ruler, conteyninge a quadrant geometricall: comprehendinge also the rare vse of the squire. And in thende a lyttle treatise adioyned, openinge the composicion and appliancie of an instrument called the profitable staffe. With other thinges pleasaunt and necessary, most conducible for surueyers, landemeaters, ioyners, carpenters, and masons. Published by Leonarde Digges gentleman, in the yere of our Lorde. 1556.

In the seventeenth century, we see an increasingly tight relationship between land measurement, speculative development, and building construction, often embodied by a single person. As a typical example of this was the carpenter James Nedam, who was appointed in 1531 as surveyor-general of the kings' works.[21] Surveyors sometimes even managed the estates which provided the wealth to build the great houses and they not only dealt with land but also with the construction and letting of buildings. In England, land measurement became particularly important with the opening and reconsolidation of land after the feudal age as marked by the Tenures Abolition Act 1660. Surveyors were often the administrative enforcers of the urban administration of its codes. In 1647 in New Amsterdam (the future New York) the city archives record:

> As we have seen and remarked the disorderly manner hitherto and now daily practiced in building and erecting houses, in extending lots far beyond their boundaries, in placing pig pens and privies on the public roads and streets and neglecting the cultivation of granted lots, the Director-General Petrus Stuyvesant and Council have deemed it advisable to decide upon the appointment of three surveyors . . . Who we hereby authorize and empower, to condemn all improper and disorderly buildings, fences, palisades, posts, rails, etc. and to prevent their erection in the future.[22]

In Engand, with the return of the king and his court from exile on the Continent in 1660, there emerged a taste for magnificence and opulence. The legions of craftsmen were enlarged by an influx of immigrants, many with special skills who could work on tombs, fireplaces, entrances, and other specialized architectural features. These pioneering and influential artisans worked on Hardwick Hall, Castle Bromwich, the Queen's House, and Belton House. But the great majority of the built work was made by contractors/tradesmen on hire by investors, particularly after the Great Fire of London in 1666 opened up huge swaths for development. Stephen Primatt's *City and Country Purchaser and Builder* (1667) dealt with valuations and rents, the business of the various tradesmen and the problems of siting, measuring, purchasing, and hiring. The building plans that he provided were of a simple rectangular shape that could easily fit onto a standard urban lot. Furthermore, beginning in the late seventeenth century and into the eighteenth, guild organizations and controls began to disintegrate in many towns and it became increasingly easy to work or set up in business without having been apprenticed, creating opportunities for the ambitious.[23] Though his book, *The Art of Sound Building* from 1725, had a frontispiece with the obligatory female personification of architecture at work on a drawing, at her feet are the more practical tools of the trade and indeed she is half gazing at the just-completed townhouse behind her, a contractor special. No architect required. The title of a book by William Halfpenny makes clear that clients wanted more than just fancy Italianate villas with expensive door frames: *Useful Architecture: Being the Last Work in this Kind of William Halfpenny, Architect and Carpenter, in Twenty-five New Designs with Full and Clear Instructions, in Every Particular, for Erecting Parsonage-houses, Farm-houses, and Inns* (1760). Just point and build.

✳ ✳ ✳ ✳

One perpetually thorny issue revolved around the framing of roofs. Floors and walls were relatively simple, but roofs were a different matter, particularly since they became increasingly complex in dimension and shape as the centuries wore on. The Latin *tectum* meant "roof" in German even into the mid-nineteenth century, demonstrating its singular position as the locus of expertise.[24]

FIGURE 3.3.6 *Frontispiece,* The Art of Sound Building, *William Halfpenny, 1725.*

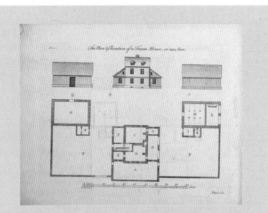

FIGURE 3.3.7 *Plate 1,* Useful Architecture: Being the Last Work in this Kind of William Halfpenny, Architect and Carpenter, in Twenty-five New Designs with Full and Clear Instructions, in Every Particular, for Erecting Parsonage-houses, Farm-houses, and Inns, *William Halfpenny, 1760.*

Batty Langley's *The city and country builder's and workman's treasury of designs* (1745) was typical in that it provided a range of roofing solutions, especially for buildings on irregular sites. Even a standard hip roof could have complex geometrical intricacies. Given the arbitrariness of apprenticeship at that time, books like *The Carpenter and Joiner's Companion in the Geometrical Construction of Working Drawings* (London: Caxton Press, 1826) were invaluable for anyone seeking to move up in the world. The book was written by Peter Nicholson, a native of Scotland and the son of a stonemason who was apprenticed to a cabinetmaker but soon abandoned his trade in favor of teaching practical geometry and writing. Though he called himself an architect, it appears that he never actually built anything. Nonetheless, the book added legitimacy to the nascent professionalization of the mechanical arts. Some of the joineries were so complex that a book like Peter Nicholson's *Architectonick: The New Practical Builder, and Workman's Companion* (1823) had at the first one hundred pages dealing only with mathematics and practical geometry.[25]

One can draw a direct connection to these practices and the how-to book, *Framing Roofs* (2002), in which the introduction points out:

> Roofs are the most complicated and dangerous part of a house framing. Geometry makes them complicated and height makes them dangerous.[26]

The architectural manifestation of this in our contemporary age can be found in the Kakasd Community Center (1987–91) by Imre Makovecz and

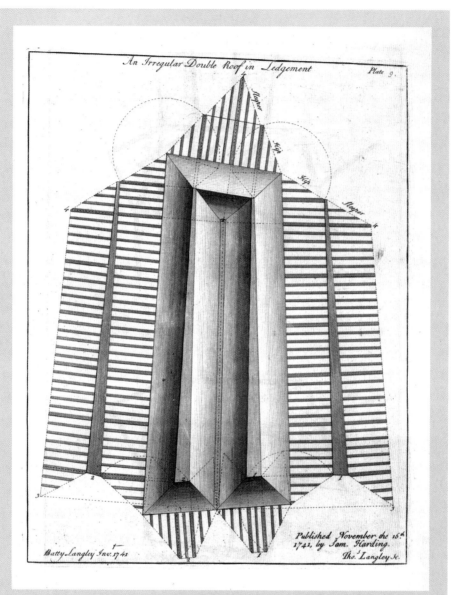

FIGURE 3.3.8 *Plate 9*, The City and Country Builder's and Workman's Treasury of Designs, *Batty Langley, 1745 (page 417).*

the top of 360 Newbury Street in Back Bay, Boston, Massachusetts (built 1918; renovated 2005) by Frank Gehry. Both structures—one more traditional, the other more abstracted—preserve the disciplinary location of the *Tectum* in contemporary practices.

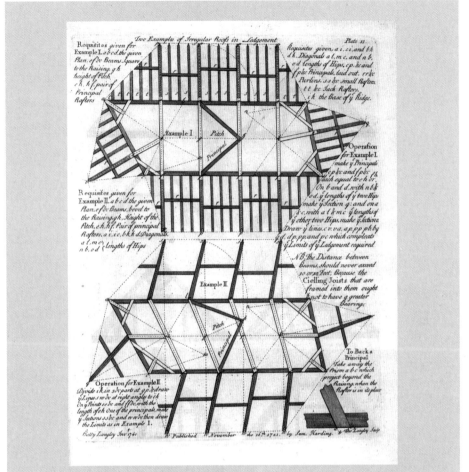

FIGURE 3.3.9 *Plate 11, The City and Country Builder's and Workman's Treasury of Designs, Batty Langley, 1745 (page 421).*

It was not just the roof that was the site of a specialized zone of recognition. In the nineteenth century, clients wanted complicated stairs to show off their wealth. In the title to *Art of Sound Building* (1725), William Halfpenny added the subtext, *Arches, Niches, Groins and Twisted Rails, both regular and irregular*, indicating the proliferation of these features. And so, beginning in the mid-nineteenth century a slew of books appeared dealing only with stairs and handrailing, from Cupper's *Hand-railing* (1849) to John V. H. Secor's *Nonpareil System of Hand-railing* on so on. A lot of ink was spent on the double-curved endpieces of the handrails, the locus of a carpenter's true mastery:

The stair builder ... was a stair builder absolutely. Not every Jack and Harry would be allowed to encroach on their territory. Occasionally some of the best joiners might have the gracious privilege of attending to the glue pot and getting out the wedges, etc., and oh, how grateful, proud and elated they would be. But when the lines were to be drawn, the face mold to be laid and the bevels to be found, the old stair builder would always be by himself. He had a secret to keep, a dignity to be guarded and he meant to do both.[27]

Illustrated Woodworker, out of New York, in its first issue of 1879, started things off with a discussion of handrails for stairs, and *Carpentry and Building: A Monthly Journal*, also out of New York, in its first issue of 1897, began with an article on roof framing followed by one of how to build stairs.[28]

* * * *

Most advanced carpenters moved from job to job and place to place as tradition would have it, but some found steady employment in the houses of the wealthy. Thomas Jefferson, for example, had several advanced carpenters in his employ, such as James Dinsmore, who originated from Ireland and was responsible for most of the elegant woodwork in Monticello. According to Jefferson, he possessed "the most ingenious hand to work with wood I ever knew." He and the assistants were responsible for the folding doors, for wall partition and window sashes, as Jefferson noted in his diary. John Hemmings, who was enslaved at Monticello, apprenticed under Dinsmore and when Dinsmore left Monticello in 1809, Hemmings became the lead master builder, working on handrails, sashes, furniture and window detailings. Letters by both men attest to the strong bond between Jefferson and Hemmings.[29]

* * * *

Mathematics, surveying, and advanced carpentry—each with increasingly specialized books and instruction manuals—allowed the upwardly mobile carpenter or builder to expand the cultural realm of occupationality into its modern form.[30] In some cases, canny contractors began to call themselves gentlemen. One commentator in 1719 even commented on "the abuse of every man's calling himself gentleman in England."[31] In fact, the period from the end of the eighteenth century through to the end of the nineteenth was the age of the *faber ingenium* with a widening register of activities from humble laborers to general contractors and overseers. There were now also building construction supervisors who, though not technically architects, could manage the more complicated projects.[32] The French art theorist Quatremère de Quincy noted in his dictionary of architecture the emergence of the word "constructor" (*constructeur*).[33] In Germany, the term *Baumeister* came to be used. These peopled mediated the triangulated spacing between the world of illiterate workers, the world of specialized, high-end craftsmen, and the world of increasingly knowledgeable and demanding clients. The contact point for all of this was the building site itself.

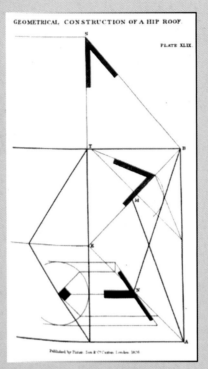

FIGURE 3.3.10 *Roof Framing Plan, Plate 50,* The Carpenter and Joiner's Companion in the Geometrical Construction of Working Drawings, *Peter Nicholson, 1826.*

FIGURE 3.3.11 *Kakasd Community Center, Imre Makovecz, 1987–91. Photograph by Dr. János Korom, 2008.*

FIGURE 3.3.12 *360 Newbury Street, Frank Gehry, Boston, Massachusetts (built 1918; renovated 2005). Photograph by Pi.1415926535.*

FIGURE 3.3.13 *Stair Case Landing, George Ball House, Galveston, Texas (Harry L. Starnes, Photographer April 9, 1936). Historic American Buildings Survey, Library of Congress Prints and Photographs Division, Washington, DC.*

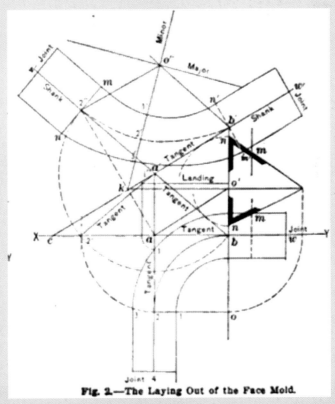

Fig. 2.—The Laying Out of the Face Mold.

FIGURE 3.3.14 *Construction drawing for a stair railing*, Carpentry and Building, *March 24, 1902, p. 70.*

* * * *

In France, in the nineteenth century, the ancient art of stereotomy got a new lease on life blending the ancient mysteries with the skills of the roofers who worked for the well-healed bourgeoisie to produce balconies and dormers. Called *guitardes*, they were designed to show the skill of the carpenter by bringing together the most difficult aspects of joinery and geometry. The complexity of the assemblies, but also their aesthetic, has created some real masterpieces. A survey in the Centre region of France has identified over three hundred still surviving *guitardes*. Many were used to signal that this was the house of a master carpenter. Some of the most spectacular examples are found on three houses located at 12, 50–8, and 72 rue de la Gare, Paris, built in 1871. Their roofs, adorned with complex dormers, were executed by Hippolyte Moreau, carpentry contractor in Châteauroux (1822–1900), built with the aid of his son-in-law, Armand.[34]

The skill of making these extraordinary exercises in joinery, along with their requisite drawings, had maintained a presence in Normandy because of a strong tradition of wooden construction and the historic role played by a theoretician of the *trait du charpente*, (line drawings of carpentry). Nicolas Fourneau was the author of a particularly famous eighteenth-century treatise. As a tribute to Fourneau, and to mark the 250th anniversary of the publication of his treatise, two young carpenters, Tourangeau le Courageux et Bourguignon Cœur-Vaillant, recreated a maquette of one of Fourneau's twisted steeples during the winter of 2016–17. The model is currently on exhibition at the Musée d'Art, Histoire et Archéologie in Evreux.[35] Another recently built *guitarde*, 2.15 meters high, was built by Alain Audrerie, master carpenter at Cénac, and started in 2005 with the help of three to four other master carpenters in the town of Brive. It is now installed in the town of Tarn in the southwest of France.[36]

* * * *

Today, stereometry is a dead field (apart from a few places of survival), complex handrails are no longer desired, and land surveying has become a separate profession. As for mathematics in architectural education, it became little more than an afterglow of that early post-eighteenth-century self-disciplining of the *tektōn*.[37] And yet, it is still a trope that students of architecture should be "good in drawing and in math," though they are never told why:

> Students pursuing a degree in architecture must take calculus courses. At the University of Illinois and Brigham Young University, students in an architecture degree program must take both Calculus I and II. The University of Illinois allows students to take beginning or intermediate physics courses in place of Calculus II, if they choose. Calculus and physics courses help students calculate structural issues, so they can design buildings that will hold up under the weight of materials and withstand interior and exterior forces.[38]

FIGURE 3.3.15 Guitardes: 49 rue des Beaumonts; rue du Faubourg-Saint-Jean, Orléans. Mazzhe; Bertrand Pierre (charpentier).

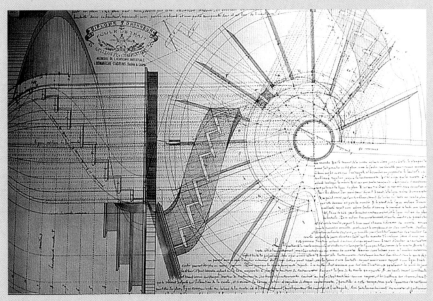

FIGURE 3.3.16 Detail of a drawing by François Guillon from the Romanèche-Thorins school of draft, 1892.

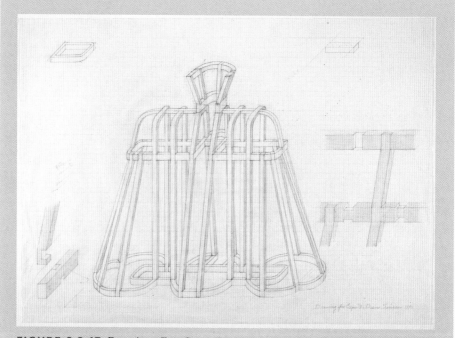

FIGURE 3.3.17 Drawings For Cape (B), *Diane Simpson, 1990. Simpson, Diane (b. 1935) © The Art Institute of Chicago / Art Resource, NY.*

Well yes, but computers do that work today. The age of the *faber ingenium* is over. This does not mean that the broad horizon of activity and creativity that developed in the eighteenth and nineteenth centuries is lacking in membership, only that it is now mostly overwhelmed by dull and more predictable avenues of professionalism. Quiet traces abound, as in the work of Simón Vélez, Elora Hardy, or Skylar Tibbits with his Self-Assembly Lab at MIT. Among those who preserve the disciplinary and cultural semiotics of the *tektōn* is also Diane Simpson, who is otherwise known for her fascination with the history of costume, as the names of some of her pieces indicate: *Sleeves*, 1996–2000; and *Bibs, Vests, Collars, Tunic*, 2006–8.[39] Though all her pieces are designed to be very conscious of their status as constructions, one piece, *Drawing for Cape (B)*, 1990, stands out. It is an open structure of wooden ribs with three cones hanging from the shoulders, with a space for the head. The structure, though it is supposed to evoke the shape of the cloth that would be placed on it, sits securely on the ground and is clearly building-like; though "architectural," it is not architecture (as opposed to "art") simply because of its scale and shape. Simpson alludes to the joinery involved in the making of this object, to its position with the discourse of "framing"— as in the framing of a roof—and in that sense this is *tektōn* without

FIGURE 3.3.18 Party Wall, *Caroline O'Donnell, New York, 2013. Photograph by Zachary Tyler Newton. © Caroline O'Donnell.*

the surfacing of architecture. It draws parallels between the skill set needed to make the ribbing for a corset and that of a joiner. Since the latter is, traditionally speaking, a uniquely male practice, it subverts gender expectations.

* * * *

Another example of *faber ingenium* was the project known as *Party Wall* (2013) that was sponsored by the MoMA in New York and designed by Caroline O'Donnell. It was composed of remaindered steel with wood for the skin recycled from a skateboard manufacturer. It was ballasted by hot-air-balloon-sized bladders of water that were part of a fountain element. *Party Wall* was a place to meet, rest, or host weddings. About 80 feet long and rising about 30 feet in the air, it is split into segments, some of which rise vertically, some of which are splayed at the bottom to about 24 feet across. Before the skin was put on, the structure, engineered by Silman Associates, looked very much like the back of a large urban billboard, except that it has two sides, like a very thick wall. With the edges exposed, the structure is not hidden away but an unusual type of inside/outside, mixing and blending notions of shed, wall, shelter, stage set, and lookout tower. Even though the skin with its skateboards—with the light and humorous touch of the *archē*—holds the

FIGURE 3.3.19 *Santa Caterina Market, Benedetta Tagliabue, Barcelona, 2005. Photograph by Zhicheng Xu.*

FIGURE 3.3.20 *Santa Caterina Market, Benedetta Tagliabue, Barcelona, 2005. Photograph by Samuel Dubois.*

keys to the narrative, the steel structure with its quasi-modular units, though not trying to overcook its role, maintains itself at least 50/50 with the skin.

* * * *

Though all buildings have roofs, Santa Caterina Market in Barcelona (2005) by Benedetta Tagliabue is one of the few buildings that brings the old virtuosity of the *tektōn* fully out of hiding.[40] It is a complex structure, floating above the outer shell of the old nineteenth-century market building. Part of the new wave-like roof rests on huge concrete beams that, rising from widely spaced posts, look like they were borrowed from a bridge design. On top of these, delicate steel and wooden struts move off in different directions depending on the graceful curve of the roof. There is an incongruous tension between the massive beams, serving as a type of elevated ground plane, and the lightweight netting of gravity-defying struts. In some parts of the building, the struts rise independently from the ground, playfully bending here and there as if reaching out toward their load-bearing assignment. Though most photos show the project from above, the real story is visible only from below. It is a masterpiece of *faber ingenium*. Though the *tektōn* in this building inhabits its traditional spaces, namely the roof, it ventures downward to the ground, but not as a manifestation of "engineering" with a semiotics of power and rationality that seeks to displace architecture, but as a semiotics of reciprocity, respect, and, one can perhaps also say, tenderness.

PART FOUR

CHAPTER ONE

"Architecture"

In Book V of *Notre Dame de Paris* (1831), Victor Hugo writes:

> Stone was laid upon stone, these granite syllables were coupled together, the word essayed some combinations . . . the pillar, which is a letter; the arch, which is a syllable; the pyramid, which is a word, set in motion at once by a law of geometry and a law of poetry, began to group themselves together, to combine, to blend, to sink, to rise, stood side by side on the ground, piled themselves up into the sky, till, to the dictation of the prevailing idea of the epoch, they had written these marvelous books which are equally marvelous edifices: the Pagoda of Eklinga, the Pyramids of Egypt, and the Temple of Solomon.[1]

The cathedrals were for him the height of this "law of poetry," whereas the Renaissance was the "setting sun which we take to be a dawn . . . [for this was] the moment architecture became merely one art among others, once it was no longer the total, the sovereign, the tyrannical art." The reason for the loss of meaningfulness was the printing press. It freed mankind from theocracy, but opened it up to a new age known for its "diversity, progress, originality, richness of design, [and] perpetual change." He goes on to famously state: "This Will Kill That."[2]

It is possible to argue that I am saying—in parallel to Victor Hugo—that "architecture" kills architecture, subverts its meanings and teleologies, pollutes its disciplinary integrity. After all, it is the printed word of Alberti's texts that allows the trans-historical, post facto wordplay to bubble forth outside of the conventions of its own space and time. It places us in a zone that is both temporally modern, historically multiple, and theoretically ambiguous. The point of difference with Hugo is that I am trying to avoid a position where there is a murder weapon, or that there is some sort of irreparable "break," or worse yet some implied "breakdown." Though it is Alberti who set off the chain of logic that frees "architecture" from its ancient locus, *archē(non)tektōn* is a prefaced origin that resides—

deconstructedly—within the word/discipline itself. "Architecture" is "broken" to begin with. Socrates and Plato made sure of that.

* * * *

Archē(non)tektōn opens itself up to a world where there is no outside to modernity. It will always repeat, rehearse, and recodify that disastrous splitting of "theory" and "practice" that we inherited from the ancient Greeks and Romans. Better stated, *archē(non)tektōn* opens a space of production where it is impossible to know where anyone who has some interest in the topic—professionally, practically, or theoretically—stands. Every inside is an outside and vice versa.

* * * *

So many things can be meant by the word architecture (without scare quotes) that one would be hard pressed to find any two people—much less two architects—who would agree on a definition, unless, of course, they had been schooled beforehand. Some might talk about shelter, others about beauty, others about place-making, others about wasteful spending, others about representation, and yet others about gestures in the landscape.

* * * *

The phrase "Department of Architecture" narrows the field of options to something academic. In these contexts, architecture (without scare quotes) declares its disciplinary status by pointing to some bibliographically-rich origin or point of departure, whether in mythology ("architecture begins with shelter"); in the field of Eurocentric history ("architecture begins with Stonehenge"); in the field of theory ("modern architecture begins with the Werkbund"); in practice ("architecture begins with community engagement") and so on. The very fact that none of these align and are themselves easily contestable only reaffirms the necessity to speak instead of "architecture." Nonetheless, architecture departments will tend to favor disciplinarity, not simply because they are watched over by the American Institute of Architecture and its accreditation regimes, but also because they must provide positive exemplars of their activities due to their location in the cultural budgets of universities. They cannot admit up front that the phrase "Department of Architecture" is nonsensical, carried forward by the banality of tradition—mostly governed by late-nineteenth-century Eurocentric assumptions—rather than by any particular set of purposes and meaning. In fact, unlike the parallel phrases "Department of Philosophy" or "Department of Art"—regardless of how wide-ranging those disciplines are—a "Department of Architecture"—despite what it might profess in a Dean's statement—might well include things that are not architecture at all. By way of contrast, it is hard to imagine a Department of Philosophy that has tenured faculty who are not philosophers, or a Department of Art that has tenured faculty who are not artists. But a Department of Architecture can easily still have faculty who are not architects (though they will have other disciplinary qualifications), and who even might be highly skeptical of the value of architecture—or at least some form of it—in the cultural world.

Architecture's shape-shifting capacity—as inaugurated by Alberti—makes the discipline pathologically unstable and the critique of the discipline almost impossible—or least a critique that assumes that there is a there there.

* * * *

Among English speakers—and, of course, in its various European translations—the word "architecture" quickly and silently essentializes. This is a consequence of the Englishification of the profession in its global dimension. The issue is not to forbid access to buildings across times and cultures, but to acknowledge that the word is a construct of a particular type. Architecture (without scare quotes) in its contemporary unreflective use in non-Anglo-Eurocentric environments carries with it not just the traces—overtly and covertly—of colonialism, but also of modernization, professionalization, and even in some cases of governmental enforcements. In other words, architecture (without scare quotes) is no harmless word. The issue in this book, however, is to look not at its external operative agendas but to its internal ones.

Architecture (without scare quotes) can never overcome the possibility that all architecture—wherever one encounters it in the semantic-theoretical world—is really "architecture"; and similarly, "architecture" can never overcome the possibility that it, too, is an apparition.

* * * *

The closer one comes to architecture (without scare quotes) the closer one comes to its spectral twin, "architecture."

Architecture (without scare quotes) is used on the off-chance that there is "a center"—or that one day, there will be a center. In that sense, architecture (without scare quotes) is pure speculation.

Architecture (without scare quotes) is used as a tautological proclamation that seeks to naturalize its teleology—to act as if the job is indeed already done.

Architecture (without scare quotes) is used to assume a mode of governance, when everyone familiar with the field can tell you that there is no such thing. And yet, from the days of the Alberti onward, that forlorn hope manifests itself as a search to maximize its teleological content—even though it was and remains scared by the structural impossibility of that mission.

Architecture (without scare quotes), by not allowing the *faber* to speak at the disciplinary table, cannot escape the sin of that exclusion.

Architecture (without scare quotes) is a concept used out of convenience to its own affirmations.

Architecture (without scare quotes) is a predicate without a sentence.

Architecture (without scare quotes) is the incomplete symbol of "architecture." (An incomplete symbol, according to Bertrand Russell, is an expression that fails to stand for a constituent of the proposition expressed by sentences that contain it or fails to stand for an entity at all.)

Architecture (without scare quotes) is predominantly therapeutic, healing over the ancient wound.

Architecture (without scare quotes) seeks to apprehended itself in the space of meanings, judgments, and communitarian obligations, performed to polite nods of the discipline's monitors. But even if we were to bring these monitors out into the open, from the profession, from academe, from pedagogy, from theory, from politics, from the ranks of the deans and dons and so on, we would easily demonstrate the lack of center. It is not that there are many opinions, many points of view, many styles, and many opportunities. Just the opposite! There are *not* many opinions, *not* many points of view, *not* many styles, and *not* many opportunities.

* * * *

The indeterminability of "architecture" should not lead us to the conclusion that there is some quasi-mystical transcendence; that only brings us back to the embrace of universalism or, just as bad, to the introduction of teleology under the guise of critique. Nonetheless, between the overdetermined word—architecture—as usually encountered in literature, a word that is pronounced without any indication of its slipperiness, and "architecture" that reminds us that its self-disciplining is an imaginary construct, there is a lot of room to operate.

* * * *

The grammatology of *archē(non)tektōn* is not freely available within the space of "experience" in some arbitrary way. It is not something that can be taught, administered, or even judged. It exists *only* within the space of disciplinary realities and brought into "experience" only through the *work* of those who engage the discipline and its paradoxes willingly or not. The nature of that work can range from a specific act to an intuition. It can be just as much a critical speculation as an accidental byproduct.

* * * *

In 1492, when Bramante designed his extension of Santa Maria delle Grazie, he also designed the pier that linked his part of the design with the preexisting medieval nave. It was an unprecedented piece of architectural wizardry composed entirely of panel-like pilasters standing shoulder to shoulder with no trace of the pier onto which they are applied. To move around the pier is to notice that one pilaster has neither base nor capital, that one has a sort of capital composed of layers of molding strips but no base, that one has both a capital and a base, and that one is in essence upside down with the molding strips at its base.

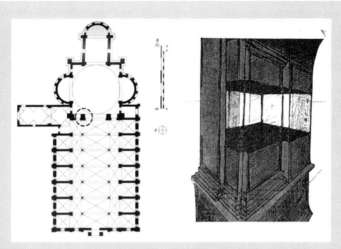

FIGURE 4.1.1 *Plan and detail: Santa Maria delle Grazie, Milan. Photograph by Mark Jarzombek.*

FIGURE 4.1.2 *Exterior elevation and detail view: Palazzo Rucellai, Florence. Photograph by M-i-k-e-v.*

It is difficult to properly assess this piece of "architecture." In truth, it could easily be dismissed as irrelevant, or as mere marginalia were it not for the fact that the pilaster as a design problem was so obviously intriguing to Bramante. And yet, the pilaster—as a representation of a column—has practically no place in the history of architecture. The book *The Dancing Column* (1996), though a majestic survey of the origins, meanings, and histories of the column, has not even a single entry dedicated to the pilaster.

But the pilaster has a distinctive history in the Renaissance where it came to be front and center in the work of Leon Battista Alberti (Palazzo Rucellai), Filippo Brunelleschi (San Lorenzo) and others. Its role is difficult to interpret.

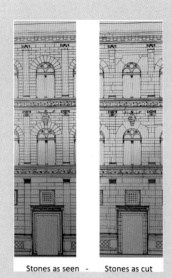

Stones as seen - Stones as cut

FIGURE 4.1.3 *Elevation drawing: Palazzo Rucellai, Florence. Drawing by Mark Jarzombek.*

As a semiotic device it points to the odd desire to "return" to Roman imaginaries as well as to the cultural overlay of "humanistic learning," and its pretensions. But the pilaster was obviously never really structure and as such the buildings of the Renaissance came to have two structural systems, one mostly of a generic, wall-bearing type of stone and masonry, and another that elevated the building into something that can be called architecture with a capital "A."

The Palazzo Rucellai—believed to have been designed for Giovanni di Paolo Rucellai between 1446 and 1451 and executed, at least in part, by Bernardo Rossellino, though probably to the designs of Alberti—is typical. The architect remodeled an existing medieval structure by adding a facade that, though skin-deep, spoke volumes about the new aesthetic sensibility. If the Greek *archē* turned wood into stone, Alberti turned a drawing on paper to stone, and then back again to "paper," for a facade like this would be incomprehensible without understanding the new relationship between drawing and erudition. The visible stone blocks of the facade are not just a few inches thick and cemented to the wall, but they are even so not really blocks, but incisions on larger flat slabs so well worked together that the joints are almost invisible. This could be seen as little more than pragmatism if it were not for the right-hand side of the facade that exposes an unfinished look as if the masons had left for a coffee break and never returned.[3]

* * * *

If Palazzo Rucellai marks the shadowy birth of "architecture" as a practice, Bramante's pier at Santa Maria delle Grazie, out of sight from the main

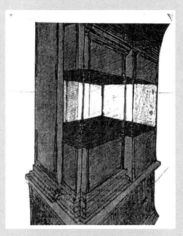

FIGURE 4.1.4 *Panel pilaster, Santa Maria presso San Satiro, Milan. Drawing by Mark Jarzombek from "Pilasters," Thresholds 58.*

space and in the forgotten corner of disciplinary control, celebrates the opening of possibilities that the tension between architecture and "architecture" provides. The pilasters that wrap the pier completely obscure its structural role. They not only obscure it, but toy with it by making it appear as if the pier were composed of non-structural things left over perhaps from the construction site and applied willy-nilly as an afterthought.

Even where Bramante is at his most classical, as in the Tempieto di San Pietro in Montorio, at the level of the drum he offers a row of panel-like pilasters without capitals. I use the word "panellike" to emphasize the ambiguous semantic role that this architectural element fulfills, as pilaster and as frame, in other words, as something solid albeit thin, and as something almost immaterial, a mere frame against the wall. At Santa Maria presso San Satiro, in the Capella delta Pieta, Bramante plays even more ingeniously with the panel pilaster theme. The geometry of the octagonal chapel is defined by splayed panel pilasters, the idea for which came from Brunelleschi's octagonal oculus of the dome of Santa Maria del Fiore, the splayed pilasters there being most probably the first such example in the history of architecture. But to make things more complicated, at the upper ambulatory level, the piers separating the two arches are pilaster-corbel hybrids that support stubby panel pilasters. These likewise read as support brackets for the entablature above. When all these features are taken together, it is clear that Bramante deliberately sought to blur the identities of frames, pilasters, dados, and brackets and yet still work within the principles of the classical system.

It would be wrong to argue that Bramante was engaged in a selfconscious play on the architectural elements of classical language even though there is something nonetheless "at play" in his architecture. What Bramante discovered was that pilasters can be embedded in traditional notions of a columnar order—living up to the exalted expectations of proportion and scale and thus to the ideology of Humanism—while at the same time existing at the margins of the permissible. In other words, although some pilasters must serve their columnar masters, others can exist in a more fluid state of definition.

****

In the seventeenth century, Pope Alexander VII commissioned Gian Lorenzo Bernini to build a monument to display the Chair of St. Peter, a wooden chair overlaid with ivory plaques depicting the Twelve Labors of Heracles and some of the constellations. Though long believed to have been used by the Apostle Peter, it was actually a gift from Holy Roman Emperor Charles the Bald to Pope John VIII in 875.[4] The chair is more than a chair. The word "cathedral" in fact derives from the Greek *kathedra* (meaning "seat") and came out of the Greek scholastic tradition of teaching *ex cathedra*—as opposed to the more ancient tradition of peripatetic philosophy. The *cathedra* is the seat of the bishop and in fact the program of the cathedral is to house the *cathedra*. The first chairs sat on an axis in the apse at the center of attention and were elevated on steps. In the age of cathedrals, it was a piece of furniture—made by that proverbial *tektōn*—that steals the show, not the work of the archē(*tektōn*), and this despite the vast difference in scale and effort between chair and building.

FIGURE 4.1.5 *Cathedra at the Basilica of St. John Lateran, Rome. Photograph by BrettLewis88.*

The backdrop to the commission was the claim by Protestants that Peter was never in Rome and thus he could not have been the Bishop of Rome. In order to reject this assertion, Pope Paul IV (r. 1555–9) reinstituted the feast of the Chair of Peter in Rome in 1558, leading to the commission by Alexander VII. After all, this was the chair of all chairs, the living embodiment of the Church as institution.

Bernini reimagined the chair as a gilded bronze throne, richly ornamented with bas-reliefs. The more humble original was intended to be housed in a niche at the base of the altar. The throne is about 15 feet tall or about five times the size of a real chair, and is flanked by greater-than-life-sized sculptures of four Doctors of the Church.

Here the *archē* has separated itself from and yet enframed the *tektōn*. In a sense, the *tektōn*—completely hidden from view—is outdone by "architecture" around it. Venerated and mysterious and supported on artificial clouds and rays of sun, Bernini even releases the chair (in its much-enlarged reimaged form) from its gravitational requirements. The only remnant of the *archē* is the two flanking columns tops, the bottoms of which are purposefully obscured by figures. Because the columns, which match those of the wall elements to the left and right of the altar, are lower in elevation, the whole seems to be descending from the heavens. But because only the upper parts of the columns are visible the viewer is uncertain where the "ground" is. The column tops, almost on the verge of being drowned by the clouds, just manage to stand resolutely against the encroachments.

* * * *

FIGURE 4.1.6 *Original Altar of Chair of St. Peter, Bernini, Vatican City, alongside Altar of Chair of St. Peter, as altered by author.*

Only occasionally do even architects understand the opportunity that is laid before them. One was Deshamanya Geoffrey Manning Bawa (1919–2003), a Sri Lankan architect and the principal force behind what is today known globally as "tropical modernism." He built religious, social, cultural, educational, governmental, commercial, and residential buildings. He also built a remarkable house for himself in Colombo known as Number 11 (in 33rd Lane). It started in 1958 when Bawa bought the third in a row of four small houses which lay along a short cul-de-sac at the end of a narrow suburban lane and converted it into a pied-à-terre with living room, bedroom, tiny kitchen, and room for a servant. When the fourth bungalow became vacant this was bought and converted into a dining room and second living room. Ten years later the remaining lots were acquired and added into the composition and then finally, the first bungalow in the row— the one along the street—was demolished and replaced by a four-story structure. Unlike the other, older parts of the house which are domestic in scale and a modernized variation on the bungalow, this one was a demonstration piece of international modernism. Bawa by this time had become a successful architect and wanted to show off his credentials in that respect. Its concrete floors, white walls, and wide windows give it the feeling of Gropius or Le Corbusier. There is, however, a remarkable feature that has nothing to do with this lineage.

The structural system of the house is made visible on the roof-terrace level with bold black columns set against the white walls. Columns, of course, must rest one on top of the other, but in the living room on the floor below, one of the columns is hidden in a closet. The other, which would have gone through the center of the room, is missing altogether! Because there are no beams in the living-room ceiling, this must mean that the column on the

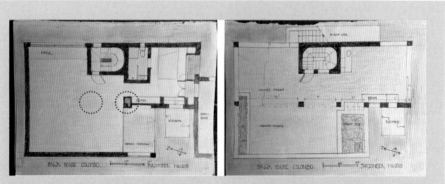

FIGURE 4.1.7 *Bawa House, Deshamanya Geoffrey Manning Bawa, Colombo. Left: Plan of second floor showing locations of the missing column and the column hidden in the closet. Right: Plan of roof terrace. Drawing by Mark Jarzombek.*

FIGURE 4.1.8 *Roof terrace, Bawa House, Deshamanya Geoffrey Manning Bawa, Colombo. Drawing by Mark Jarzombek.*

roof is in essence fake and not load-bearing. There is a possible practical reason in that on the main floor below the living room there is a garage, and a column there would have messed things up. But pragmatics is insufficient to explain this unusual play with columns.

If we assume that Bawa wanted the visible modernity on the roof terrace to look structural—even if one of the columns was technically unnecessary—he wanted the domestic areas to not be organized around mandates of structure. This means that the official modernism of the roof—where he held his receptions with his clients—needed to fit the norms of disciplinary expectations, as well as the more conventional expectations of his clients. His *own* expectations were of a different order. He did not need to remind himself in his own living room that the roof was held up by columns. He was after all an "architect." Instead, he wanted the columns to withdraw not just from visibility, but from service—the one removed physically, the other hidden in the closet. Whether this was an autobiographic commentary is something that cannot be easily determined, but what is clear is that this play of signifiers allows one to (not)see structure in order to come to better terms with "architecture." He was probably fully aware that few people, even perhaps fellow architects, would notice this sleight of hand.

FIGURE 4.1.9 After ALife Ahead: *Pierre Huyghe, Münster, 2017. Floor detail.* © *2021 Artists Rights Society (ARS), New York / ADAGP, Paris.*

****

Pierre Huyghe, for his *After ALife Ahead* (2017), excavated an abandoned former ice-skating and hockey rink tucked behind a Burger King on the edge of Münster in Germany. Since the site was slated for destruction, he could act on it as he wanted.[5] The concrete floor was cut away to reveal below it the gravel and below that the dirt, and even some old pipes. The thinness of "architecture" is apparent throughout. As one walks through it in the valleys, the remnants appear like mesas.

Though the tradition of operating in spaces that were soon to be destroyed dates back to Gordon Matta Clark, here Huyghe replaces architectural determinacy with biological indeterminacy. At the center of the space, up on a cement platform, is an aquarium with glass that can shift from clear to black. It contains a venomous sea snail, a conus textile, which sports a shell with an intricate pattern that is an example of cellular automata. An incubator holds cancer cells whose rate of growth is determined by various measurements that sensors are taking of the space. Rain flows in, feeding the algae in the soil. There's no telling what it will look like at the end. "I'm interested in letting, in a certain way, self-organizing systems try either to find or to not find a symbiosis . . . I try my best not to intervene within it." Large apertures in the roof automatically open and close without any apparent logic.[6]

The project exchanges one completeness for another that is a new beginning, except that it is no longer humans who are in charge, but fungi, animals, and cells, planted there not by nature, but by an artist and

FIGURE 4.1.10 After ALife Ahead: *Pierre Huyghe, Münster, 2017. Skylight view.* © *2021 Artists Rights Society (ARS), New York / ADAGP, Paris.*

yet—doing what nature does—turning a landscape into an environment. In a Piranesian manner, the visitors walking through the alien site are uncertain of their scale. Water, the bane of everything architectural, flows in freely through the roof.

The labor of making this intervention is nowhere visible and in this is different from the works of Gordon Matta Clark who reveled in dust and danger. This piece proclaims itself as an "artwork." It is a stage set. The floor slabs are not ruinous, but meticulously cut by diamond-tipped saws (presumably) along straight lines as if reinvoking the ancient geometry by which the floor was scored by its original contractors. In that sense, the artist addressed the architecture architecturally, not smashing it to bits, but elegantly slicing it as if with an X-Acto knife. In making "architecture" out of architecture (or is it the reverse?), the work shores up the disciplinary status of architecture while yet exhibiting it as a "construction." Instead of a primitive hut, it is the primitive slab, the primal semiotic of architecture as the artificial crust of the earth. It is held in place not to protect man from the proverbial elements, but as a functional platform for the outsized humans to observe the natural world. The hint that these ancient tropes might be under interrogation is that one mound has its lid slid off as if moved by some ancient force, perhaps a huge deluge that had come from the opening to the sky above that had now drained away, leaving the ocean floor exposed.

CHAPTER TWO

Anamorphic Realism

When Plato in *Statesman* separated the *tektōn* from the *arche-tektōn*, the consequence, as it developed in our more modern world, was not just in the nature of labor, occupation, and status, but also in how the two sides operate in the domain of representation. Before Alberti's times, representation was mostly in the hands of the *tektōn*, who deployed geometries that were inward-focusing. They were not meant to be seen by the layperson; at best they were a curious, ghostly trace left on a cathedral wall or floor. Perspective was a different matter altogether. Controlled by the architect, it became an instrument of its own. Alberti even famously wrote a treatise, *De pictura* (1435), to explain its operations. Perspective is not a representation *of* reality, as is often understood, but a "construction" with its own set of instruments, papers, rulers, compasses that include, of course, the eye itself, the organ that is the most easily deceived. When it comes to perspective, for every ounce of method there is an ounce of magic.

The architect could now represent the world, the future world, the imagined world, in a way that allied itself with optical naturalism. It was the locus of a particular type of magic that dislocated the "real" and that opened up the cognitive space of visual imperialism. And it was, like good wine, associated with a particular class of people and a viewpoint inaccessible to the standard conventions of the *tektōn*.

Perspective lies between *ratio et via* and *mente animoque*. Based on rules and on the necessary comparative associations with "reality," it has to carry the sanctioning of natural vision. And yet its undisguised illusionistic practices leave plenty of room to abandon its legislative requirements. Book One of Alberti's treatise on painting is about the geometry needed to make a perspective drawing; Book Two opens with the sentence, "Painting contains a divine force which not only makes absent men present as friendships is said to do, but moreover makes the dead seem almost alive."[1]

* * * *

FIGURE 4.2.1 *Altarpiece of San Esteban, Jaime Serra, 1385. National Art Museum of Catalonia, Barcelona.* © *J. Enrique Molina / Alamy Stock Photo.*

Before the advent of perspective, architecture when it was represented in Europe in murals and painting came in small doses, just enough to tell a story or serve as backdrop. The front of a palace served as indicator that the story revolved around an emperor. A room cut open served as backdrop for the annunciation or portrayed a manger for the birth of Christ. Rarely, as in T*he Allegory of Good and Bad Government* (1338) in Siena, do we see a more elaborate architectural spread, but even then it is an assemblage of different elements. Perspective allowed, for the first time, architecture to have its own disciplinary presence with floors, walls, roofs, windows now part of coherent structural systems. Though sometimes here, too, parts were cut away or left open, there is no mistaking architecture as a disciplinary world unto itself.

∗ ∗ ∗ ∗

The structure of perspective's teleology is perfectly expressed by Irwin Panofsky in his book *Perspective as Symbolic Form* where he argued that perspective was the central component of a Western "will to form" and that it linked social, cognitive, psychological, and technical practices into harmonious and integrated wholes. It provided a "full vision of the world." Panofsky saw the history of perspective through military terms of conquest and victory:

> The *conquest* over the medieval representational principle begins with this achievement of Duccio and Giotto.

p. 55

The *conquest* of this new and at last "modern" standpoint appears to have been carried out in the north and in the south in two fundamentally different ways.

p. 59

Thus the history of perspective may be understood with equal justice as a *triumph* of the distancing and objectifying sense of the real, and as a *triumph* of the distance-denying human struggle for control

p. 67 (my emphasis)

But all is not well in Panofsky's tale of conquest. In Footnote 74 we read:

Botticelli, despite his every more clearly emerging disinclination for the perspectival view of space, nevertheless, had thoroughly mastered perspectival construction.

One wonders why the sentence was not be written in reverse:

Botticelli, though he had thoroughly mastered perspectival construction, became ever more disinclined toward the perspectival view of space.

In other words, Panofsky wants to reinforce the winner's perspective, seeing problems with the adaptation of perspective as, literally, a footnote in the grand narrative. He reinforces this in the following footnote, the last of the book, where we read that Mannerism, with its anti-perspectival spaces, was basically a backward-looking movement that constituted the "reawakening of a religious and dogmatic worldview, one which in many respects reestablishes contact with the ideas and creations of the Middle Ages." Panofsky sees the negative reactions to perspective as reactionary and unenlightened.

If we take away Panofsky's ideological bias, and move into the history of "architecture," which I might have to remind the reader is not the same as the history of architecture, perspective mostly stands as an outer shell that gives only false readings of what is inside.

* * * *

Perspective is the special condition of anamorphism. Anamorphism is an image distorted in such a way that it becomes visible only when viewed in a particular place.

Though Panofsky tries to keep the history of perspective *in perspective*, foreclosing perspective around its own special teleology, we can see behind the curtains a different world. In Panofsky, history's anamorphic reality is repressed into the footnotes.

In 1988, Jean-Max Albert (1942–), a French painter, sculptor, writer, and musician, laid out *Un carré pour un square*, that takes the form of white

FIGURE 4.2.2 Un carré pour un square, *Jean-Max Albert, Paris, 1988.*

lines that outline a square when seen from the correct vantage point. The lines extend over various parts of the plaza (18 x 25 meters). Since the park in French was called *un square*, Albert designed by means of a linguistic pun an illusionary square, "*un carré* (square) for a *square*."[2] Some of its elements are narrow slabs of Carrara marble placed in the walls of the buildings. Others are painted lines; an old building was preserved to serve as "support" for the design of the virtual square. The ground is covered with an asphalt inlaid with fine steel lines which converge on a small post located on the sidewalk, at 61, rue de Belleville, the "obligatory point of view" from which the visual coincidence can be registered.

Whereas perspective wants us to think that the world "out there" is not anamorphic, the anamorphic potential structures its construction at every turn.

✳ ✳ ✳ ✳

In 1631 Cardinal Bernardino Spada hired Giovanni Borromini to help renovate his palazzo, which he bought and which had been built in 1540. Tightly constrained by neighboring structures, there was not much space for large gardens. Spada was eager to show off his connections to the Vatican and so wanted a corridor—as was newly fashionable—where the power elites would enter and exit. The problem was there was no room, so Borromini made a faux corridor. The Augustinian priest Giovanni Maria da Bitonto worked out the mathematics and Borromini did the rest. To make the illusion work he reduced the dimensions at the entrance from 6 meters high and 3 meters wide to 2 meters by 1 meter at the end. He also sloped the floor upward and the ceiling down. The two-deep rows of columns are built smaller

FIGURE 4.2.3 *Borromini Corridor, Palazzo Spada, Rome, c. 1635. Photograph by Livio and Ronico 2013.*

FIGURE 4.2.4 *Plan: Borromini Corridor, Palazzo Spada, Rome. © Relevé d'architecture.*

toward the end of the passage. They frame a statue of Mars, the Roman god of war, that looks as big as any Bernini sculpture in the Borghese Museum. In reality the statue is a mere 31 inches tall. Borromini was able to do here what no perspectivalist painter could do, give the viewer both a reality and its falsification. Though the piece is often described as an "illusion" or as a "garden curiosity," Borromini's corridor broke the spell of perspective. It revealed in all sharpness its awkward teleological claim that is all or nothing.

Borromini's corridor embraces the simultaneity of perspective and anamorphism. The unbuildable had to be built to give the illusion of delivery.

* * * *

San Carlo alle Quattro Fontane (Saint Charles at the Four Fountains, 1646, Rome) was designed by Francesco Borromini and is one of the standard exemplars of baroque architecture. I would like to focus on the walls of the church. First, there are the overly tall Corinthian-esque columns. But that is hardly the strangest part. It is what is in between the columns, an assortment of aedicules, panels, niches, and moldings. The whole is set around two horizonal bandings. The lower one is mostly implied whereas the upper one looks more like an actual entablature. That upper one pinches the columns at shoulder height but leave a vertical scotia gap running all the way up and down the columns. This creates the sense that the walls between the columns do not touch the columns, even if they come extremely close. In comparison to the upper entablature's aggressive posture, the lower one is regressive and appears in and out of the composition. The niches with tri-lobed vaults in these areas, however, are oversized, leaving only a relatively narrow band of framing at the perimeters. Above them and above the entablature is a simple panel. In other words, nowhere in the space between the columns is there anything that one might call "wall."

The shocking compression of all the elements—entablatures, moldings, niches, and framings—only comes to fore if we compare it with the work of Michelangelo, whose Palazzo Senatorio and Palazzo dei Conservatori in the Campidoglio designed almost a hundred years earlier in 1538 are clearly referenced. There we see the lower order of columns that flank openings paired with grand pilasters. We even find here vertical scotia molding that makes Michelangelo's architecture so distinctive. But there is no doubt that there is also something that one can call "wall" and, compared to San Carlo, the facade seems relaxed and even lacking in tension. In the Albertian sense, the facade of the Palazzo dei Conservatori looks like a built version of a flat drawing—a grand exemplar of Humanism's requirement for conspicuous erudition.

FIGURE 4.2.5 *Interior altar of San Carlo alle Quattro Fontane, Francesco Borromini, Rome, c. 1635. Photograph by Livio and Ronico 2013.*

FIGURE 4.2.6 *Palazzo dei Conservatori, Michelangelo Buonarotti, Rome, 16th century. Image courtesy of https://www.michelangelo.org/.*

One can also compare San Carlo alle Quattro Fontane with the more contemporaneous Sant'Andrea al Quirinale (begun in 1658, completed in 1670) by Gian Lorenzo Bernini, which is just a few hundred feet down the street. It also references Michelangelo in respect to the relationship between the large and small columns. Here we see the Michelangelo-esque lower-order entablatures and the strategic use of minor pilasters and paneling. The upper entablature and the spaces between the arches and entablatures are all bits of conventional wall architecture that had been part of classical architectural form language for ages.[3] The design may be curved, but it, too, is basically a curved drawing. What then do we make of Borromini's

FIGURE 4.2.7 *Interior: Sant'Andrea al Quirnale, Gian Lorenzo Bernini, Rome, 1670. © F1online digitale Bildagentur GmbH / Alamy Stock Photo.*

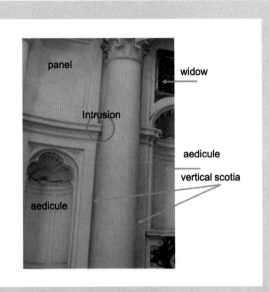

FIGURE 4.2.8 *San Carlo alle Quattro Fontane, Francesco Borromini, as modified by author. Photograph and modifications by Mark Jarzombek.*

wall-less architecture, leaving the impression—if one were a critic—of a crowded mess of architectural components?

There is no answer to the question. To relegate it to "the baroque" is to assume stylistic coherency. We should see it as an anamorphic structure where the appropriate viewing point is designed to remain allusive. Is it from above, below, from an angle? This "wall-less" anamorphism brings "architecture" to the very edge of possibility.

* * * *

Mies van Rohe deployed perspective throughout his career with great effect as in this drawing from 1950, making everything he designed rendered as a line drawing, as if it were all floating in air and contrasting with the robust volumetricity of the outside world.[4] But to make the drawing more legible, Mies moved the two chairs against the window to the right-hand side of the drawing, the seat he also moved to the right, and the two chairs on the left he moved further to their left toward the curtains. The clean symmetry implied by the table is, therefore, an illusion. If people were sitting, they would be talking at unusual angles across the space. Along the left edge of the drawing, one can make out a mysterious wall that seems to have no real place in the design. This compression toward the lower right corner and left side of the drawing opened up a space in front of the viewer that allows the floor and roof to be seen together, making the whole more airy. Otherwise,

FIGURE 4.2.9 *Interior Perspective, Mies van der Rohe*, Architectural Forum, *January 1950, p. 76. Drawing by Mies van der Rohe.*

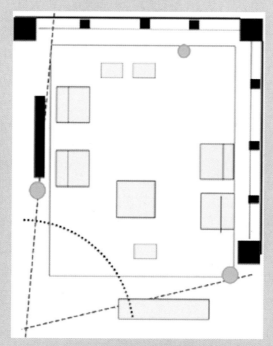

FIGURE 4.2.10 *Plan based on the drawing by Mies van der Rohe. Plan by Mark Jarzombek.*

the roof would seem all too empty. It is clear that Mies is not interested in the banal illusions of perspective, but wanted to counteract one set of seductions with another.

The anamorphism here is at its most cunning, since, unlike with Borromini's Spada Corridor, where we are given both the perspective and the anamorphic "reality," and unlike San Carlo alle Quattro Fontane where we are given the anamorphic but not the perspectival key, here we are given a perspective that disguises the hidden anamorphic within.

* * * *

In 1951, work was completed on Mies van der Rohe's Robert F. Carr Memorial Chapel of St. Savior on the Illinois Institute of Technology (IIT) campus in Chicago. His only ecclesiastical work, it is a simple, unadorned rectangular box-like structure with a thin concrete roof sitting on a steel frame. The walls are of a sand-colored brick with large, glazed openings in front and back. Though nondenominational, there is a thin stainless-steel crucifix set against Shantung silk curtains. The cross can be obscured by the curtain if need be. The altar is a solid piece of Roman travertine. The building's elegance and simplicity have been remarked upon repeatedly in the literature, as has its industrial aesthetic. Innovative was the absence of a portal and the building feels almost like an outdoor shrine. But there is reason to pause.

The great opening on the front is a perspectival window that focuses directly to the top of the altar. It forms a 30-degree angle that is of course

FIGURE 4.2.11 *Robert F. Carr Memorial Chapel of St. Savior, Mies van der Rohe, service in progress, Illinois Institute of Technology, Chicago, c. 1950s, with pictorial additions by author.* © HB-16676-B, Chicago History Museum, Hedrich-Blessing Collection.

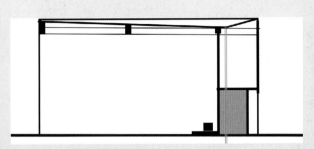

FIGURE 4.2.12 *Plan and roof and section: Robert F. Carr Memorial Chapel of St. Savior, Mies van der Rohe, Illinois Institute of Technology, Chicago. Section by Mark Jarzombek.*

one twelfth of a circle and thus embeds in the building an allusion not just toward perspective, but to the ancient attributes of *archē*. But there is more at play. The roof is not flat, but sloped in such a way that water flows to a drainage hole with groins describing the same 30-degree angle. The drainage pipe is located just behind the altar.[5] This can be no accident, as it makes visible—albeit from *above*—the perspectival key to the building. Humans, of course, will not register this, but rather focus only on the ocularist tug of religion.

Here the anamorphic is inverted. It is the real world, the world of you and me, who, unbeknownst to us, make up an anamorphic mess that can only resolve itself in the absolute compression of the perspectival point.

* * * *

Though these examples outline conditions where the anamorphic has broken through into the creative tissue of "architecture," all "architecture" is anamorphic in the context of its disciplinary landscape. The Rotch Library of Architecture & Planning at MIT, like many architectural libraries, embodies the anamorphic in that it requires a specific position to be recognizable: the Library of Congress System. Here the disembodied "perspective" comes from the Enlightenment and its desire to control discourse through its privileging of mind over body. It is, therefore, predictable that when a philosopher (Heidegger) or a sociologist (Sennett) speaks about crafts, their work is ranked higher than when a real builder speaks.

Sample of the anamorphic location of "Architecture" in the Library of Congress System:

B 3279: *Bauen Wohnen Denken*, Martin Heidegger, 1952.

BJ1498.S46 2008: *The Craftsman*, Richard Sennett, 2008.

BF353.B44 1996: *Environmental Psychology*, Paul A. Bell, 1996.

HD9715.G72.N277: *The Construction Industry*,1964.

N6537.M57.A4 2004: *Mary Miss,* Mary Miss, 2004.

NA1123.A334.B67: *Leon Battista Alberti*, Franco Borsi, 1975.

ND237.S683 A66: *Frank Stella: Irregular Polygons, 1965–66*, Brian P. Kennedy, 2010.

T59.7.H337 2013: *The Hand, an Organ of the Mind: what the manual tells the mental*, Zdravko Radman, 2019.

TH4818.W6.W65 1988: *Wood frame house construction*, Gerald E. Sherwood, Robert C. Stroh, 1988.

S870.W55 2017: *Plywood: a material story*, Christopher Wilk, Elizabeth Bisley, 2017.

VM321.B57 1984: *Boat building techniques illustrated*, Richard Birmingham, 1984.

What we see is the incommensurability between the reality of the discipline, as shaped by the Library of Congress that we in the field use without a thought, and the metanarrative that operates to unify the whole into an artificial singularity. The library is nothing more than the alienation of incomprehensibility.

The figure of the discipline is profiled in the metaphysics of Reason.

*	*	*	*

An afterthought: A quotation from *Woman, Native, Other* (1989) by Trinh T. Minh-ha, a Vietnamese filmmaker, writer, literary theorist, composer, and professor, has always stayed with me:

> A conversation of "us" with "us" about "them" is a conversation in which "them" is silenced. "Them" always stands on the other side of the hill, naked and speechless, barely present in its absence. Subject of discussion, "them" is only admitted among "us," the discussing subjects, when accompanied or introduced by an "us," member, hence the dependency of "them" and its need to acquire good manners for the membership standing. The privilege to sit at table with "us," however, proves both uplifting and demeaning.[6]

PART FIVE

CHAPTER ONE

Arche-Socio(~~Arche~~)ology

Alberti and Filarete are today mostly thought of as irrelevant to the core issues of modernity. Between the two, however, it is Alberti that steals the show. Filarete is still overlooked in the conventions of the discipline. If we look again, we see that they started, or better stated, placed into disciplinary formation, a culture war that is still fundamental. Only by integrating Filarete more fully into the discussion can we recognize the expanded field of grammatological possibilities of the *archē-tektōn*.

* * * *

Filarete's enthusiasm for the building site is infectious. He tells us about heading out in the early morning on his horse to a quarry to meet the masons, having lunch with the carpenters on a hillside to discuss wages, observing the mixing of mortar and even participating in arcane, shamanistic rituals that were significant to the builders as well as to the patrons. He understood that world and was not afraid to talk about it. In one passage, he goes out searching for wood for the beams. After several exhausting days of riding, the group finally comes to a forest:

> While riding through the forest we kept seeing a straight and beautiful wood for making anything a man could wish. When we arrived at the place where these men were working, we greeted them. They replied pleasantly and asked what we were looking for. We told them and they replied that there was plenty of wood of many kinds. We asked them if they knew how we could proceed to have this wood cut. After our explanation they replied yes. We would find [men] enough and, if there were no other, they would do it themselves both for the money and to help us.

> "Yes, but we want it done quickly."

> "In the name of God, we will do it as fast as we can. You can also get other [men] from the village, for there are plenty there. It will all be done in good time. Now you are invited to eat [with us]."

Since we were light on food, we accepted their invitation. [We] also [wanted] to see how [their work] was done. We dismounted from our horses. The horses would gladly have eaten hay if they had had it, but we gave them instead some sort of straw. We drew around the fire and put a part of the pig to cook. When it was cooked, we all ate together. This revived us a little. We looked at their lathes to see how [their work] was done.[1]

It is a remarkable text; though designed to make Filarete look good, it is nonetheless the first narrative from a builder's point of view in the history of the discipline! It is also the first and probably the last time an architect will write about having lunch with some of his workers! Even more astonishing is that Filarete acts quasi-ethnographically. During one sojourn into a sparsely settled area, a local shepherd offers him a place to stay in their camp. After dinner he took a stroll and observed:

Even though it was a shepherd's place, it was pleasant and beautiful. It was slightly elevated. There were three oak trees here that seemed to have been planted by design, for they were in the shape of a triangle. In the middle there was a space of perhaps 25 or 30 braccia between them in such a way that their branches all touched. This made a beautiful roof. They had built a hut in front of each of these oaks.[2]

Based on these experiences, he began to imagine the origin of architecture making drawings that aimed to depict the moment humans first began to make shelters, which he calls variously *habitatione* or *cabbanne*. Though Filarete had been in Rome from 1433 to about 1447 and took great interest in its ruins, liking in particular the richness of detail, the various types of marbles and porphyries, and the colors in the mosaics and frescoes, his origin story does not begin in the antiquity of imperial Rome and the pretensions of humanistic facadism. We see normal people busily going about the activities of house-making. In one drawing, a man brings a sapling to the site and begins to bend it while his compatriot is working on a branch. In another drawing, a man is pounding a stake into the ground, while another nearby is preparing a rectilinear structure with a thatched roof.

Cesare Cesariano (1521) showed a more elaborate situation portraying a gradual development starting with a rudimentary triangular structure, in the upper right of the woodcut, and proceeding to a more advanced type of hut made of wattle and daub. In the foreground to the right, we see men quarrying out blocks of stone meant to show the future tradition of stone-building.

Alberti, of course, also recounted an origin story, except that he links it directly to the teleology of architecture which developed "through experience and skill . . . with the introduction of various building types, of which some

FIGURE 5.1.1 *Drawing*, Libro Architectonico, *Filarete, Book 1, folio 5r.*

FIGURE 5.1.2 *Drawing*, Libro Architectonico, *Filarete, Book 1, folio 5v.*

are public, others private, some sacred, others profane," etc.[3] In this Alberti is following Vitruvius who makes it clear that developing skilled labor was a necessary step:

> Furthermore, as men made progress by becoming daily more expert in building, and as their ingenuity was increased by their dexterity so that from habit they attained to considerable skill, their intelligence was enlarged by their industry until the more proficient adopted the trade of carpenters [*fabros*].
>
> Vitruvius, *Ten Books on Architecture*, 2.1.6

The difference between Alberti and Filarete is not to be missed. Whereas Alberti moves quickly to the issue of skill and expertise, thickening the story in a way that then becomes nothing less than the discipline of architecture— leading to the important question for Alberti of who speaks for it—Filarete, oddly, does not bridge the gap between rustic craftsman and urban master builder.

Filarete describes the rustic house not just as the beginning of architecture's history, but as one step removed from Adam and Eve:

> It is true that Vitruvius says that the first to invent habitations were those first men who lived in the forests and made themselves huts [*cappanne*, i.e., cabins] and grottoes as best they could. However, it was, I believe, that Adam was the first.[4]

* * * *

Alberti, though acknowledging the primordial role of the house, sees the city, and Rome in particular, as the place where architecture comes into its disciplinary fullness. The art of building, he writes in Book VI of *De re aedificatoria*, underwent three stages of development during antiquity: it experienced *adolescentia* in Asia under despotic kings, flourished with the Greeks, but reached *maturitas* in Italy, the point at which, Alberti believes, it showed its greatest potential.[5] It is in the context of the city, he implies, that we see the codification of knowledge and precedents, a process in which the field "grew with practice and skill" (*excrevisse usu et arte*) where *excerno*, deriving from Latin *ex-* ("out of, from") + *cernō* ("separate, sift; discern") implies a mental sifting and ordering.[6] And indeed the first line of the book reads:

> Since we are to treat of the lineaments of buildings, we shall collect, compare, and extract into our work all the soundest and most useful advice that our learned ancestors have handed down to us in writing, and whatever principles we ourselves have noted in the very execution of their work.[7]

Whereas Alberti's project is cumulative, connecting the present with the past through a thousand stitches, Filarete's connects the present to the past in a single and powerful leap of imagination.

* * * *

Whereas Alberti perpetuates the ancient, urban-based class distinction of the *banausos*, Filarete—in direct opposition to Socrates—portrays village craftsmen as dignified and reasonable. He addresses them with respect, has dinner with them, and sleeps in their huts. They are the glue that holds everything together. Truth be told, the easy relationship that Filarete evokes between himself, the patron, and the builders was more fantasy than reality. All the buildings that he worked on in Milan, namely the Cathedral, the Castello Sforzesco and the Ospedale Maggiore, were never finished, due to disputes both between the Duke and the local aristocracy, and between the Filarete and local master builders.

* * * *

For Alberti, labor is a necessary ancillary to architecture. The making of great buildings would be unthinkable without skilled labor as a field of expertise— of making and knowing—that carries deep cultural memories of successes and failures. For Filarete, labor is so integrated into the fabric of society, it exists without independent structure. There are in his descriptions no discussions about apprenticeships, complex tools, or seniority, and to not mention them is to purposefully falsify the image of building.

Whereas the Albertian world acknowledges the *tektōn*, albeit through silencing, the Filaretian world sees the *tektōn* as a "natural" within the social structure of civilization.

Alberti's treatise outlines the dialectics of progressive approximation; Filarete's, the dialectics of mythological extrapolation.

* * * *

A more recent example of the dialectics of extrapolation was posted by none other than the *Journal of the American Institute of Architects* which let it be known:

> Over time our ancestors also learned to make simple huts using stones, tree branches, bones, and other materials found in nature—humanity's first step toward the development of architecture.[8]

The joke, of course, is on them. In *that* world, there would be no professional architects, and not even master builders.

* * * *

The Filaretian model became particularly valuable from the 1970s onward when architects and intellectuals began to try to heal the perceived split between the architectural profession and social realities. It was especially foundational for those who advocated for "vernacular architecture," a term that became fashionable beginning in the mid-1970s. Bernard Rudofsky's famous exhibition *Architecture Without Architects: A Short Introduction to Non-Pedigreed Architecture* (1964) serves as an early example. In the press release for the exhibition that accompanied the book, Pietro Belluschi, the Dean of the school of architecture at MIT, wrote that the book is

> an exhilarating glimpse of architecture as a manifestation of the human spirit beyond style and fashion, and, more importantly, beyond the narrows of our Roman-Greek tradition.[9]

Filarete would probably say, "Right on."

* * * *

But it was not just vernacularists who were chasing the elusive, happy socio-. Died-in-the-wool modernists, like Alison and Peter Smithson, also began to make their orientation to the presumed authenticity of ancient life part of their rhetorical strategy:

> We see architecture as a direct statement of a way of life and in the past, ordinary prosaic life has been most succinctly, economically, tersely expressed in the peasant farms and the impedimenta of Mediterranean rural life that Le Corbusier had made respectable.[10]

We can also draw a line from Filarete to home improvement retailer, The Home Depot. There are differences, of course. The Filaretian model operates without the idea of a supply chain. Materials are local and readily available to anyone with initiative (an illusion, of course). Although The Home Depot operates in the context of advanced capitalism and is at the center of a vast global system of procurement and delivery, it posits the materials for its consumers in its shops as if they were freely available in a state of nature. For the consumer, the supply chain does not exist. Just as the Filaretian builder would go to the nearby forest to get some timber, the modern-day consumer goes to The Home Depot to get some 2×4s or load up on plywood. And in the one that is close to where I live, you can get a hotdog and chat with an associate on how best to mix the concrete.

* * * *

Though Filarete uses the word "architect," as far as I can see he never uses the word "architecture," except in the title. Although we can easily call his writing a "theory of architecture," that would be to falsify its distinction from the Albertian project, and not just because his *Libro Architettonico* is presented as a transcription of an oral presentation to Francesco Sforza, Duke of Milan. We might also be tempted to say that Filarete is describing something like a

FIGURE 5.1.3 *Author stocking up at The Home Depot. Photograph by Mark Jarzombek.*

"building practice," but that would be to undercook its narrative and theoretical armature and return to the conventions of skills and trade. There is no word in the dictionary that fully embraces the Filaretian project.

One can imagine it as an *archē*socio(*archē*)ology, a word that opens up a range of grammatological possibilities that work their way through all the way to the present day. *Archē*, because Filarete embraces the magic of the discipline; *socio*, because of its quasi-sociological grounding; and *archē*, because it critiques the more formally trained "experts" of the age. The tension between *archē*, an architect oriented toward that *socio-*, and *archē*, an architect who is more formally trained through books, lies just under the surface of his writing.

Unlike *archē(non)tektōn*, *archē*socio(*archē*)ology does not divide the world between knowing and making, but between two different types of knowing, a true one and a false one. The true one is represented by Filarete, the master builder, and his friendly village craftsmen; the false one is represented by the aristocratic clients—in this case, Sforza—who, if left untutored, would make all the wrong decisions.

Filarete's *Libro Architettonico*, almost more so than Alberti's *Ten Books on Architecture*, marks the more official beginning of architecture's quixotic search for disciplinary (dis)integrity.

CHAPTER TWO

Arche-²

Giorgio Vasari, who thought that Filarete's book was "the stupidest book ever written," would be shocked to know that its influence extended into our contemporary era. Its contribution to our grammatological history was, however, not linear, but one that morphed in numerous ways, which brings us to Marc-Antoine Laugier, who authored the *Essai sur l'architecture* in 1753. He was no insignificant Jesuit abbé. In 1754, he took the pulpit in the chapel at Versailles to thunder against the Louis XIV's doubtful amusements, entreating the king to give religion its due and to confound the rebels. He depicted an indolent ruler, ministers who abuse their power, and a people who become disobedient because more is exacted from them than they possess.[1] After a few such sermons, the king had had enough. Laugier was ordered by his superiors to leave Paris. Laugier must have had some time on his hands for in this same period he authored his *Essai*, believing that he had determined the irrefutable first principles of architecture.[2]

Like Filarete, Laugier imagined an alternative history, but with a profound difference. Instead of starting at zero, he wanted to *re*start the clock, famously portraying a primitive hut, or to use his phrase, *la petite cabane rustique*, in the frontispiece of his book. In this he was not completely counterfactual, but inspired by the buildings of the Native Americans, the Iroquois in particular, whom the Jesuits had been attempting to convert. That the Native Americans were not godless, but imbued with the potential for Christianity was borne out, so the Jesuits argued, by their ordered lifestyle and their buildings. In comparison to the decadent French aristocrats, the Native Americans seemed indeed like a lost moral world.

Though Laugier was suspicious of the aristocratic class, he, unlike Filarete, was not going out to have lunch with the workers. Laugier's goal was not to guide builders, but to define the tastes of the architect:

There are several treatises on architecture which explain measures and proportions with reasonable accuracy, enter into the details of the different Orders and furnish models for all manner of buildings. There is no work

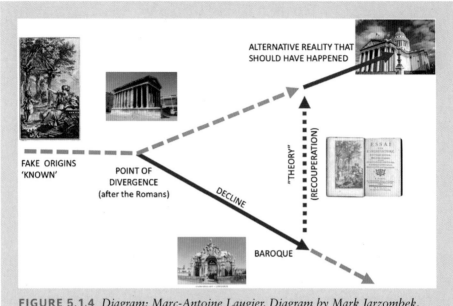

FAKE ORIGINS 'KNOWN'

POINT OF DIVERGENCE (after the Romans)

DECLINE

"THEORY"

(RECOUPERATION)

ALTERNATIVE REALITY THAT SHOULD HAVE HAPPENED

BAROQUE

FIGURE 5.1.4 *Diagram: Marc-Antoine Laugier. Diagram by Mark Jarzombek.*

as yet that firmly establishes the principles of architecture, explains its true spirit and proposes rules for guiding talent and defining taste. It seems to me that in those arts which are not purely mechanical it is not sufficient to know how to work; it is above all important to learn to think.

Unfortunately, that space of learning, for him, had its problems, for it was cluttered by designers who gave in to capricious whims, used precepts indiscriminately, and followed rules randomly. His target in all of this was the theatrics of the baroque and whimsicalness of the rococo. The more subtle tension in Filarete between *archē* and ~~*archē*~~ is now brought out into the open:

Only architecture has until now been left to the *capricious* whim of the artists who have offered precepts *indiscriminately*. They fixed rules at *random*, based only on the inspection of ancient buildings. They copied the faults as scrupulously as the beauty; *lacking principles* which would make them see the difference, they were bound to confound the two. Being servile imitators, they declared as legitimate everything which has been authorized by examples. They always confined their studies to fact and deduced from them, *erroneously*, the law: thus, their teaching has been nothing but a *source of error*.

my italics

✳ ✳ ✳ ✳

In this context, after the Greek and Romans,

> [t]he barbarism of succeeding centuries, having buried the fine arts under the ruins of the only empire that had preserved taste and principles, called forth a new system of architecture in which neglected proportion and ornament childishly crowded produced nothing but stones in fretwork, shapeless masses and a grotesque extravagance—a new architecture which for too long has been the delight of Europe.

> p. 8

To which he then concludes:

> It is to be hoped that some great architect will undertake to save architecture from eccentric opinions by disclosing its fixed and unchangeable laws.[3]

If the moral imperative could be imposed on the Native Americans, it might just work on the out-of-control architects back in Europe.

* * * *

The *Essai* is often seen as characteristic of the rationalist thinking of the Enlightenment. But that is not accurate. For the first time we have a clear example of the superfluidity of an "architecture" that aims to supersede normative practice as its administrative agency. This type of "architecture" is not embedded within the careful stitching of an Albertian disciplinary framework, but rather is to be located in a torturous confusion of objectives: it is a theory that does not see itself as theory (i.e., as written and handed down in codices), but as with Filarete, as grounded in the presumed factuality and immediacy of natural history. This anti-disciplinarity finds its resonance with Jean Jacques Rousseau's *A Dissertation On the Origin and Foundation of the Inequality of Mankind*, (1755): "O man . . . behold your history, such as I have thought to read it, not in books written by your fellow creatures, who are liars, but in nature, which never lies."[4] Rousseau writes that in the end, all of his arguments benefit only a few readers, namely "those who know how to understand."[5] Laugier, like Rousseau, presumed that the spread of "lies" has not reached its hegemonic state. There is still time to restart the engines of practice.

* * * *

When Laugier recounts the origin story of a savage who seeks to protect himself by making his *petite cabane rustique* (made, in his narrative, by one man), it is to suggest that we do a cultural rebuild, one building at a time. We do not even have to go all the way back to Adam and Eve, as Filarete did, but only as far back as the Maison Carrée, a Roman temple in Nîmes in southern France and one of the best-preserved Roman temples to survive in the territory of the former Roman Empire. The difference between the two tracks—the false Now and the suggested Now—is that the new one is armed with a particular script, his own *Essai sur l'architecture*. Without this explicatory gospel, the recuperation of architecture—and its ~~history~~/"history"—is impossible.

This innovative ~~history~~/"history," opposed to the presumed evils of contemporary practice, imagined a history that *should* have happened in contradistinction to real history that has only one goal, to show how architecture got cluttered up in the transition from oral to textual. The new "history" focuses on the beginning/endgame, that, of course, can never manifest itself as real except in a dialectic that finds self-righteousness in its own pronouncements and abjection in the outside world. It is in fabricating and obscuring that gap where theory—to use that all too dull word—begins to operate and find its audience and defenders as separatists fighting not just against the proverbial builders, but against members of their own profession. There are now two historical points. One of origins and the other of divergence.[6]

It is not the deeply learned *archē* who is going to restore confidence in the discipline (Alberti), but an *archē* who accepts myth as reality. All the numerous codices and writing of the ages past can be thrown away. The new discipline rests on a single book, the job of which—in all its presumptive paradisciplinary glory—is to champion a restorative architecture while openly denying the problem of its own simulacral faults. Learning does not come from the deep trough of antecedents held dear in the bindings of codices, but in the presumed legalism of nature that operates to target, expose, and ultimately purge the unnatural within its ranks.

Laugier, in Jesuit fashion, dislocates the subject from the discipline, torments it in the affectations of self-righteousness, and then exorcises from it the long tentacles of history.

✳ ✳ ✳ ✳

The Enlightenment is often thought to have opened up the avenue to the modern inner Self; if so, that was not true for Laugier. Whatever opening there was toward imagination and design in the phraseology of *mente animoque* is squashed in Laugier. The architect draws nourishment from the outside—and a very particular outside at that.

We must not lose sight of its violence as therein lies the core of architecture's disciplinary modernity.

When Derrida, in "No (Point of) Madness—Maintaining Architecture" (1986), writes of "architecture" and elsewhere writes of "modern architecture" we can hear the deep echoes of the Laugierian split. The unmarked violence that produced "modern architecture" assumes that the word "architecture" by itself is insufficient to carry its semantic meanings. And yet, "architecture" is written to assume in reverse, like Laugier, that it can magically erase that which was post facto added to it.

***

But one does not need to always dig so deep to find the ghosts of Laugier. If there was a Laugier Prize in Architecture, the Oslo Opera House (2007) by Snøhetta would certainly win it, even though there would hundreds of contenders. Fiercely ascetic and clearly expressing its "construction" as a way to demonstrate honesty, it operates as if there was no rhetoric. Glass is glass, structure is structure, roof is roof and so on. It exalts in the standard modernist obligations to whiteness and cleanliness, and shimmers in the dust-free dialectics of completion. Laugier's insistence on a reference to nature as the guide is here translated into a regional variant of snowy fields.

In 2009, the building won the European Union Prize for Contemporary Architecture—Mies van der Rohe Award. Perhaps that should be conceived less an honor than a sign of the scandalous perpetuation of the Laugierian ethos by certain European elites who think that the mission of architecture is to perpetuate the cult of self-abnegation.

****

The Laugerian ambition of disciplinary self-disciplining is that of figure/ground, the "figure" of a theory that stands over the "ground" of reality, the former oriented toward the logos and the metaphysics of delivering the promised land of orderliness, the latter oriented only to the emptiness of meaning in a chaotic world of quotidian production. Unfortunately, the promised land is built on the thin ice of self-deception, producing something quite new: *archē*(~~archē/ tektōn~~), or *archē²* for short.

FIGURE 5.1.5 *Oslo Opera House, Snøhetta, Oslo, 2007. Photograph by Chuthulu975.*

Filarete imagined an easy and happy flow between the Then and the Now. Laugier wanted to violently jump-start the whole process, creating two Nows—the false one and the true one—and yet end somewhere in a cultural space of peace and order. The tension is unmistakable. For the converted architect, shamed into submission, there is little room to maneuver. He was condemned to embody an ambition-less social/historical/empirical ontology that had to deliver the grand narrative with no shred of ambiguity.

* * * * *

Once the gap between the false Now and the true Now had been opened up as a sliding signifier, there was no turning back. It became the hallmark of modernity. As the century progressed, archaeology and ethnography would become the thickening sauce. Soon even "history," designed as a story of origin, divergence, and recuperation, became a mythology of its own making.

* * * *

Joachim Winkelman's *Geschichte der Kunst des Alterthums* (The History of Art in Antiquity, 1764) marks the intensification—and increased stressing—of that message. The *terminus post quem* is not Adam's house, not the primitive hut, but the temples of ancient Greece that belonged to a imagined period where political freedom flourished in the context of an ideal Mediterranean climate. If architecture was to have relevance, it would have to take its cue from Greek art:

> What generally characterizes the excellence of Greek masterpieces is finally a noble simplicity and a calm greatness, both in the pose and in the expression. Just as it always remains calm in the depths of the sea, however much it may rage on the surface, so the expression of Greek figures, whatever passions they may be subject to, reveal a great and placid soul.[7]

With the Greek temple, Winkelman brought the story of architecture's mythologically imagined socio away from colonial-era fascination with the primitive and into the immediacy of "civilization."- Imaginary trips through the forest in search for lumber became long and difficult trips to archaeological sites in search of valuable details. The resultant classicism was far different from Alberti's. For Alberti, columns, pilasters, and entablatures spoke of noble aspirations, the esoterica of learning and the separation of the elites from the lower classes. Classicism was meant to be publicly pronounced, even if for show. Winkelman's classicism, though it maintained many of those features in silence, proclaimed itself on the broader front as the potential model for the modern German. "The only way for us to become great, or even inimitable, if possible, is to imitate the Greeks."[8]

Classicism now promised an architecture (and, of course, its associated ontolo-nationalist imaginary) that was self-regulatory; an architecture (without scare quotes) that transcends the "architecture" that it sees lurking around every corner.

* * * *

The post-Winkelmanian search to upgrade the pedigree of the Euro-socio- by infusing it with the material substance of its "history" is exemplified by the Panthéon in Paris (1790) designed by Jacques-Germain Soufflot, and known, as one scholar phrased it, for his "strictness of line, firmness of form, simplicity of contour, and rigorously architectonic conception of detail."[9] That is one way to put it. Another way is to see the building as a box with an updated version of the Pantheon of Rome for the front and a similarly updated version of Donato Bramante's Tempietto at San Pietro in Montorio (c. 1510) for the dome. Its referentiality to ancient Rome and to the Renaissance was meant to make sure that its ideological position was unambiguous. The former pointed to Roman imperial might and to early Christianity (since the Pantheon was the only Roman temple directly converted into a church), and the second to Christian martyrdom (San Pietro in Montorio was built on the spot of Saint Peter's crucifixion). As a play of semiotic referentialities, the building spells out the logic of origins and recuperations where the architect needs to do little more than cut and paste in order to tell the story.

The architect, dislocated from a subjectological position into a presumed objectological one, performs its evacuation in the name of cultural depth. The logo of architecture could now become more properly the logo of empire.

* * *

If it was not the Greeks or Romans, it was something else. When the Royal Institute of British Architects in the 1830s was established, it adopted a seal that featured a Minoan-esque column flanked by Egyptoid/Assyrian-esque lions (slightly modified over the decades). The Then—defined by its

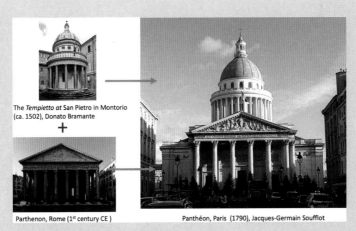

The *Tempietto at* San Pietro in Montorio (ca. 1502), Donato Bramante

+

Parthenon, Rome (1ˢᵗ century CE)

Panthéon, Paris (1790), Jacques-Germain Soufflot

Figure 5.1.6 *Panthéon, Paris, 1790, with additions by the author. Diagram by Mark Jarzombek.*

FIGURE 5.1.7 *Royal Institute of British Architects insignia as stamped on a leather book cover. © Royal Institute of British Architects.*

colonialist gaze of appropriation—was now the official imprimatur of the discipline's Now.

* * * *

In an attempt to pursue the elusive socio- from a different direction, Gottfried Semper in *Die Vier Elemente der Baukunst* (The Four Elements of Architecture, 1851) moved away from archaeology to a more promising and universal anthropology.[10] Protection against rain makes the roof, protection against fire makes the hearth, and protection from enemies the earthen mound and walls.[66] The Caribbean Hut, he argued, was a place where "all elements of ancient architecture appear in their most original and unadulterated form: the hearth as center, the mound surrounded by a framework of poles as terrace, the roof carried by columns, and mats as space enclosure as wall."[11] Though Semper looks closely and intensely at the walls, colorings, and stone courses of ancient buildings in ways that clearly show him "on the building site"—even if often metaphorically—the closer he got in his writings to the modern age, the less the connection between past and present becomes apparent. As with Laugier, Semper's theory of "origin" is posited within a culture in decline. After seeing the 1851 world exhibit in London, comparing it to the Tower of Babel, he wrote:

> This seeming confusion is nothing more than the clear emergence of certain anomalies in current societal interrelationships, the origins and effects of which could not be recognized until now in such a general and clear way to the world.[12]

＊＊＊＊

Architectural history as a way to obscure the structural violence within the discipline is not a thing of the past. In 2016–17, OMA designed an exhibition called "Pan-European Living Room" for the London Design Museum. Viewers saw a domestic living room that answered the title of the exhibition, "Fear and Love: Reactions to a Complex World" (2016–17). The view through the window of a bombed-out urban scene from World War II was filtered through blinds that were colored vertically to look like a sliced-up version of the famous EU barcode that OMA had designed as the symbol of the European Union fifteen years previously. The project wants us to imagine Europe as a *tabula rasa*, cleaned of the historical detritus and now "prepped" for the arrival of modernity. In this, OMA is dramatizing the already much-circulated rhetoric about modernity as a struggle against the old, but we see not the usual housing projects that came to dominate our understanding of post-World War II modernity. Instead, we are offered an alternative history as told by its avatar, the furniture. Although OMA's "object catalogue" that lists the furniture in the room was meant to show in more detail the first modest restorative touches of humanity following the terrors of the war, it points in reality to the private sector and the unknown elite clients who could afford designer chairs. There was a set of Cesca Chairs by Marcel Breuer that stood in for Hungary, a Dining Table by Eero Saarinen that celebrated Finland, while Mies van der Rohe's Barcelona Table represented Germany.

Everything had the look of the twentieth century, except for one piece, the Traditional Coffee Table, as it was titled, that represented Slovakia, the designer of which was listed, with bureaucratic precision, as "unknown," as if it were some anthropological object from a distant land.[13]

OMA's message was the following: The Slovakians, still wallowing in decorative craft, have a long way to go before they reach the equation: Europe=modernity. In that sense, Slovakia—the last of the various countries of the group to have entered the EU (2004)—was the token fall guy for all the orientalist Others even further beyond the border. However, the fact that this table is unfamiliar to the two people from Slovakia that I know and asked about it, makes me wonder if the table is a cultural fantasy concocted for the convivence of the argument. This suggests that the Slovakian table had a second meaning, serving as the mythological—and fabricated—beginning point from which modernity establishes itself. It was Laugier's primitive hut in furniture form, a four-posted, natural corrective against the lure of excess, the arch-reminder that the world—in its originary moment—was not arbitrary, but sourced in the (imagined) stability of anthropological primitivism. Just as Laugier's fake hut served his Catholic, hyper-moralizing tendency to see a world that "derived" linearly from all that was authentic, OMA's "hut," no less moralizing, points backward to a presumed, mythical point of origin. Both huts exemplify the Eurocentric invention of an anthropological Other.

Laugier's *cabana rustique* and its neomodernist reincarnation by OMA in the form of a *table rustique* only pretend to acknowledge the ancient *tektōn*. Both instead cheat the system not only by emptying out the signifier of origin, but also by heading straight to a teleological exit that elevates "the good" over "the bad," the classical over the rococo, the modern over the postmodern, and the false Now over the true Now. Both make extreme moralistic claims, fictions meant to turn architecture away from the sensory and disciplinary overload of the "outside" world. Both look for architecture to kill off "architecture," and yet both circle around to the repressed. The Pan-European Living Room would be another winner of the Laugier Prize.

* * * *

The contemporary architect who most sought to return to the tension of the Laugierian *archē²*—not by trying to solve the puzzle (as had been done through the nineteenth century in the form of anthropology and/or historicism), but to demonstrate its originary, cruel, if not sadistic, efficiency—was Peter Eisenman, who set his sights on Palladio. It was for him not a building as such that was important (for that would just return us to the conventions of the primitive hut and its avatars: the Greek temple or the Roman Colosseum, the Slovakian table), but the architect as ontological proposition. Eisenman's Palladio was not a singular being, but two people:

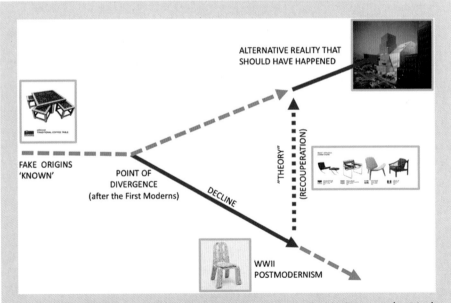

FIGURE 5.1.8 *Diagram: Pan-European Living Room, OMA. Diagram by Mark Jarzombek.*

the *tektōn*, Andrea di Pietro della Gondola, and the upstart "architect," namely Palladio. Eisenman registers that split in Palladio's *own* drawings where he sees a ghosted virtual Palladio, a "Palladio" of hidden lines that doubled up the designs, as if seen through two lenses. The Albertian drawing, as the singular performance of humanism's *ratio et via*, is here confounded. The spatial, anamorphic dislocations in the drawing give the lie to the inherited image of Palladio as a classical figure of the Renaissance working with clean and orderly geometries. Eisenman also intended to dislocate the idea of the modern as well, giving it a starting point in the "real/fictional" world of an imagined Palladio.

Palladio's onto-disciplinary split performs directly on a psycho-symbolic register of modern architecture. The track of Eisenman into the problem thus begins with the recognition that the split *archē²* is *already* in place, as its own mytho-historical construction, one that is "debilitated and disturbed," as Eisenman expresses it, at the get-go.[14] It is a model without a model.

The ideology of fracture as inaugurated by Alberti and the ideology of violence as inaugurated by Laugier are now both in the open, instead of being secreted away in disciplinary protocols or self-righteous moralism. There is in all this no progress toward the teleological cleansing of the ground that the modernists and neomodernists promise. The result is a new strange creature—an Andrea di Pietro della Gondola and a "not Andrea di

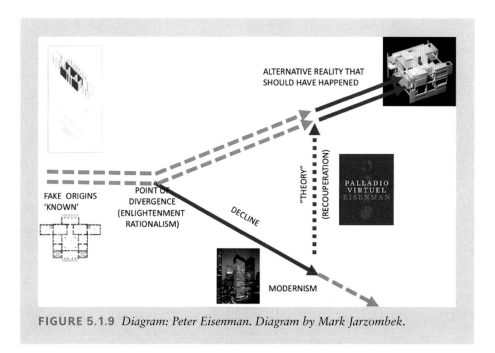

FIGURE 5.1.9 *Diagram: Peter Eisenman. Diagram by Mark Jarzombek.*

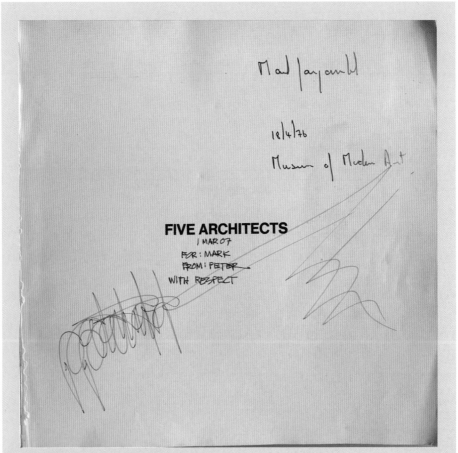

FIGURE 5.1.10 *Autographed page of* Five Books of Architecture, *Peter Eisenman. Photograph by Mark Jarzombek.*

Pietro della Gondola," a Palladio and a "Palladio"—that forecloses against any anthropological, sociological "prehistory." Architecture has no choice but to operate in the post- of that new origin/origin. There is no there there to go back to. There is also no future except to revisit and replay the split to it illogical end. With his figuration of "Palladio" in mind, Eisenman even came to sign his name with two pens.

CHAPTER THREE

Laugier's Haunts

The English translation of Laugier's book from 1755 had a frontispiece drawn by Samuel Wale (1721–86) that shows a hut under construction with men busily going about their work.[1] One of the walls has been built with an opening for a rather conventional window. Though the posts have been left

FIGURE 5.2.1 *Frontispiece*, An Essay on Architecture, *Samuel Wale, 1755. Courtesy of archive.org, accessed October 9, 2020, at https://archive.org/details/ essayonarchitect00laugrich.*

rough, the beams have been neatly plained, presumably only with an axe as no adze is visible. A hearth is set out in front and some of the men are preparing lime for plaster. A woman with her playful young child dominates the center of the composition and it is presumably her husband and relatives who are doing the work.

The more famous French version offered something quite different. It was drawn by Charles-Dominique-Joseph Eisen (1720–78), a French painter and engraver known for his illustrations of lovers in the forests, cherubs, and an occasional erotic scene; he is not the illustrator that one might imagine for the moralist Laugier. He was chosen for the job, however, by the publisher, and perhaps because of Eisen's connections to the court, or perhaps because of it was thought that his reputation might spruce things up. What Laugier thought of the etching is not known, but one cannot doubt that the image has played an outsized role in shaping narratives about the discipline.

The astonishing thing about the image is that the four columns are actually trees. Only the roof structure is man-made and even then the branches are barely worked. There is no suggestion of carpentry or of the emergence of skill. It is almost as if the builders had scavenged the forest

FIGURE 5.2.2 *Frontispiece:* Essai sur l'architecture, *Charles-Dominique-Joseph Eisen, 1755.*

floor for usable branches. There are no people, apart from the rather youthful goddess of architecture sitting to one side with a somewhat confused cherub standing nearby. The hut is empty and open, without the hint of partitions, walls, or even a hearth. It lacks the traits of domesticity, of inhabitation, and even of construction. No ladders or instruments are lying about.

But the makers of the structure certainly did not willingly abandon their efforts, even if rather rudimentary. In good colonial fashion, Eisen seems to have expelled them from the forest, opening up the structure of appropriation. The silent, empty structure is intertwined with the silent, emptied-out forest.

Laugier/Eisen's pavilion tries to capture the moment of disciplinary formation, the moment when architecture (without scare quotes) appears as sprung directly from the mind of the goddess. But not only is there no one making the structure, it is impossible to imagine anyone even living in it. The violence of exclusion figures forth an *oikos* without habitability, exorcizing habitation, in fact, in order to clean out the ground for some new unknown form of socio-, one presumably unhindered by its former banality. It is a masculinist fantasy, rendering the old socio- as either irrelevant or invisible to the making of a new one. It is a socio-~~socio~~, the enhanced *modern* version of *archē(non)tektōn*.

****

The Biomimetic Research Pavilion 2018 was built at the University of Stuttgart in Germany to demonstrate a special interlocking system that could generate a lightweight and material-saving architecture. It was inspired by diatoms, a type of algae that usually live in water and which are able to form colonies in the shape of filament ribbons. That system was then translated into an architecture made out of birchwood-based, middle-density fiberboard plates.

FIGURE 5.2.3 *Interlocking Shell: Biomimetic Research Pavilion 2018. Bachelor thesis of Arzum Coban and Victoria Ivanova, supervised by Prof. Dr.-Ing. Arch. Hanaa Dahy. Photograph by Coban, Ivanova, BioMat@ITKE/University of Stuttgart.* © *Arzum Coban and Victoria Ivanova.*

Pavilions like this bring the dialectics of (in)completion into extreme form. They display the prowess of completion in the real world, the pride of new-*oikos*, as imagined through the process of its materials and its making, in this case simulating its presumably corrective alliance with "nature." They also point backward to the mythological moment of architecture's disciplinary emergence as a form of habitation-without-habitability.[2] The assembly of these pavilions, usually made by students, unpaid interns, and friends, is sometimes part of the story, as if reliving/reviving/reenacting some faux, ancient communitarian moment. But to gain this advantage these structures leave the gap between the Then and the Now, and between the Now and the Future as part of a *mysterium* of some soon-to-be-imagined disciplinary project.

* * * *

The presence of a statue of a woman in the park in the photograph was not accidental. It references the statue of Morgen ("Morning") by Georg Kolbe at the Barcelona Pavilion by Mies van der Rohe, which in turn references Eisen's goddess. The figure serves to smooth over the disjuncture between the socio- and the ~~socio~~. Its femininity hides the wound of alienation by pointing to an anticipated socio-, a socio- in representation only, though obviously no one knows when or where that socio- will emerge.

The statue is the windowless view onto the displaced socio-.

* * * *

The pavilions that now feature in various exhibitions and biennales, promise a tactical detachment from the pulls of convention. They are a satisfying illusion as they refresh the critique of bourgeois expectations. They try to outfox the idea that architecture is somehow a reflection of society (whether for better or worse). They are also not utopian in that they do not deliver the script for its future. Pavilions refuse the title architecture (without scare quotes) and would readily adopt the title "architecture." And yet, though they signify the desire to break free from expectations, they cannot call themselves into question, as they stand before the observer as alpha and omega.

The aesthetic unity that they establish crashes apart almost instantly when even the most prosaic, functional questions are posed.

* * * *

In 2017, Gilles Retsin designed a pavilion for the Tallinn Architecture Biennale. The structure is based on sheets of plywood (3.3 × 1.35 meters) cut by a robotic machine to be assembled into elements that are capable of bearing structural loads. Martin Tamke of the Royal Danish Academy described the pavilion as "characterized by outstanding aesthetic and intellectually challenging, as it questions current beliefs and trends in architecture."[3] That is certainly true, but the project also updates, if not

FIGURE 5.2.4 *Tallinn Architecture Biennale Pavilion, Gilles Retsin Architecture, 2017. Photograph by NAARO.*

actually celebrates, habitation-without-habitability into the realm of high-end computation, proclaiming, yet again, the rebirth of a new discipline.

※ ※ ※ ※

Jean Baudrillard in his essay, *Architecture: Truth or Radicalism*, bring us even further into the Laugierian haunts. Baudrillard begins with the mythology of emptiness—mistaking this "emptiness," like Laugier, as "primal," when it is an emptiness that expresses a violent, predecessorial emptying out of the construction site and the removal of the human subject. It is a colonial project:

> Let's start with the space that constitutes the primal scene of architecture, and with the radical nature of that space, which is emptiness. Is it necessary, even possible, to structure or organize this space other than through an indefinite horizontal and vertical extension? In other words: is it possible, given the radical nature of space, to invent a truth of architecture?[4]

The cruel disenfranchisement of the socio- is carried even further:

> An entire architecture is made, and has been made for millennia, without even any notion of architecture. Human beings have conceived and constructed their environment according to spontaneous rules, and this lived space was not made for contemplation. It had no architectural value nor even any properly aesthetic value. Even today, what I like about certain cities, especially American ones, is that a person can go right through them without even thinking of architecture.

One should not put the naivety or the arrogance of the claim aside; maybe Baudrillard was driving too fast through these towns; and apparently, he did not stop to talk to anyone. In his mind he didn't need to. He has already applied to the people their absence. Is he saying that without architecture these people were better for it? Is he saying that these people, unaware of their invisibility, are in the fortunate condition of representing the objectification of authenticity?

His focus, however, is not on this non-architecture, but on Architecture with a capital A, the architecture of the metropole and its proliferation of arbitrary monuments like the Beaubourg which bring out, involuntarily, both "culture and the thing to which culture succumbs more and more . . . the perfusion, suffusion, and confusion of signs." In the metropole, where Architecture rules, it does so in the torturous embrace of civilization as a symptom of a problem with no solution:

> There is a future for architecture for the simple reason that no one has invented a building, an architectural object, that will put an end to all others, that will put an end to space itself—nor the city that will be the end of all cities, nor the thought that will be the end of all thoughts.[5]

In Laugierian manner, Baudrillard posits two types of architecture. In the distant towns of America there is to be found a non-architecture-architecture, still existing in some quasi-anthropologically pure, socio-nativeness. He even has some admiration for it, as it allows—not for him, presumably, since he identifies himself as a man of the metropole but for some unknown other thinkers—the possibility of "strong thinking":

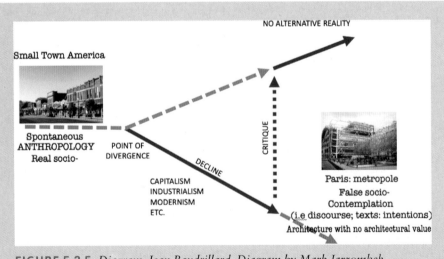

FIGURE 5.2.5 *Diagram: Jean Baudrillard. Diagram by Mark Jarzombek.*

It is the very perfection of architecture that removes its own traces, and where space becomes thought itself . . . the only strong thinking is that which no longer performs the comedy of meaning or of profundity, of the history of ideas, the comedy of truth.[6]

In the metropole, we see an architecture disconnected from these supposedly naive sources. Laugier thought he had the answer to this problem: a morally-inflected, Bible-thumping, Nature-oriented classicism. But in *this* day and age, that would be absurd—at least officially since it is quite alive and well by those who have replaced classicism with modernism. Baudrillard is Laugier without the answer, a moralist without a morality. For him a true *archē* can never materialize. It is to be found neither in the urban center nor in the rural peripheries. We are left with in a vertiginous nowhere land.

* * * *

In 1978, Mary Miss designed an outdoor installation at the Nassau County Museum outside New York called *Perimeters/Pavilions/Decoys*. It consisted of three tower-like structures, two semicircular mounds, and an underground courtyard, a 16-foot-square hole in the ground with a ladder protruding. Upon descending, a person became aware that the ground that one walked upon to get to the ladder was actually the roof of the spaces around the courtyard. The towers and the courtyard are made of simple 2×4s on regularized grids. The beams sticking out from the edge make it clear that the earth has been hollowed out. The soil that was dug out was used to make the nearby burms.

FIGURE 5.2.6 *General view:* Perimeters/Pavilions/Decoys, *Mary Miss, Nassau County Museum, Roslyn Harbor, New York, 1978.* © *Mary Miss.*

FIGURE 5.2.7 *Interior:* Perimeters/Pavilions/Decoys, *Mary Miss, Nassau County Museum, Roslyn Harbor, New York, 1978. © Mary Miss.*

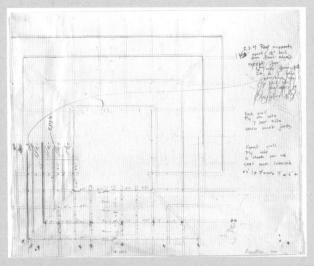

FIGURE 5.2.8 *Study for Tower in* Perimeters/Pavilions/Decoys, *1977. Pencil, colored pencil, and correction fluid on paper. 18 1/4 × 22 1/4" (46.4 × 56.5 cm). Digital Image © The Museum of Modern Art/Licensed by SCALA / Art Resource, NY. Gift of the Gilbert B. and Lila Silverman Instruction Drawing Collection, Detroit.*

FIGURE 5.2.9 *A reconstruction of a pit house at the Step House ruins in Mesa Verde National Park, Colorado. Photograph by Elisa Rolle.*

The prototype is not the hut but the ancient typology known sadly as the pit house, examples of which go back to 20,000 BCE if not earlier and that can be found from Japan to the southwest US. No architect would, however, dare claim that a pit house has any disciplinary legitimacy in the contemporary world. Pit houses are a thing of the past. Here, however, it is advantageously deployed as an anthropological alternative to the Eurocentric fascination with the "hut." As a simulated/real construction, Miss's pit house is a rationalized environment, placed in the domain of the everyday carpenter. Its wooden elements are not cleaned-up pine trunks, but Home Depot 2×4s, the grid serving as the semiotic indicator of "architecture" and its *ratio et via*. But this is not just a handyman's special. The roof was grassed over to look like it was continuous with the real earth and this illusion brings us back to the magic of the *archē*. The illusion is not just between roof plane and the surface of the earth, but between not being able to figure out if the anthropological reference is a homage to a lost way of knowing the world, or whether its rationalization embodies the loss itself. The piece points to an ancient and obsolete origin and yet the grid points to the triviality of reason.

The artist's photographs, in good "architectural" fashion, however, are without people. Whereas for a conventional building we know that habitation is to follow soon enough, here there will be no post-teleological phase. As with Laugier's hut, there are no people who will magically show up and live in this place, except that here the pit house is not presented as the promissory re-beginning, but a dead end. The socio- has all but vanished both in the "anthropological" past and in the contemporary present. It undercuts Laugierian negation into a semantics of loss.

The piece never went through the obligatory phase of maintenance and repair. When the exhibition was closed, the whole thing was quietly and with no documentation erased from the site. It was a completion with no (in)completion. Its emptiness—and its loss—is absolute.

FIGURE 5.2.10 *The Green Corner Building, Anne Holtrop, Muharraq, Bahrain, 2019–20. © Studio Anne Holtrop.*

* * * *

The Green Corner Building in Muharraq, Bahrain, by Studio Anne Holtrop, has walls made from concrete slabs cast on the ground next to the building. Inspired by a visit to a quarry in Cairo, the cast concrete makes a mess of semiotic signifiers: of the earth and yet a negative of its shape; formless and yet formed; rock and yet man-made. It is chthonic (from Greek *khthōn* meaning "earth") and yet floats overhead. The referent to the Then is not the "hut," but its predecessorial variant, the primal cave. It awaits its first barefooted occupants.

* * * *

Archē(non-socio)~~*archē*~~ takes on promising intensity with *I'm lost in Paris*, a shed/house hidden in a Parisian courtyard. It was designed in 2008 by the architectural firm R&Sie(n) of François Roche with Stephanie Lavaux and Gilles Desevadavy and New-Territories in 1999 with François Perrin. The name R&Sie(n) results from the contraction of the names of the group, but it also refers to RSI, the event "Real, Symbolic, Imaginary" of Jacques Lacan in 1972. It is an altogether different *cabana*—what the architects call a "Duck Blind cabana"—in which a house, covered in plastic, is layered with 300 glass beakers that contain bacterial culture. The house's shroud of 1,200 ferns is fed by hydroponic tubes which carry water from the roof to the plants. The 300 glass "beakers," as Roche calls them, contain a solution of water and rhizobia, a kind of bacteria. These "brew" in the sunlight and are harvested in summer. The rhizobia are then fed in small quantities into the ferns' substrate, where they assist the plants in fixing nitrogen from the atmosphere.[7] The beakers are held in place by metal pipes that stick out from the concrete wall and are held together by tension cables.

    Unlike Laugier's forest hut—where architecture is first tamed and then instrumentalized—here nature is unleashed to its own devices, while at the same time operating within the framework of some quasi-scientific experiment. Underneath all the fuzz is a research project that turns the greenhouse inside out and thus plays on the Enlightenment/colonial obsession with plants and gardens. The building is basically a concrete box covered with high density PU sprayed-on foam insulation that is then covered by green geo-textile. It is literally a "green" house covered in "greenery" mediated by exquisite reasoning and instrumentalities of a "green" science. The building internalizes its refusal to be read as architecture not because the concrete box is invisible, but rather because of the fabricational surfacing, the site of the (non)*tektōn*.

There is still something moralistically Laugierian about the project. According to Roche, "To territorialize architecture is certainly not to drape it in the cheap finery of a new tendency, of a style which is by nature as out of sync and 'separate' as those that have just been consumed." In other words, the project stands against the business-as-usual superfluidity of "architecture." It stands against the supposed shallowness of the rococo as well as against bourgeois platitudes, which is why it cannot be anything more than a *cabana*, for anything more would slide it back into the normative world of excess. And as a "cabana" it cannot have any of the usual attributes of domesticity. In this, the building aims its gaze at a moralized *archē*, except with a twist. "To territorialize architecture, so that the site reweaves a social, cultural and aesthetic tissue, is to enshrine it in what it was preparing to destroy."[8] The fearsomely stark white floors and walls, and the absence (at least in the published images) of carpets, photographs, books and shelves produce a hyper-asceticism that is meant to focus on the great windows that are filled with ferns and the green luminous bottles of ooze.

This is less a *cabana* than a cave/shrine of purification that allows the alienated male/human to find his deepest spiritual nature that only after much isolation and asceticism, presumably, leaves him worthy of contemplating the isolating beauty seen through the plate-glass openings. There is nothing to soften to tone. One would be shocked if the inhabitant of this cabana even wore clothes.

The logic of display is itself on display, performatively shaming the architecture into a flagellational attack on its own standard, corporeal desires. Here the *archē* lies not just in the inextricable metaphysics of "nature," which exists as a false semiotic reference—a smokescreen for its neighbors—but also in the immanent future of nature-destroyed; but first, along the way, architecture has to withdraw into the aesthetics of passivity to recapture the possibility for a guilt-free human. It was to be architecture (without scare quotes) but in the end, perhaps almost accidentally, brings out the repressed of "architecture."

✳ ✳ ✳ ✳

The pavilion as a locus of disciplinary cogitation about the all-important socio- as repressed, removed, and reimagined points also to the *Ghost*

FIGURE 5.2.11 *Franklin Court Museum, Robert Venturi, Philadelphia. Photograph by Elisa Rolle.*

Structure (1976) in Robert Venturi's Franklin Court Museum in Philadelphia that memorializes Benjamin Franklin's home demolished in the nineteenth century. The building's shape is approximated in the outline form with white box steel tubes. It is not architecture (without scare quotes) and is rarely discussed as one of the great theoretical projects of the age, but it is "architecture" of the highest order. It is not some fetishized "re-beginning" of the discipline. If the *archē* lies in its (faux])axonometric precision, in other words in its representation of representationality—a magic of appearance out of thin air—the *tektōn* lives in its steely incarnation, a frame dutifully waiting to be filled. But these frames do not hold up a floor or even a screen or reference anything other than the building. They are literally and symbolically "a fabrication." The cruel emptiness of Laugier's *cabana* is replaced here with a never-to-be-filled emptiness. And it is not just because the house is lost, but because the past itself might be lost, available to us only in a sketch form that points not to the teleological future of completion, but to an imagined beginning that once was.

* * * *

FIGURE 5.2.12 *Restored CMU block chair, Mark Mack, 1983. © Mark Mack. Photograph by Mark Jarzombek.*

FIGURE 5.2.13 *CMU block chair, Mark Mack, 1983. © Mark Mack. Photograph by Mark Jarzombek.*

Mark Mack, a Los Angeles architect, designed a chair out of cinder blocks that was exhibited under the heading, "Restored CMU block chair dates to 700 B.C. and found outside of Sacramento, California."[9] It was positioned in front of a partially built house.

The whole is a witty play on architecture's disciplinary obsession about origins. The unfinished building reflects the technological "advances" of that "ancient world," its construction interrupted for some unknown reason and now "restored" in the gallery space. This is not the angry-modernist, Laugierian primitive that magically becomes the (restorative) modern, but a productive-primitive that was displaced by architecture's industrialized afterlife. The chair is not some steely artifact that speaks to our desire to bring (dis)comfort to the modern house, but made from various building blocks lying around on the construction site. It is in that sense temporary and of the construction site, pointing to the unfinished site of future habitation. The master builders—ancient and lost in time—made it for themselves in a few minutes' time and would have used the chair only temporarily. And yet it is undeniably monumental and is now, cleaned and restored, a museum-grade masterpiece.

The dialectics of completion comes to brilliant and stuttering halt. Will the future be a place where we restart the processes lost in this imagined antiquity/antiquity, or is the ancient *faber* a purely ghostly figure in archaeological recreations.

****

The Philippines Pavilion at the 2021 Venice Biennale was curated by Framework Collaborative, the members of which include GK Enchanted Farm and the architects Sudarshan Khadka, Jr., and Alexander Eriksson Furunes. Khadka, Jr., is from the Philippines and Furunes from Norway.[10] Working together, the pavilion is designed on interlocking the principle of "bayanihan" (pronounced: buy-uh-nee-hun), a Filipino custom derived from the Tagalog word "bayan" that means "nation, town, or community," and the Norwegian concept of "dugnad" (pronounced doog-nahd), a Norwegian cultural tradition where members of a community work together toward a common goal for the greater good. Today, bayanihan refers to the spirit of communal unity, work, and cooperation to achieve a particular goal. It is traced back to the times when townspeople would lend a hand to a family when they moved to a new place and would literally carry the old house on their shoulders using bamboo poles. The bayanihan spirit has also taken more modern forms especially when calamities or disasters strike.[11] Dugnad dates as far back as the Vikings, when villagers worked together to bring ships back to land after their excursions. Over time, dugnad evolved as rural farming communities applied the concept to making preparations for harsh winter conditions so they could survive together.[12] Bayanihan, like barn-raising, is one of the great words in the lexicon of the *tekton*'s tradition of occupationality.

This project moves away from the Eurocentric essentializing of the primitive hut. Ignoring the lure of habitation-without-habitability, it changes the core terms of socio-*tektōn*-ology. This pavilion begins and ends in the socio- and in that sense speaks of a whole different way of understanding the modern, something almost completely lost in the developed world where we often imagine an abstracted, happy socio- as a mythological enhanced recipient of the architect's efforts. Here the issue was on working together across geographies, cultures, and languages, seeing these zones of contact not as something that has to be manufactured by purifying tradition into the culturally-protective mysteries of *oikos*, but as something that gets worked through at the community level and that has already been tried out in the form of bayanihan. The narrative starts with village-making not house-making. The *archē* is not to be first driven out of the picture to then magically return in a supposedly pure form, but folds itself into the village-making world.

PART SIX

CHAPTER ONE

Tekton-Topia

Histories of the long nineteenth century in Europe and the Americas often feature banks, libraries, parliaments, train stations, palaces, offices, tall buildings, department stores, and government institutions. The narrative focuses on industrialization, the rise of steel and concrete and large-scale commissions, and, of course, the important architects and theorists who gave voice to the concerns of the day. This can give us a false impression. This period saw the emergence of a broad cultural space that one can call *tektōn*-topia. It is defined preeminently as a space where the architect plays a secondary or negligible role, or in some cases even a negative role. This space had always existed in the form of traditional practices associated with the proverbial *faber*, but it was only in the nineteenth century that it developed a socio-disciplinary-economic integrity of formidable scale, one that has at least four vectors that emerged in staggered form, each with its own historical determinants.

HOME BUILDING
When Bernard Rudofsky published his book *Architecture Without Architects: A Short Introduction to Non-Pedigreed Architecture* (1964), the buildings he talked about were from China, Africa, and the Mediterranean. He did not have to go that far. Probably 99.9 percent of the built world in the nineteenth century in Europe and the colonized zones of the Americas was made by non-architects. The main element in the story was, of course, the small-scale, independent carpenter/contractor who still today in many parts of the world operates at their own speed and within the low- and medium-range delivery-conscious environment of the capitalist system. They specialize in making the thousands of houses and other similarly scaled projects that proliferate across the landscape. One of the first books to chart the expansive boundaries of this space of operation was authored by John Carter and produced between 1774 and 1778 as a set of monthly publications that came to be known as *The New Builder's Magazine, and Complete Architectural Library for Architects, Surveyors, Carpenters, Masons, Bricklayers, &c. As Well as for Every Gentleman who Would Wish to be a*

Competent Judge of the Elegant and Necessary Art of Building. Consisting of Designs in Architecture, in Every Style and Taste, from the Most Magnificent and Superb Structures, Down to the Most Simple and Unadorned: Together with the Plans, Sections, and Elevations, Serving as an Unerring Assistant in the Construction of Any Building, from a Palace to a Cottage. The full range of the portfolio was even more brilliantly expressed in the title of a book authored in 1862 by Louis F. Allen, a land speculator in Buffalo, New York: *Rural Architecture—Wood Houses, Workshops, Tool Houses, Carriage and Wagon Houses, Stables, Smoke and Ash Houses, Ice Houses, Apiary or Bee House, Poultry Houses, Rabbitry, Dovecote, Piggery, Barns and Sheds for Cattle, etc.,* in which he noted:

> Why it is, that nothing of the kind has been heretofore attempted for the chief benefit of so large and important a class of our common as our farmers comprise, is not easy to say, unless it be that they themselves have indicated but little wish for instruction in a branch of domestic economy which is, in reality, one of great importance, not only to their domestic enjoinment, but their pecuniary welfare.[1]

* * * *

In Philadelphia, one of the city's more storied historic buildings is the headquarters of the Carpenters' Company that was built in 1770. The company was organized in 1724 for the benefit of the area's craftsmen and provided an educational and support network. The hall was designed to showcase the technical skills of its members, much of which is still visible today. Many founding members were alumni of London's Worshipful

FIGURE 6.1.1 *Postcard showing the Carpenters' Hall, Philadelphia, 1905.*

FIGURE 6.1.2 *Two Men and a Boy with Outside Calipers, Backsaw, Square, and Frame Saw, 1860s. Tintype with applied color. Metropolitan Museum of Art, New York.*

Company of Carpenters and modeled their new guild after it. The hall is still owned by the Carpenters' Company. These and other such organizations proliferated in the major urban areas. As for London's Worshipful Company of Carpenters, in 1886 it opened an evening institute on its estate in Stratford, London, offering classes in carpentry, joinery, plumbing, geometry, mechanical drawing, and cookery. In 1891, the Carpenters' Institute had become a day school for boys. (The school closed in 1905 when the local authority opened its own school.)

As we have seen, the designation "carpenter" has, of course, to be understood very broadly to include everything from finish carpenters to surveyors and contractors. Increasingly, many of these began to call themselves architects.[2] Some even began to teach architecture. John Nevell, a prominent Philadelphia carpenter who taught at a school that opened in the mid-1760s, offered to teach any person "of common capacity" the rudiments of architecture "in two months at most."[3] The book *The Young Carpenter's Assistant* (1805) by Owen Biddle, a prominent Philadelphia carpenter, was geared toward young men who had already swung tools and formed calluses, who knew how to build, but not how to draw or design, which was critical to attracting a higher level of clientele.[4]

The risks in the building trades were innumerable. Nonetheless, those who were ambitious, already by 1860 had a growing list of books addressing their needs: *The American Cottage Builder* by John Bullock; *Specifications for Practical Architecture* by Alfred Bartholomew; *Brown's Carpenter's Assistant*; *Examples of Ornament in every style* by Joseph Cundall; *Designs for Cottages and Rural Buildings* by T. D. Deam; *Improved Farm* by Professor Donaldson; *Cottage Residences* by A. J. Downing; *City Architecture* by M. Field; *Modern Builder's Guide* by N. Lefever; *Guide Book for Carpentry and Joinery* by Peter Nicholson; *The Builder's Pocket Companion* by A. C. Smeaton; *Designs for Cottages and Villas* by E. W. Trendall; *Rural Architecture* by R. Upjohn.

And increasingly, owners were admonished to hire carpenters who had done their reading. An article in *Genesee Farmer* out of Rochester, New York, from 1846 notes:

> The improvement or alteration of houses requires to be done judiciously and skillfully—harmony and proportion must be observed in all. Without these, every dollar spent is worse than thrown away ... An ordinary country carpenter, who has no opportunity for acquiring either, will as certainly spoil it.[5]

* * * *

A new element entered the system: journals. Improvements in paper manufacturing with cylinder paper machines in the 1830s, the development of iron plates instead of copper in 1830s, and the development of cloth binding in the 1840s not only made so-called carpenter books affordable, but also trade journals, a testament to the increased readership and to the increased literacy of members of the various professions. The opening paragraph of the first edition of *Illustrated Wood-worker* (1880) states in plain language the growing nature of practice as a discipline unto itself:

> Three hundred thousand workers in wood confess the want of a cheap illustrated journal. This initial number must be taken as the indication of a purpose, not as an average sample of the *Woodworker*. If this number is favorably received, we can vouch for those that are to follow. It is our

purpose to cover a wide field. The house-joiner, the car-joiner, the cabinet-maker, and other mechanics who work in wood will always find profitable suggestions in these pages. Every man who feels rich enough to subscribe for this journal, by paying one dollar may depend on. We have ample facilities for obtaining the best examples of modern design, and no pains will be spared in making the *Woodworker* worthy of the support it seeks. The objective point of this journal is the workman, not the employer. We wish this to be distinctly understood at the outset. The *Woodworker* is specially and solely for men at the bench.[6]

Some of the journals were:

Dublin Builder (Dublin: 1859) (In 1867 it changed its title to *The Irish Builder and Engineering Record*]
The Building News and Engineering Journal (London: 1864–1926)
The Architect, Builder and Woodworker (New York: 1868) Absorbed by *National builder* (Chicago: 1896)
Illustrated Wood Worker (New York: 1879)
The Illustrated Carpenter and Builder (London: 1877–1923)
The American Contractor (Chicago: 1879–1922)
Carpentry and Building (New York: 1879–1909)
Wood-Working Tools: How to Use Them (Boston, MA: 1881)
The Carpenter (Philadelphia: 1881–)
The National Builder Magazine (Chicago: 1885)
Work; an illustrated magazine of practice and theory for all workmen, professional and amateur (London: 1889)
The Craftsman (Atlanta: 1898–1916)
Builders' Magazine (New York: 1899–1911)
Building World: an illustrated weekly trade journal for builders, carpenters, joiners, bricklayers, masons, plasterers, painters, glaziers, plumbers, sanitary engineers, brickmakers, gasfitters, locksmiths, decorators, hot-water fitters, paperhangers and for all engaged in allied trades (1896–)
American Carpenter and Builder (Chicago: 1905–17)
Building Age (New York: 1910)

At stake was more than just the need for information. The journals added powerful layers of cohesiveness to the building trades. In 1843, an editor for *Builder* out of London wrote with confidence that the magazine "will never lose sight" of the fact that "there are some five hundred thousand working builders in this United Empire," who, especially when one adds in the mix all their families, influence "the working of events and changes in our commercial and civil polity."[7]

Given the nature of the work and its dependency on oral arrangements, it is difficult to get a full picture of the life of the carpenter/contractor in the nineteenth century. One exception is Jacob Holt (1811–80), as researched by

FIGURE 6.1.3 *Street sign in Warrenton, North Carolina, commemorating the work of Jacob W. Holt.*

Catherine W. Bisher.[8] The son of a carpenter, he slowly built up a practice in Prince Edward County, Virginia, but he left and reopened his shop in Warrenton, North Carolina, seeking out better opportunities for the up-and-coming community of plantation owners who were looking to upgrade their lifestyle. A street sign acknowledges Hunt's contributions. As one resident later recalled: the town "embraced the callings of architecture, carpentry, brick-laying, lathing and plastering. They [the new arrivals] were all experienced and capable managers or workers. The individuals, without exception, were religious, sober, honest, truthful, orderly, and industrious."[9]

Later, after the American Civil War, Hunt moved again, this time to Christiansville, Virginia, adapting to the changed social conditions, and to the new technological and economic environment. In all of this he kept abreast of the latest publications so as to offer his clients the best in terms of fashion and sophistication, becoming a much-sought-after builder yet again in his new area of work. His remodeling of Emmanuel Episcopal Church in Warrenton from the 1850s closely followed the drawing for "A Village Church" in Samuel Sloan's *Model Architect* from 1852. But he was no mere copyist. Most of his houses, many of which were expansions and renovations, showed a range of approaches reflecting the typical flexibility that contractors developed.

* * * *

William Ware, born in Cambridge, Massachusetts, and the first American to graduate from the École des Beaux-Arts in Paris viewed all this with a rather dim eye: "The [architectural] profession is, at present, in the hands of . . . contractors and superintendents, who are mechanics with a talent for affairs, and many of whom take the name of architects."[10] Ware went on to found the school of architecture at MIT in 1868 that is celebrated as the first such institution in the country. Its significance in the history of the profession, however, overshadows the fact that in the nineteenth century builders had become a class unto themselves integrated into ever expanding and demanding epistemological, cultural, and economic horizons.

Ernest Newton, a London-based architect at the end of the nineteenth century, and president of the Royal Institute of British Architects would have sided with Ware. Writing in 1892, the "architect-surveyor," he argued, had taken over the profession. Out of about 1,100 persons in the London Directory, who are identified as "architects," about "550 describe themselves as 'surveyors,' of whom [only] about 230 are members of the Institute," so he laments. Lawyers, he argued, "are largely responsible for this. For legal purposes an architect is a surveyor; he is dragged into cases to give evidence as an expert on points having no connexion whatever with architecture." To this he concludes:

And yet the "architect and surveyor" flourishes in our midst. The secret of his claims to the title of surveyor are in his own keeping, but in many cases the possession of a drawing board and a box of French curves is considered a sufficient claim to the title of architect. [11]

The English architect and archaeologist John Thomas Micklethwaite was even more colorful:

If there is say a slaughter house or a coal store to be built, and there is a man who knows exactly what is wanted and how it may best be had, by all means let him have the work to do, though he be absolutely ignorant of design. But do not call him an architect— "a prosaic building director" . . . if you like, but not an architect. The work he produces is not architecture, and he has no more claim to be called an architect than the man who sounds the fog horn on a Thames steamboat has to be called a musician. [12]

Another architect wrote about driving in New Jersey:

A drive through the summer cities that fringe the coast of New Jersey reveals very little of interest to the architectural instinct. In the older settlements, such as may be seen at Ocean Grove and Asbury Park, the houses and hotels are practically a jumble of boards set on ends, perforated without mercy by the inexorable jig-saw, and painted all the colors that it were possible to crowd into the paint pot . . . Dwelling houses, however, are, as a rule, designed, plans drawn and executed by the average carpenter, and, like most all designs conceived over a carpenter's bench, bear evidence of crudity of thought, grossness of proportions and garishness of details which have made such designs open to general criticism. In fact, planing-mill architecture, with jig-saw details, is an inconceivable conglomeration, but one has only to land somewhere on the Atlantic coast in the dusk of evening and in the morning wake to find it blooming all about him.[13]

A new word came into existence at the end of the nineteenth century: "jerry-builder," which developed from the popularization of "Jerry" to mean disreputable. Sir Thomas Graham Jackson, RA, considered to be one of the most distinguished British architects of his generation and a person who helped lay the course of events which resulted in the passing of the Architects (Registration) Act 1931, had this to say about jerry-builders:

> In his own bad way the jerry-builder is a master of construction, and if he did not know how to build well he would never be able to build so badly. He has little to learn from those who would teach him, and very likely could tell his examiners a good deal that would be new to them. He would pass the examination with flying colours, and come out with glory, and go on jerry-building as before with your certificate in his pocket.

> Jerry-building will only disappear when the demand for it ceases, when public taste improves, when there is more simplicity in domestic life, when we acquiesce in more modest ways of living, when we delight in solid and honest workmanship, and rejoice in beauty rather than ostentation— when in fact the public sense is once more alive to the influence of art . . . [The Jerry-builder] is but the creature of a vicious system, and the system and he will stand or fall together.[14]

Not all jerry-builders were amused. In the article from the *Liverpool Mercury* from 1877, a man named Walter Pierce took objection to being described as such at a meeting with the mayor:

> I am indisposed to believe you intended a personal insult. The term "jerry builder" is low and coarse, and to my mind unbecoming a gentleman and I think all such expressions should be avoided, as they do no good, and when used by persons of position set a bad example to those under them . . . I shall be glad for your sake if you withdraw the words used.[15]

Well said, but obviously not heeded by Sir Thomas Graham Jackson.

The emergence of professional class of *architects* at the end of the nineteenth century with its own strands of pedagogies, requirements, institutions, cultural affirmations—and later with its own celebratory histories—was designed to offset the blurring of class distinctions that were taking place in the building trades in the nineteenth century. It might not be unreasonable to argue that it was *only* in the late nineteenth century with the professionalization of architecture and the creation of the Library of Congress cataloguing system that codified the young discipline's cultural claims that *archē(non)tektōn* could be more effectively instrumentalized by the architects.

The trade journals were not mute on the problem and the tone of the following letter to the editor of *The Builder* from 1843 would certainly have received a thumbs-up among the trades:

> The master builder is too often subject to the bad debts and actions at law, arising either from the tyranny of the architect employed, or from the rigid and impartial enforcements of some despotic, capricious, or ill-defined clause in the specifications, or from some disputed accounts relating to alterations from the original drawings ... The experienced practical builder, in addition to the evils already adverted to, has to combat with the poppyism ... and practical inefficiency of the heartless architects, who are too frequently supported by building committees not as they ought to be, principally from the excellence of their qualifications, but from the personal influence of family connections.[16]

****

ENGINEERING

My intention is not to tell the history of the upwardly-mobile carpenter class of the nineteenth century, a history that is yet to be adequately acknowledged in our textbooks, but to link it to the broad cultural space of *tektōn*-topia that was shared, though on different registers, not just by carpenters, builders, and contractors, but also by engineers, whose history is usually told as if it were on a separate plane of reality. In actuality, engineering expanded the space of *tektōn*-topia even if it took it into a different dimension. The critical distinction was the rise of steel and, of course, its early use and development in transportation infrastructure and long-span architectural spaces. The emergence of complex calculations played a critical factor, insinuating itself into the space between design and delivery—from the mid-nineteenth century onward—through an ever expanding regime of analysis, codes, laws, investment risks, and contracts, squeezing architecture into the ever thinner space of relevance, mostly around the alleged primacy of "design."

In Europe, technical universities began to proliferate: Polytechnic School of France, 1794; Technical University of Berlin, 1770; Royal Polytechnic Institute at Vienna, 1815; Federal Technical University, Zurich, 1854; Technical University of Munich, 1868. The United States saw the rise of engineering societies such as the American Society of Civil Engineers (ASCE) (1851) and the American Society of Mechanical Engineers (ASME) (1880).

Unlike the world of contracting and carpentry which was filled with economic risk for all involved, engineers in France and then soon elsewhere had a more secure social footing. In France, as explained in 1843 by an observer, graduates from the engineering schools were "admitted into the lower grades [of governmental administration] where they acquire at the same time the practical experience that they lack and the right to actual

pecuniary advantages of this system are not great; but, in general, the position of engineers is honorable and secure. Members of a well-run administration, they enjoy the public respect that is attached to it as well as what they might merit individually."[17]

Because engineers had to be licensed, and their work had to be inspected, they gave to *tektōn*-topia a powerful voice that played itself out through the twentieth century and even integrated itself into the foundations of nation-building across the planet. Any number of architects, as is well known, began to look to engineering as the core voice of modernity. In many places in the world even today a Department of Architecture will lie within a School of Engineering. And yet, even when Viollet-le-Duc, in *Dictionnaire raisonné de l'architecture française du XIe au XVe siècle* (1854–68), pronounced: "Architecture and construction must be taught and practiced together," he added that "construction is the means; architecture the end result." A commonsensical enough proposition that tries to produce a conflict-free zone of interdependency, it is quite obvious that he wants the *archē* to remain in the traditional dominant position as set out by Alberti. The title of the mid-nineteenth-century *Architectural Magazine* put Engineering at the very bottom of the long list of subdisciplines. Though requiring a vastly different set of preparations than the traditional master builder, both the master

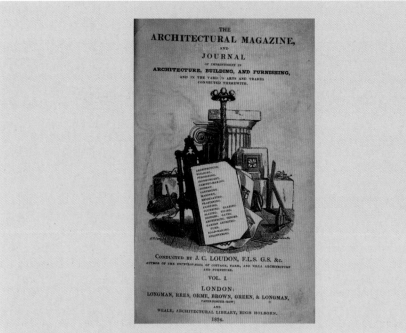

FIGURE 6.1.4 The Architectural Magazine, *1834.*

builder and the engineer were in essence deprived of membership in the creative class. Or as explained in 1888 in *The Iconographic Encyclopaedia of the Arts and Sciences: Architecture*:

> ...the term "Architecture" has been applied to artistic building, in distinction from the constructive art of Engineering. Just as the ideal and material tendencies develop hand in hand in civilization as a whole, so in the ordinary course of things must Architecture and Engineering be considered as distinct yet closely-linked departments ... The separation of *the more material, constructive part of the vast domain of the building art*, under the name of "Engineering," from more ideal part, which we assign to Architecture, is therefore based more upon custom than upon theory, but, since the division has been made, there is no reason why we should depart from it.[18]

It was repeated endlessly. In a recently published article in an architectural journal, note the difference between the architect "consumed by art and creativity" and the engineer who "executes" the project:

> Engineers and architects are programmed differently. An architect is always consumed by art and creativity during design, the spatial functionality, as well as the user's comfort; a theoretical thinker one might say. On the other hand, an engineer designs construction and facilities systems, as well as building management systems. He executes the design on site considering several technicalities of the construction process.[19]

One university has this on their website:

> Architects design the space to meet client needs, as well as the *aesthetic appearance* of the inside and exterior of the building. Engineers' main responsibility is to ensure the *design is safe and meets all appropriate building codes*.[20]

> my italics

Occasionally one finds the voice of critique from the side of the engineer. In 1913, William Welles Bosworth, a French-trained, American, Beaux Arts architect, had been called in to make a design for the new MIT campus in Cambridge, Massachusetts. John Ripley Freeman, a noted civil engineer and professor at MIT who would go on to design the Panama Canal, complained that Bosworth was nothing but a "beauty doctor."[21] Or more recently, as explained by Dino NG, a New York Department of Transportation engineer:

> I always tell my staff that this is a never-ending job. I mean, it's a profession that people outside may not understand. They may not even miss us if we go away for a year or two. But if we don't exist, I don't think the society

will last for any length of time. Does the public understand what we do? We're not like architects. Architects love flamboyance. "Look at my building." Engineers don't do that. They don't say, "Look at my sewer."[22]

* * * *

An early attempt to bring the two vectors, the master builder and the engineer, together was developed by Jean-Nicolas-Louis Durand (1760–1834), who was a professor of architecture at the École Polytechnique in Paris. His book *Précis des leçons d'architecture données à l'École Polytechnique* (Précis of the Lectures on Architecture Given at the École Polytechnique) first appeared in 1802–5.[23] In it he presented a wide range of plans derived from historical precedents, consciously modifying some to make them appear more regular and geometric than they actually were. In the plates that correspond to the Roman ruins, for example, it can be seen that the drawings are not so much a faithful description of some old buildings as cleaned-up versions of them.

His reductivism has been duly noted by historians. Michel Gallet calls him "The theorist of an impoverished architecture."[24] Similarly, Alberto Pérez-Gómez sees here the loss of meaning and the beginning of architecture's downfall into the pathologies of rationality: "To his way of thinking, character was nothing but a sign, or the result of a direct mathematical relation postulated between the final form of a building and the organization of its plan . . . [His architecture] speaks only to a technological process, not to the world of man."[25] I would like to see Durand in a different light, as the first attempt to theorize a pure *tektōn*-topia.

Unlike the pattern books of the day which laid the groundwork of simplification and implementation, but that operated apologetically in the

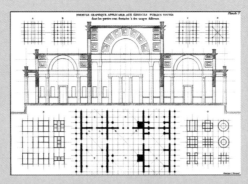

FIGURE 6.1.5 *Sheet of drawings,* Partie graphique des cours d'architecture faits à l'École Royale Polytechnique depuis sa réorganisation [. . .], *Jean-Nicolas-Louis Durand, orig. ed. Paris 1821. Reprint Unterschneidheim: Uhl Verlag, 1975: pl. 3.*

domain of the practical or mechanical arts, Durand imagined a clean and definitive break further up the food chain. Here the builder/engineer becomes the architect. Durand accomplishes this sleight of hand by following a series of methodological moves that are easily learned and applied. History, which by this time had become the secret language of the elites, is here simply a matter of following the convention of easy-to-use patterns except that instead of houses, builders are making grand edifices, libraries, courthouses, and parliaments. Point and make. The learned Albertian architect simply dies out.

Even the graph paper played a role, becoming the representational medium by which the *tektōn* speaks of its desire to be made comprehensible after being hidden away for so long.[26] Unlike his predecessor theorists he did not see the ancients as infallible. If an ancient building did not quite conform, no problem. The mistake was theirs and it can easily be corrected.

****

Durand, like Winkelman, took *archē* out of the equation, except that whereas Winkelman wanted to sharpen the focus and restrict the possible answers to the Greeks, Durand proclaimed the end to the game of history altogether. All that was left was to deploy its various references wherever appropriate. In the hands of Durand, the *tektōn* cuts the Gordian knot of elitism, punches through the smoke and mirrors to fully embrace the place of anonymity in the making of buildings. Ornery debates about origins, divergences and recuperations disappear. The books and codices on architecture and architectural history could now be put into storage. Society no longer needs to worry about its ever-so anxious desire for deep meaning, as those can be culled and simplified from its communal wisdom. Disciplinary depth has been replaced by a studious facile-ology. All that was left was implementation.

It is the revenge of the *tektōn*.

****

The attempt to place the engineer's rationalizing capacity at the center of an architect-less world and, simultaneously, to imagine that world without a complex, academic, and disciplinary structure was carried through into more recent times by Christopher Alexander with his *A Pattern Language: Towns, Buildings, Construction* (1977) and *The Timeless Way of Building* (1979). In good Laugierian manner, Alexander thinks that the world is a mess:

> The languages which people have today are so brutal, and so fragmented, that most people no longer have any language to speak of at all—and what they do have is not based on human, or natural considerations.[27]

Moving then effortlessly from the Then to the Now, he wanted builders to produce harmonious works that unify the physical, emotional and practical dimensions:

> Without the help of architects or planners, if you are working in the
> timeless way, a town will grow under your hands, as steady as the flowers
> in your garden.[28]

The pitched roof was one among many elements that would restore our
connection to our inner social nature. It evoked, he argued, a "primitive
feeling."[29] But Alexander was no regressive traditionalist. A mathematician
by training, he aimed in *A Pattern Language* to regularize and formalize the
efforts of the builder so as to rationally dismantle the architect's privileged
position as author figure.[30] The book introduces 253 design rules and
solutions, called "patterns," to suggest guidelines for creating spaces. Within
these patterns, a single pattern may be chosen or even group of patterns as
a solution to a particular problem. Alexander writes:

> At the core ... is the idea people should design their homes, streets, and
> communities. This idea ... comes from the observation most of the wonderful
> places of the world were not made by architects, but by the people.[31]

It is not clear who these mysterious "people" are or how they were to do this
without the expertise of the building trades, without the oversight of codes
and regulations, and without even a rudimentary infrastructure of
investment.[32]

We have moved past Durand's *tektōn*-topic purism into a *tektōn*-utopia.

* * * *

TRADITIONAL ARCHITECTURE

The space of *tektōn*-topia expanded in the 1970s in yet another powerful
direction with the development of a field that came to be known as
Traditional Architecture or Vernacular Architecture. Though traditions have
existed in the building arts since the proverbial dawn of time, of which the
faber is the very embodiment, the elevation of tradition into the status of
academic discipline was quite recent. Admittedly, already at the end of the
nineteenth century, John Ruskin praised the Swiss cottage, proclaiming
"the joy of peasant life, continuous, motionless there in the shadows of its
ancestral turf—unassailed and unassailing."[33] Edward S. Prior, a noted Arts
and Crafts architect influenced by Ruskin, spoke more precisely of what he
called the "unarchitected building":

> The certainty with which natural unarchitected building has in all ages
> developed the characteristics of good art, suggests that there is in mankind
> in the aggregate an instinctive capacity for good architecture.

The longevity of "natural unarchitected building" suffered, so he argued,
with the emergence in the nineteenth century of styles and of the rise of
architect as professional, the symptom of which was the creation of the

"Institute of British Architects as a learned Society." But "unarchitected building ... endured so long as the provinces could still develop a provincialism which was not a mere diluted edition of Metropolitan fashion."[34] It was a basic argument that has lasted the ages, and as we have already seen, one that seeped its way into the thoughts of even Baudrillard.

****

What Filarete started, and what nineteenth-century ethnography enhanced, and what in the mid-century was often known as "primitive architecture," the post-1970s discipline of Traditional Architecture completed, producing a type of prehistory to socio(*archē-tektōn*)ology. The main point of difference between the conventional world of house-building and the new one of Traditional Architecture hinged around the role of the building trades. Whereas the great craftsman-contractor tradition could accept the portable skill saw, sheetrock, unionization, and any number of other modernizations, defenders of tradition were skeptical, seeing value in forgotten or ignored techniques of production.

Since the 1970s, a vast amount of research has been conducted on the topic. Paul Oliver's *Encyclopedia of Vernacular Architecture of the World* (1998) is only the tip of the iceberg. Much of it is salvage research pieced together against the grain of tragic cultural collapses within the maw of modernization. And yet, in many places, an ideological component—overtly or covertly—can be detected that went hand in hand with national or ethno-centric interests. This was apparent already in the pathbreaking book, *Katsura: Tradition and Creation in Japanese Architecture* (1960) by Kenzo Tange, in which the author championed the Jomon (Japan's original pre-rice, hunter-gatherer culture from *c.* 14,000 to 500 BCE) as the ancestors of Japanese modernism.

FIGURE 6.1.6 *Reconstruction of Jomon hut, Goshono Archaeological Site, Japan. Photograph by Qurren.*

The book presented the case that the seventeenth-century villa is a fusion of a tough, simple farm aesthetic rooted in the world of the ancient Jomon and the elegant aesthetic of detachment that came from Japan's aristocratic tradition. These two horizons, Tange claimed, stand as the backdrop to a uniquely Japanese understanding of modern architecture. The designers of Katsura, however, had never heard of the Jomon, who were discovered only in the late nineteenth century. In fact, most postwar Japanese might have never have heard the word "Jomon" either. But after Japan's defeat in 1945, something had to supplant the imaginary of an emperor and the history of his lineage as the focus of national consciousness. With the Jomon, a largely young, Marxist-oriented generation of Japanese archaeologists saw an opportunity to stress the values of "common people."[35] Allied with this was the change of the phrase "imperial Japan" to "cultural Japan."[36] The term "bunka" (culture) emerged as a prominent element in the rhetoric about rebuilding the nation. By reaching back to an imagined Jomon and tracing Japan's subsequent rice-farming history, Tange was trying to nativize the idea of a populist, agrarian tradition. He was also placing modernism firmly into the post-Filaretian disciplinary domain, but doing it one better. If the Filaretian man in the forest was an imaginary, the Jomon were not. Their place in history was grounded in archaeological evidence.

With Katsura, the word "tradition" became a semiotic indicator of a type of disciplinarity in which archaeologically legitimated ancient-ness served to empower a nation's relationship to history. This was amplified in books like *Traditional Sukiya Architecture* (1969), *Impressions of Japanese Traditional Architecture* (1972), and *Traditional Domestic Architecture of Japan* (1972). Though nothing was left of the Jomon apart from postholes, it was not long before full-scale reconstructions were created in many places across Japan.[37] Tradition as retrieved through scholarship was not a photorealist anamorphism.

* * * *

The elevation of the concept tradition was not limited to Japan. It quickly became a global phenomenon and was even given its own theoretical polish. The German Catholic philosopher Joseph Peiper (1970) argued that, in the modern world of constant, unrelenting change, tradition was that which must be preserved unchanged. More important was Edward Shils (1910–95), professor of sociology at the University of Chicago, who argued in his book *Tradition* (1981) against the old modernist notion, as defined by Max Weber, that saw it as a type of uninspired, automatic reaction to habitual stimuli. In contrast, Shils believed traditions were characteristically meaningful and motivated. All of this helped transform tradition to the level of a disciplinary project.

A Survey of Traditional Architecture and Related Material Folk Culture Patterns in the Normandy (1976), *The Traditional Architecture of the*

Kathmandu Valley (1977), *An Analytical Study of Traditional Arab Domestic Architecture* (1979), *African Traditional Architecture* (1978), *Arsitektur tradisional daerah Sulawesi Utara* (1981), *An Introduction to Nigerian Traditional Architecture* (1990), *Temples in Traditional Environments* (1992), *The Traditional Architecture of Mexico* (1993), *The Traditional Architecture of Indonesia* (1994), *The Traditional Architecture of Saudi Arabia* (1998), *Traditional Buildings of India* (1998), and so on and so forth.[38]

All of which was reinforced by dozens of museums and reconstructions: Heritage Park Historical Village (Canada, 1964), Rumšiškės Wallenberg (Switzerland, 1968), Giorgi Chitaia Open Air Museum of Ethnography (Georgia, 1966), Taman Mini Indonesia Indah (Indonesia, 1975), Hagen Westphalian Open Air Museum (Germany, 1970s), Korean Folk Village (South Korea, 1980s), Khokhlovka (Russia, 1980), Sirogojno (Serbia, 1990s), West Stow Anglo-Saxon Village (England, 1970s), etc.

Though trying to accurately represent and protect an endangered cultural heritage, reconstructions are inevitably used for civic pride and national identity.[39] And while this is not an unreasonable expectation in the face of modernization, it does bring "architecture" into the vortexes of representation in a way that normative architecture does not. The issue is not how these buildings fit into the discipline of "architectural history" but rather how these buildings represent "architecture's history" within the increasingly complex contexts of ideological interests.

* * * *

ONTO(TEKTON)OLOGY

The *tektōn*'s proliferating modalities took on a more philosophical turn as intellectuals began to envision a place for building not through the support mechanisms of archaeology but from within the individualized space of the emerging modern Self. This is the fourth space of *tektōn*-topia. Building on the figure of Joseph, the carpenter father of Christ, and reinforced by the moralizing tendency of the nineteenth century, the act of making came to be seen by some as intrinsic to the now universalized individual. An early indication of its possibilities can be found in Viollet-le-Duc's *Dictionnaire raisonné*, where we read the following astonishing claim, not about architects, but about builders:

> [A] builder must have not just knowledge and experience but also a "feel" [*un sentiment naturel*] for building. Builders are born and not made, in fact. The technical knowledge and science of construction can only be based upon elements already present in the brains of those who are going to fashion for practical use and give durable form to brute matter. Moreover, it is as true of peoples as it is of individuals that some are born builders from their cradles on, while others will never become builders under any circumstance.[40]

The idea of "born builders" or more literally "builders from the cradle" (*dès leur berceau*) is clearly different from the Albertian proposition of the builder as "mere instrument." It suggests something quite remarkable, an onto(*tektōn*)ology.

Viollet-le-Duc did not flesh out this onto(*tektōn*)ology beyond these few sentences. If he had, he would have had to explain that these "born builders" probably had few advantages at birth, as they would have to work their way through the complex system of apprenticeships and guilds. He would have had to point out that such a person probably worked with and employed journeymen and laborers under a variety of short-term or contract wage agreements, and only slowly developed a reputation for honesty, organization, and management. He would have had to note that such a person would be a master builder at one site and a hired contractor on another. And finally, he would have had to admit that this so-called "born builder" would have acquired pattern books and trade journals and would have been expected to know mathematics and geometry. And had Viollet-le-Duc followed the life of this builder from cradle to coffin, he would have noted that once the builder got old and could no longer engage in manual work, he probably lived a life of poverty at the margins of society.

As it turns out, Viollet-le-Duc is not really interested in the life of the born builders. He uses the reference simply as a foil to help the reader better understand the world of the architects who in Viollet-le-Duc's writings do not live on the presumably easy street of ontology. The architect has to engage in laboriously study. He (and it in this case certainly still a "he") is also the victim or beneficiary of cultural or national realities outside of his control. He must also make sure to issue his ideas "from out of their own intelligence ... in keeping with their possession of the faculty of reasoning." And if he fails somewhere along the way the "work will be nothing but an accumulation of borrowings" (234). Viollet-le-Duc's architect, embedded in the changing and turbulent cultural world, bears all the stresses and risks. If the Albertian *archē* could hope to work with a mind cleared and prepared by the controlling methodologies of perspective, his path oriented toward the *dignissimis hominum*, by the time we get to Viollet-le-Duc, *mente animoque* had become almost lost in the mess of reality, in the impossibilities of success, and even in the inevitability of shame and failure.

* * * *

Henry Thoreau's *Walden; or, Life in the Woods* (1854) paved the way for a more robust ontology, except—in an astonishing move—he stripped the builder from his ancient connection to the trades.

In the text, we first encounter the usual Filaretian mythology, except that instead of a grown man foraging in the woods to find material to make a

FIGURE 6.1.7 *Reconstructed Thoreau Cabin, Walden Pond, Concord, Massachusetts. Photograph by RhythmicQuietude.*

shelter, Thoreau sees evidence of this "natural yearning" in the playacting of children:

> We may imagine a time when, in the infancy of the human race, some enterprising mortal crept into a hollow in a rock for shelter. Every child begins the world again, to some extent, and loves to stay out doors, even in wet and cold. It plays house, as well as horse, having an instinct for it. Who does not remember the interest with which when young he looked at shelving rocks, or any approach to a cave? It was the natural yearning of that portion of our most primitive ancestor which still survived in us. From the cave we have advanced to roofs of palm leaves, of bark and boughs, of linen woven and stretched, of grass and straw, of boards and shingles, of stones and tiles.

But when Thoreau wanted then to build his hut, we learn that he did not own an axe, so he had to borrow one from a local farmer.[41] Later on, he admits that he had to borrow other tools as well:

> Near the end of March, 1845, I borrowed an axe and went down to the woods by Walden Pond, nearest to where I intended to build my house, and began to cut down some tall, arrowy white pines, still in their youth, for timber. It is difficult to begin without borrowing, but perhaps it is the most generous course thus to permit your fellow-men to have an interest in your enterprise. The owner of the axe, as he released his hold on it, said that it was the apple of his eye; but I returned it sharper than I received it . . . So I went on for some days cutting and hewing timber, and also studs and rafters, all with my narrow axe, not having many communicable or scholar-like thoughts . . .

I hewed the main timbers six inches square, most of the studs on two sides only, and the rafters and floor timbers on one side, leaving the rest of the bark on, so that they were just as straight and much stronger than sawed ones. Each stick was carefully mortised or tenoned by its stump, for I had borrowed other tools by this time.

* * * *

There is a problem in Thoreau's narrative. This is not easy carpentry. Where he learned the skills he never says, presumably from the time he spent working in his father's pencil factory or maybe from his time in the house of Ralph Waldo Emerson (1841–4) where he served as the children's tutor, earning his keep as an editorial assistant, repairman, and gardener. That said, Thoreau's primary employment as a surveyor is not to be overlooked; he was responsible for dozens of plot plans for individual clients and towns, producing documentation of properties, towns, and roadways.[42] But though it familiarized him with buildings of various types, it did not in itself prepare him to be a builder as such, unless there is part of the story that he is not telling us.

Not only did he disguise how he learned carpentry, he does not even mention how the acquisition of advanced carpentry skills assisted him in his philosophical quest, even though these skills were clearly just as metaphorically important as they were real. Things went so smoothly throughout the construction that I suspect that some of those smiling angels that once helped Joseph might have been on hand.

The point is simple. Here, in a book that heralds a philosophy of independence, we see the disappearance of the occupationality of the building trades. There is no one to help lift the beams, no one to help set the dowels, no topping-off ceremony, no obscene banter about past lovers. Thoreau acted as if making the hut was natural to him and beyond that natural to any man, and—beyond even that—natural to mankind's ethos of well-being.

The making of a hut was no longer relegated to architecture's quasi-anthropological beginnings, the pro forma starting point for a story of European civilizational progress, but was front and center of a performative philosophy. The old equation of hand and tool that had been controlled by a politics of silencing overlayed by a theology of dutifulness had now a new element, the Enlightenment-era mind staging its search for spiritual healthiness. The hut as the stand-in for simple construction, clear purpose, and transparent social position came to integrate itself, in the United State especially, into the ideological formations of the so-called Protestant ethic, one that held that man was a sturdy and responsible individual, responsible to himself, his society, and his God. For a time, anybody who could not measure up to that standard could not qualify for public office or even popular respect. For public officials, fixing their birthplace in or near the "log cabin" was de rigueur.[43]

* * * *

WikiHouse is a digitally manufactured building system that can be downloaded for free and used by anyone with access to the right materials and machinery. According to its website,

> It aims to make it simple for anyone to design, manufacture and assemble beautiful, high-performance homes that are customised to their needs.[44]

The designers of WikiHouse assume a completely *archē*-free sense of onto(*tektōn*)ology. But it is not that simple, since making the elements involves complex robotic tools and programming—in other words, a production facility. The physical elements of the assembly also require special materials. And even though the house is ostensibly easy to assemble, it does require a good sense of planning and oversight. The rhetoric belies the reality, and as always with the mythology of the hut, the assumption is that a happy socio- can be magically squeezed out of an otherwise dreary and overdetermined world.

> Can I build it myself? Yes, and it's a lot of fun. But it's important you do so in a competent, safe way, and comply with any relevant health & safety regulations and insurance obligations.[45]

* * * *

The removal of both *archē* and the *tektōn*'s occupationality from the idea of building was particularly attractive to philosophers trying to express their disillusionment with modern life. In *La Poétique de l'Espace* (Poetics of Space, 1958) by Gaston Bachelard, we read:

> For our house is our corner of the world. As has often been said, it is our first universe, a real cosmos in every sense of the word. If we look at it intimately, the humblest dwelling has beauty. Authors of books on "the humble home" often mention this feature of the poetics of space. But this mention is much too succinct. Finding little to describe in the humble home they spend little time there; so they describe it as it actually is, without really experiencing its primitiveness, a primitiveness which belongs to all, rich and poor alike, if they are willing to dream.
>
> It is body and soul. It is the human being's first world. Before he is "cast into the world," as claimed by certain hasty metaphysics, man is laid in the cradle of the house.[46]

Nowhere in Bachelard's description of a house is there any recognition that this house is something that was built, and that needs to be maintained and cleaned, that the floors need to be dusted, windows polished, gutters scraped, and walls painted. The *tektōn* has been so removed from this person's consciousness that its inhabitant would be completely puzzled if the roof sprung a leak.

✳ ✳ ✳ ✳

One of the most forceful attempts to integrated ontology with building was Martin Heidegger's *Bauen Wohnen Denken* (1951). To understand his fascination with *bauen* ("to build") we have to recognize that he associated the word "architecture" with the Greco-Roman civilization that was introduced with the Roman occupation of ancient Germany. In current times, from a Heideggerian point of view, architecture relates to ugly cities, big buildings, the economy of trade, and the top-down culture of expertise. To counteract architecture's invasiveness and pervasiveness, Heidegger produced an elaborate, Ponzi-scheme-like etymology to link *bauen* with *bin* ("to be"). His argument goes like this: In some ancient time, a man awoke in a forest and said the word *bin*; after a while his grandchild presumably heard *beo*. Then after some time and losses and gains of comprehension, *beo* became *bahn* and then *buar*, which led to *nachbahr* or "neighbor" which then led—when the "h" became and "u"—to *bauer* ("farmer") and then with more losses and gains to *bauen*.

There are no women in the story or, for that matter, family. The single male in the forest produces the socio- out of his language when, at some

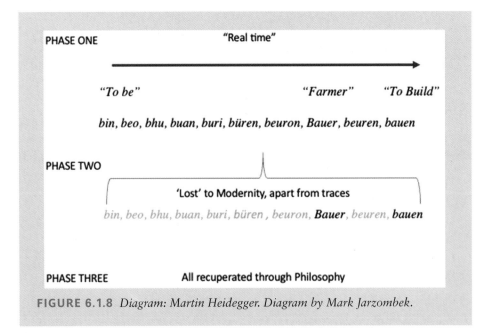

FIGURE 6.1.8 *Diagram: Martin Heidegger. Diagram by Mark Jarzombek.*

time, he first recognized the presence of "neighbors" (*nachbahr*) and maybe has something to say to them, or not. For Heidegger it does not matter. All that happens is that people began to acknowledge others *in language* when they started to make declinations "I am," "you are," "he/she is," "we are," and so forth. Grammar becomes the sole instrument by which the "I" recognizes the presence of the societal. It is not intimate, nor is there much of a world past the outer reaches of the neighbor's property. Only through the plasticity of language in combination with its conjugations is the socio- , for him, properly evoked.

The thrust of his argument is that *bauen* still contains—fortunately, he would say—the ancient ontological centeredness of being ("I am") despite the twists and turns of language as it developed over time. Modernity, however, has interrupted the built-in comprehension of the word, at least among Germans—the radio was for him particularly problematic in that respect—meaning that Germans now have to read the etymology—as foggy as it might be—backward to the originary *ich bin*.

For Heidegger, language is the register of the socio- without that philosophy has to do the hard work of sociology. It points to the result, not the actual human processes of encounter and exchange. We do not build because we have a family, or because we need a barn for the cows. We do not need special skills or training; we do not need family or friends to join in a barn-raising. We build because we—*men*—can supposedly recreate in our minds our grand awakening of consciousness in the forest.

The absurdity of it all turned out to be its lure. *Bauen* became the pet project in theory circles for generations, especially in the 1970s, and often in the context of phenomenology, despite its complete rejection of society's anthropological origins, despite its masculine centrism, and despite the fact that there was no clear project that could explain how one goes from the act of *bauen* to an actual modern architect, except to say that such a person would have to have some inner natural connection to ancient ways. But how that is to be ascertained—apart from self-proclamation or academic indoctrination—is unknown.

* * * * *

The above was a quick sketch of a vast cultural landscape where the ambitions of *archē*(non)*tektōn* face the realities of *tektōn*(non)*archē*. Since this entire cultural landscape works with limited or no input from architects, none of it belongs—in the narrow sense—to the history of architecture, which only goes to show how the term "architecture" has imperialized itself over the disciplinary field. But there is no alternative.

Each of the four vectors has its own internal dimension from the small scale to the most extreme.

Home-building today can involve a local contractor with a few people working out of a front office, but it is also a multibillion-dollar industry controlled by huge corporations. In the US in 2019, they were: D. R. Horton

(1978): revenue: $17.4 billion, closings: 58,434; Lennar Corp (1954): revenue: $20.6 billion, closings: 51,491; PulteGroup (1956): revenue: $9.9 billion, closings: 23,232, etc. The top ten corporations in the US in 2019 had $80 billion in revenue with over 200,000 closings.

> D. R. Horton: "We Are America's Builder"
> Lennar Corp: "A Simpler Way to Buy"
> Ryan Homes: "Homes Built to Live Better"
> KB: "Homes for the way you Live"
> Taylor Morris: "Inspired Living"
> Meritage Homes Corp: "Life.Built.Better"
> Century Communities: "A home for every dream"
> LGI Homes: "We don't just build houses, we build homes"

The vector of engineering can span the scale of small businesses to huge corporations like ARUP with their managerial model of control and collaboration. "We are Total Design" is their rather frightening corporate motto. At the small scale, there is the much-ballyhooed world of the makers whose perspective was elegantly summarized by David Lang in *Zero to Maker*:

> In a way, makers are the guardians of this industrious self-reliance I had hoped for, but together they're so much more. They understand and respect their place in history, as part of a long line of toolmakers and tool users. Although they keep traditional knowledge alive, they are also busy inventing and bringing new technologies into the world. And these are not your grandparents' tools.[47]

Traditional Architecture, though the most academic of the various vectors, has its own extreme formation in the reconstructions of ancient buildings, collapsing the Then into a Now. Tedious forays into the complexities of histories can hardly compete with a single gulp of fulfillment.

The vector of onto(*tektōn*)ology, though often proclaiming itself in righteous opposition to the evils of capitalism and other forms of mercantile exploitation, imagines a world of isolated purists who magically need neither money nor skill. Buildings seem to emerge out of an auto-poetic, *tekton*-ology.

The space of *tektōn*-topia is thus not a singular space of resistance to the overbearing instrumentalities of *archē*. In some places, as in the home-building industry, it is embedded in the core workings of capitalism. In engineering, it sides with the exclusionary practices of corporate power, mostly hiding behind the now de rigueur narratives of multidisciplinarity and collaboration. In the world of Traditional Architecture, it has become increasingly allied with the tourist and cultural industries and fantasies of nostalgia. Furthermore, each of the four quadrants has built-in opposition to the other three and thus often mistakes its disciplinary self-positionality for legitimate critique.

It is also a world, as we have seen, with its own specialized banter of affirmations and put-downs, a grammatology all unto itself: "non-pedigreed architecture," "unarchitected building," "vernacular architecture," "bauen," "dwelling," "shelter," along with "architect-surveyor," "carpenter-architect," "planning-mill carpenter," "country carpenter," "jerry-builder," "maker," and "beauty doctor." What we see by the end of the nineteenth century—and still in play today—is not just the proliferation of code words that fill the ancient gap between *archē* and *tektōn* but a graphology of intonations and insinuations. These words, even the words such as "architecture," "master builder," and on down the line, are part of the discipline's slang. They all have referential intent, but giving that intent its historicity can prove difficult and indeed often counteracts the very nature of usage itself. They are not "definitional," but embody particularly charged scenarios that seek to play themselves out as partisan actors on the disciplinary stage.

* * * *

As with anamorphic realities of architecture (without scare quotes), here, too, in the frictional space of *tektōn*-topia, a creative practice can only happen in the loopholes of foreclosed realities.

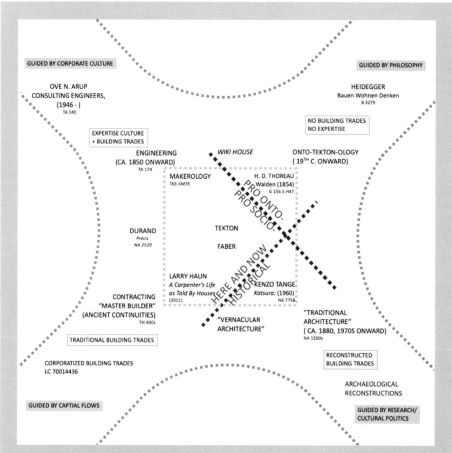

FIGURE 6.1.9 *Diagram: The primary zones of* tekton-topia. *Diagram by Mark Jarzombek.*

PART SEVEN

CHAPTER ONE

Master Builder

In *Design and Crime (And Other Diatribes)* (2002) by Hal Foster, there is a chapter entitled "The Master Builder" which was a not-so-veiled put-down of Frank Gehry, whom he described in the very first sentence as "the master architect" (27). In other words, Gehry was *no* master builder.[1] This is, of course, a familiar dualism. In good Laugierian manner, Foster states that he is "opposed to a computer-driven version of a Potemkin architecture of conjured surfaces" (38). He is, of course, no moralizing champion of classicism, but posits his claim as part of a quasi-leftist critique of the excesses of capital. He lets it be known that instead of bringing "elite design in touch with common culture and renew stale architectural forms with fresh social expression" (what that might mean I am not sure), Gehry is content to use "a readymade image or commodity object" (32). Gehry first went wrong, Foster argues, when he tried to become an artist and made "projects that simply go Pop, such as his Chiat Day Building . . . This object may suit the client, but it manipulates the rest of us, and reduces architecture to a 3-D billboard." The messy integration of architecture, art, information, and computation creates a clear cultural loss:

> This integration, that erasure, is a deterritorializing of image and space that depends on a digitizing of the photograph, its loosening *from old referential ties* (perhaps the development of Photoshop will one day be seen as a world-historical event), and on a computing of architecture, its loosening *from old structural principles* (in architecture today almost anything can be designed because almost anything can be built: hence all the arbitrary curves and biomorphic blobs designed by Gehry and followers—see Chapter 3). As Deleuze and Guattari, let alone Marx, taught us long ago, this deterritorializing is the path of capital.[2]
>
> my italics

If the goal, for Foster, is to fuse art and life—or to at least hold that out as a possibility—Gehry stands as the negative. Even his personality is under attack. Gehry is at times described as witty, manipulative, inflated, willful, strained, swollen, extravagant, gestural, perverse, oppressive, and exclusive. It makes for difficult reading. Foster is implying that it was a disturbance in Gehry's personality that produced his false consciousness, a position which seems to suggest that Gehry was no "born builder," but just the opposite a "born architect"—one who at birth was destined to soak in all that was wrong with modern society.

One would think that Foster would work just as hard to theorize the world of the *tektōn* as he does of the architect. But for him the "Master Builder" is little more than a trope of some imagined wholesomeness. Foster thus misses the very thing that identifies *archē* as such, namely its primal orientation toward the art of magic, even if fueled now by a modernist subjectology that places *archē* into ever bolder positions. To hold out for the "Master Builder" an *archē-non-archē* is to falsify—but also to play out yet again—the tension that marks the entire history of post-Albertian discourse. I wonder what Foster would have to say about the architects of the Parthenon or about Alberti, Borromini, or for that matter Mies van der Rohe, magicians all.

* * * *

Theodore Adorno in *Ästhetische Theorie* (1970) is less worried about the presumed excess of *archē* than about the presumably more entrenched dangers from the side of the *tektōn*. In a discussion on "construction," which for him is both a metaphor for the Enlightenment's cult of Reason and an attitude that comes out of the building trades, he worries about what he sees as the "reification of technique" that "trends towards the 'savage,' the barbaric, the primitive, the artless." It could lead to a frightening "descent into sheer routine."[3] If construction becomes autonomous, its ostensible alliance with mindless bureaucracy leads to the "emaciated subject." In architectural terms, he would put Durand in that world: banal, mindless, and, above all, "artless." There is nothing more fearsome in post-Enlightenment theories than laboring bodies unleashed from guidance, even for a Marxist.

At the other end of the spectrum of possibilities, there is a form of construction that has what Adorno rather mysteriously calls a "prosaic provenance." Here we can insert the track made by Filarete and Laugier in the sense that they would value a type of construction that was untroubled by self-reflection. But, so Adorno seems to be reasoning, since we have to work *within* the modern, and thus within the space of self-reflection, this track does not bring us into the problematic of the current situation which for better and worse is defined by self-reflection. This would return us to Durand, who, as we have seen, leads us downward, however, to estrangement. In the end, he suggests a way through this tangle:

> Construction is able to do two things: it can codify the resignation of the emaciated subject, and promote absolute estrangement by incorporating it in art; or it can project the image of a reconciled future situated beyond static and dynamics. There are many linkages between the principle of

construction and technocracy, linages that reinforce the suspicion that construction belongs inevitably to the administered bureaucratized world. Yet it may also terminate in an as yet unknown aesthetic form, the rational organization of which might point to the abolition of all notions of administered control and their reflexes in art.[4]

What he is saying is that if only we can insert and manage construction through the dynamics of reason, but not allow reason to take over the job of administration, then the rational would give us some possibility for hope. The clever twists and turns of the argument lead to an implausibly utopian proposition: construction without administration—a non-artless artlessness—made by people without an occupation (as that would require administration) but still guided by reason whose agent of enforcement has yet to be determined.

* * * *

Stated differently, the track through Laugier does not adequately upscale into modernity and so would exist in a quiet dead end. The track through Durand aligns more consistently with modernity, except that it ends in the false rationality of artless administration. Is there an alternative?[5] Apart from promising some "yet unknown aesthetic form," it is hard to know what Adorno would have wanted in more concrete terms. A more positive solution would go under the heading "tectonics," a term that emerged in the nineteenth century and is still current in architectural discourses to this day. There were several key figures: Karl Bötticher (1806–98), Gottfried Semper (1803–79), and Kenneth Frampton (1930–). All of them, it can be argued, sought to resolve the separation of *tektōn* from *archē* by returning to *tektōn* a semblance of authority and even dignity that had been denied it by Alberti. Bötticher in *Tektonik der Hellenen* (Greek Tectonics, 1844–52) argued that every detail of a Greek temple not only had a specific working function, but also satisfied a higher symbolic function— its art-form. This relationship of part to whole was defended as late as by Adolf Heinrich Borbein in 1982 when he writes, for example:

> Tectonic becomes the art of joinings. "Art" here is to be understood as encompassing tekne, and therefore indicates tectonic as assemblage not only of building parts but also of objects, indeed of artworks in the narrow sense. With regard to the ancient understanding of the word tectonic tends toward the construction of making of an artisanal or artistic product.[6]

These interpretations—in some Hellenic-centric way—want to seek out the conceptual grounding of architecture (without scare quotes) and thus assume that by beginning with "tectonics" in isolation we can come more directly to the nature of architecture and revise it against the grain of our modernity (without, of course, falling into the world of "architecture"). As it turns out, solving the problem in this way does not solve the problem. Just as Derrida overshot the mark by trying to detach *archē* from architecture, the defenders of "tectonics" overshoot it, but from the opposite direction, as they were not out to free *tektōn* from the rulership of *archē*, but to constrain *tektōn* all the more. Bötticher states:

> [A] concept of each part [which] can be thought of as being realized by two elements: the core-form and the art-form. The core-form of each part is the mechanically necessary and statically functional structure; the art-form, on the other hand, is only the characterization by which the mechanical-statical functional is made apparent.[7]

Admittedly, the *tektōn* and the *archē* are asked to collaborate, but the *tektōn* still has to do its duty. Though tectonics reaches back to the *tektōn*'s ship-building and furniture-making days, it is ever more the slave to *archē* as it stands in for a type of work that is thought to be in love with its own labor. Just as the detail is not allowed to step out of line, so, too, presumably the worker. Frampton reaffirms this moral mandate when he critiques shallow capitalism, which he calls the "scenographic" and the superfluidities of "global modernism":

> The primary principle of the autonomy of architecture resides in the tectonic rather than the scenographic: that is to say this autonomy is embodied in the revealed ligaments of the construction and in the way in which the syntactical form of the structure explicitly reveals the action of gravity . . . The tactile and the tectonic jointly have the capacity to transcend the mere appearance of the technical in much the same way as the place-form has the potential to withstand the relentless onslaught of global modernism.[8]

In his essay "Rappel à l'ordre: The Case for the Tectonic" (1990), Frampton was hoping to rescue architecture from the influence of pop culture as well as from the likes of Robert Venturi and Denise Scott Brown. He called for revisiting a set of essential distinctions such as those between ground and building, and between column and beam.[9] This approach, as one defender explained, "declares to be a proposition for disclosing the inherent meaning of things depending on the quality of their objecthood through the fundamental revelation of technique taken beyond mere instrumentality."[10] From that point of view, "tectonics" requires the outside agency of guilt as enforcement. As Bötticher wrote,

> It is in the nature of things that this simple law will restrain any subjective and arbitrary desire to cover the core-form haphazardly with symbols . . . The essence and idea of a structural part prohibit arbitrary decoration and do not allow one to deal with the decorative elements as one pleases.[11]

* * * *

Tectonics works through the imaginaries of the morally stabilized human body in that it wants architecture to self-identify with itself as *constructum*. Buildings are not meant to be put together through the abstract determinations of reason or because of the arbitrary impositions of the construction industry.[12] Nor are they meant to be the reservoir of some sleepy tradition. There has to be a certain custom-tailoring of the parts. The tectonic is thus a site of resistance to the modern world, a type of counterfactual factuality.[13] Tectonic does not change architecture and its goals or messages, but is a type of value-added that makes the building more expressive and quite likely expensive. The tectonic is thus also the location of the discipline's claim to thoughtfulness. But because it is a hidden moral order, it constrains more than it frees.

The *tektōn*, as I am discussing it, is something altogether different. At stake is not how an imagined Hellenic, dignity of labor (without laborers) can be used as leverage against the unruly, industrialized world of today, but rather its role in the play of disciplinary signifiers. If anything, the *tektōn* seeks to free itself from the compulsions of good behavior, whether imposed on it from within (either in the form of unreflective "tradition" and hyper reflective "tektonics") or from without (as in the form of "good design" and contractual behavior).

Whereas tectonics assumes that one can inhabit—ideally at least, though it is never clear how—a space of both being and becoming, the *tektōn*, as I am discussing it, cannot be represented as such, but by virtue of its rescuable encounter with its negating other, an encounter that makes us aware that there is something that cannot be represented. The *tektōn* as discussed in this book can only be represented as an "after" to its own predecessorial place in the teleology of production.

* * * *

The word *tektōn*, as I am discussing it, has multiple semiotic registers. Though it refers back to an actual person (ship maker, for example), it is also an occupation (contractor, for example), an occupational place (roof, for example), and even to a place in the Library of Congress cataloguing system. It is also a figure of architecture's identity-of-difference, since it is *always* also a -tektōn and so is never anything purely autonomous, but, when possible, seeking out a space of resistance.

The point is not to make the unconscious of the *tektōn* speak (for it does so already in any number of different ways), or to render the *tektōn* as a practice (for it does so already in any number of different ways), but to locate it more legitimately as a necessary alien and sometimes disturbing and yet also sometimes creative force in architecture's disciplinary landscape.

* * * *

When Frank Lloyd Wright designed Marin County Civic Center in California (1957), it was overnight clearly a magnificent piece of architecture and rightly deserves it place in the history books. In designing external colonnades, Wright apparently faced a quandary. Instead of doing a more regular column, Wright decided to float the column and have it seem to rest precariously along the flank of a "rock" that rises like a mini-monolith from the walkway as if it were some natural feature. The column seems to be made more of wood than metal, looking very much like a gilded 2×4. To

FIGURE 7.1.1 *Exterior: Marin County Civic Center, California, Frank Lloyd Wright, 2008. Photograph by Fizbin.*

FIGURE 7.1.2 *Column detail: Marin County Civic Center, California, Frank Lloyd Wright, 2008. Photograph by Mark Jarzombek.*

FIGURE 7.1.3 *Column detail: Marin County Civic Center, California, Frank Lloyd Wright, 2008. Photograph by Mark Jarzombek.*

make sure the viewer pauses and reflects, he added an elegant slopping capital to transition to the arch.

These columns do not fall in line with the conventions of tectonics as they not only want to look like they defy gravity, but they also defy the expectations and even the material properties of concrete and steel. They even defy the constructional principle set out by the building itself. They are a curiosity and a flourish, but also a puzzle to be figured out, one that begins with the decorated temples of the Greeks.

Compare these columns with a detail from Borre Skodvin's Mortensrud Church in Oslo (2002). There, a rock from the earth protrudes into the space. The architects shifted the columns to accommodate its girth tilting them to emphasize the rock's location in the design. It is without doubt an example of subtle contextualism. Frank Lloyd Wright's rock is, of course, not real and yet it serves as an imagined piece of "bedrock." In 2003, Mortensrud Church was given the European Steel Design Award and in 2007 was designated one of the most important postwar buildings in Norway. And even though the Marin County City Hall is no less an example of excellence, these columns bring us to the creative borderlands of "architecture."

FIGURE 7.1.4 *Mortensrud Church, Oslo, Jensen & Skodvin Arkitekter AS, 2002.* © *Jan Olav Jensen.*

* * *

In 1945, Mies van der Rohe designed the S. R. Crown Hall at IIT in Chicago. There is no doubt that the presence of the main column is represented by the metal cladding placed over the corner and develops the continuity of the corner from one mullion around to the other mullion, as one commentator expressed it.[14] But the covering over of the concrete column in which there is embedded a steel I-beam can also be read as the transfiguration of concrete into steel, giving the illusion that this is a steel building. Although the "tectonics" may be in the careful drafting of the detail and in the integration and legibility of the parts, the suppression of the concrete is where I locate the (non)*tektōn*. In other words, the concrete is both invisible and dutiful, falling with the Albertian disciplinary protocol. The steel covering, deployed for expressive and semiotic purposes, serves the *archē* to erase the issues of structural load altogether. "Tectonics" here obscures its dissimulative practices, the core attributes of post-Albertian *archē*. To make this more visible, I would add weepholes in the steel covering so that one could see the covering for what they are: pilasters. I would then make it appear as if the concrete were indeed leaking out of the holes to create the effect that the concrete behind might no longer be as stable as one might think.

Mies van Rohe, IIIT, Chicago   with weepholes for concrete

FIGURE 7.1.5 *Corner detail: S. R. Crown Hall, Illinois Institute of Technology, Chicago, Mies van der Rohe, c. 1955, with changes by author. Photographs and additions by Mark Jarzombek.*

* * * *

Occasionally one finds an architect who sees in tectonics a fetish in its own right—as at the building known as the McCormick Tribune Campus Center on the main campus of IIT on the south side of Chicago (2003), designed by Rem Koolhaas. Among its many well-known features is the "unfinished" ceiling in part of the entrance. We see the naked sheetrock, and the places where the sheetrock attachments are located and patched over and, of course, the patching itself. It might be a wry commentary about the budget. But it is also a poke in the eye of tectonics. And yet in showing the "space" of *tektōn* it admits for all to see that at least here *archē* has purposefully violated the sacred insistence of completion. He has placed on exhibit not the unfinished building, but the unfinished labor of the contractor.

* * * *

Neither *archē* nor *tektōn* have permanent identities rooted in their imagined Hellenic etymological pasts. They will only support their configurations as theoretical propositions through the relations that each maintain with the other. Each occupies and occasionally even preoccupies the other.

Each—as the abstract material of content—undermines the capacity to see either heterogenous systems or systems of smooth synthesis. The first is

FIGURE 7.1.6 *Ceiling detail: McCormick Tribune Campus Center, Illinois Institute of Technology, Chicago. Photograph by Mark Jarzombek.*

usually done in the name of critique (and its various teleology disguises), the latter in the name of the bourgeois taste (and its own set of teleology disguises). The first is done to produce and enhance tension outside of the system, the second is done to produce and enhance an absence of tension within the system. The first argues that modernity is unfinished and would work "only if . . ."; the second argues that modernity is finished "if only we could get on with it." The first celebrates the desire to destabilize the normative (as in tectonics), the second celebrates the desire to deliver (as in the work of large architecture/construction firms). Both sides would reject the prioritization of "architecture" over architecture.

FIGURE 7.1.7 Seven White Hammers, *Jim Dine, 2008. Etching, aquatint and drypoint, with hand-coloring in acrylic and charcoal.* © 2021 Jim Dine / Artists Rights Society (ARS), New York.

* * * *

In the prints of Jim Dine, tools feature in many of his works. They provide a link, so he writes, "with our past, the human past, the hand." There is an autobiographical resonance, as Dine's family owned a hardware store in Cincinnati, the Save Supply Company, where as a young boy he played in the aisles. His work represents, according to one critic, "an intense search for his own identity, using everyday objects and accessible imagery to carve out his autobiography."[15] I would like to see his drawings in a different light, since they provoke a question about where to locate the real of the tool.[16] It might well be that these drawings are not a celebration of tools, but rather of an evocation of the voicelessness of the (non)*tektōn*. The hammers in *Seven White Hammers* (2008) are removed from the clean instrumentalities of their purpose. They speak of their nightmarish independence, taping, scratching, grinding, and clawing, but not achieving the clarity that is embedded in the grand idea of "tool." Though oriented to some presumed task to the left of the frame, they are lost in the neither/nor: neither fully of the *tektōn* anymore—with modernity having turned them into symbols of obsolescence— and yet not fully of the art world, except as representations of a former ideal. In both conditions they represent the crisis of the unspoken within the "non."

FIGURE 7.1.8 Born from Each Other, *Bhuvanesh Gowda, 2016. Image courtesy of Chemould Prescott Road, Mumbai, India. © Chemould Prescott Road and Bhuvanesh Gowda.*

* * * *

Bhuvanesh Gowda (b. 1976), based in Mumbai, India, was born in the small town of Kadaba, on the slopes of the Western Ghats, a mountain range in southern India. He has remarked that in his hometown "almost everyone knew how to handle wooden implements and build wooden structures."[17] But even there, that tradition is dying out. Most of the wood he uses is salvaged from dismantled houses and elsewhere. He also draws on the imaginaries of "Vishwakarma," the master carpenter and divine architect-engineer of the gods, who is celebrated in ancient hymns and is supposed to have built the city of Dwarka overnight. *Born from Each Other* (2016) is a carved sculpture of two pieces connected by a dovetail joint and presented horizontally on a steel frame. One piece is left its natural color, the other is charred black. From a disciplinary point of view, this is an artwork that, as one critic states, deals with "the unknown, the unexplained, and the mystical."[18] From the point of view of the narratives of "architecture," we see here a work that straddles two worlds. On the one hand, there is the ancient world of the *archē-tektōn* where the ethos of the *tektōn* has been restored from discarded bits of old houses. On the other hand, the piece looms large as a homage—a memorial even—to the lost majesty of woodworking and joinery.[19]

FIGURE 7.1.9 *Zoma Museum, Addis Ababa, Elias Sime, 2002–9.* © *Zoma Museum.*

****

The Zoma Museum, in Addis Ababa, Ethiopia, opened its doors in 2019. It was founded by Elias Sime with Meskerem Assegued, an anthropologist and art curator who lived in the US for seventeen years before moving back to Ethiopia in the late 1990s. Sime, an artist and the project's architect, worked with a team of masons to build the houses on the grounds of the museum. Since it was not possible to apply for a building permit for constructions in mud, the decision was taken to maintain the foundations of preexisting buildings and use them to support the new structures, with the argument being that the project was one of restoration.[20]

The exterior walls are hand-designed with swirling patterns and built with wattle and daub (locally called "chikka"), a building material that mixes sand, clay, straw, and animal dung. The patterns were inspired by different events of Ethiopian culture and environment. One incorporates the numerical system of Ge'ez, one of the oldest written languages in the world, while several units depict the four stages of the mysterious life cycle of the butterfly. The patterns on the main gallery walls resemble both the lines of a thumbprint and a very windy road, inspired by the ups and downs the builders experienced in trying to pull off such an ambitious project.

Here labor tells a broader story about the site, about earth and about the processes of making, especially since it shows what can be accomplished without the overbearing presence of *archē*. There is a fine line between this and a vast array of architects who work with traditional materials, but usually in a way that seeks to mimic a form of abstraction compatible with neomodernist tastes. The emphasis in these cases is almost always on the "finish." The results do not engage the simulational and multidisciplinary ethos of the ancient *archē*. Stated more directly, though the buildings at the Zoma Museum might seem more humble than a Greek temple, they are of the same order.

* * * * *

What if there was a delay mechanism between idea and result, where the intentionalities of the *archē* and operations of *tektōn* could both come into play. This is the argument of Zach Cohen, who works with robots to pour concrete. Several labs are now trying this out. There are a range of difficulties. It is hard to maintain consistency; the concrete can clog the nozzles; and, once poured, there is no easy chance of repair if something goes wrong. But what if to all those problems one adds a delay between when the instructions are entered into the computer and when the robot acts. The results are not going to be

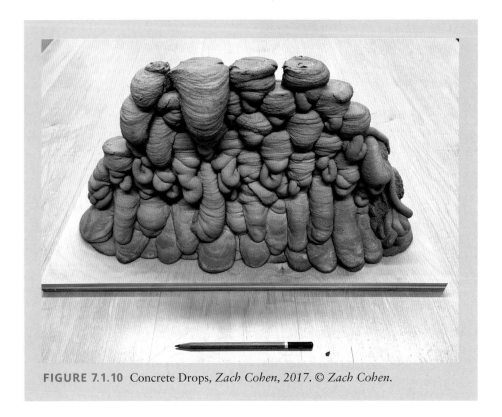

FIGURE 7.1.10 Concrete Drops, *Zach Cohen, 2017. © Zach Cohen.*

satisfying to the construction industry. But "real-time techniques have negatively distanced architectural designers from material, temporal, and instrumental understanding. Further, the current dependence on real-time points to a future of *anti-anticipation*: a time in which architectural designers—and human beings, in general—will not have to anticipate what happens next." The gain in convenience is a loss in improvisation and speculation. So, for example, by using a dripping technique, Cohen can produce work that would technically be called "failures" but that can range from new ways to make walls to new ways to make ornamental components. Here the *tektōn* is not asking to supersede its relationship to *archē* and promise a world liberated, but rather to be acknowledged, if not in space, then at least in time. This project begins to dismantle the logic of equivalence produced in the exchange relations between capitalism and industry.

* * * *

It would be wrong to assume that the metaphysics of dutifulness lacks externality, for the bourgeois world will always exploit its track toward dutifulness to keep the world of the *tektōn* in its silent mode, asking it to perform and disappear. For that reason, things that go under the heading of "contractor mistakes" should also be fully integrated into the theoretical speculations of the grammatology of *archē*(non)*tektōn*.

The builder of this house added an extra column base for the porch before he realized his mistake, so he left it unfinishedWhen he decided to raise the roof a bit, he left the facing of the gable dangling in the air. It did not really bother him.

FIGURE 7.1.11 *Mistake House? Photograph by Mark Jarzombek, with alterations.*

FIGURE 7.1.12 *Telephone pole near Boston, Massachusetts (contractors/builders unknown by author). Photograph by Mark Jarzombek.*

This project makes no one happy. The advocates of critical theory would fail to see any orientation toward some hoped-for emancipation from capitalism. If everyone just left their mistakes out to rot, what does that say about "critique." The post-Criticalists would see a failed attempt at the basic level of construction.[21] The teacher of architecture would see this simply as silliness and note that such a building's resale value has been damaged. The pro-tectonic advocates would cringe at the carelessness of the carpenter and perhaps see it as even a statement verging on the immoral. The museum curator would think that this hardly rises to the level of "an installation."

And yet I would say that the builder of this house has made a political statement, modest but powerful, not about some future world of improved justice and not about the superficiality of capitalism, but about the tyranny of the ideology of completion and about the pathology of dutiful conformity to expectations. This builder did not need to prove his morality to his bourgeois observers by making a "beautiful detail."

* * *

The "contractor unleashed" not only from the tyranny of the *archē* but also from the compulsion of its own desire to conform, gives us insights into the limits and possibilities of the (~~non~~)*tektōn*.

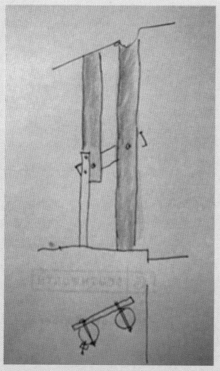

FIGURE 7.1.13 *Sketch of elevation: Telephone pole near Boston, Massachusetts. Drawing by Mark Jarzombek.*

FIGURE 7.1.14 *John H. Daniels Faculty of Architecture, Landscape, and Design Addition, Toronto. © Nic Lehoux, Daniels Faculty.*

* * * *

Driving to work I passed a telephone pole under repair. One will never find this solution in textbooks on structure because here the subversive nature of *tektōn* was allowed to manifest itself, if only for a while, presumably, until a new pole would be planted.

* * * * *

The master builder—slipping and sliding in the cultural semiotics of desire, as well as in the performativities of imagination and the subversion—may soon be a thing of the past. In 2018, Nader Tehrani [NADAAA] added an extension to an older building for the John H. Daniels Faculty of Architecture, Landscape, and Design in Toronto.[22] The building is located on a large traffic circle on Spadina Avenue. The fabrication lab with its imposing robot sits directly on the ground floor on an axis with the avenue as a type of chapel at the end of a grand allée. Moving about in graceful arcs, and visible through the orifice-like door, this animated/mechanized tongue speaks its coded language in silent gesticulations to the world. On stage is the autoerotic transcendence of "architecture" into a cybernetically oriented, Nietzschean future. The *tektōn* can now remove the hated (non), remove even the pressing obligations of the socio- and demand reversed equivalency.

The building celebrates a new disciplinary world with the robot serving as the icon of a new devotionalism. It is the new "master builder." The old one, dehumanized by Alberti into an *instrumentum* and falsely naturalized by Filarete and struggling to find a voice of its own, morphs here into a post-humanized divinity: an *über-tektōn*(non)*archē*.

CHAPTER TWO

Tekton Libidinalism

In *Civilization and Its Discontents* (1930), Freud argues that the primary friction in the world stems from the individual's quest for instinctive freedom and civilization's contrary demand for conformity and repression of instincts. Civilization from that perspective is on the side of the *tektōn*—as the core embodiment of tradition, caution, conformity, and safety—whereas the *archē* pulls itself toward the subjectological. *Tektōn*'s normative association with stability, structure, and longevity is, however, by no means a stable one and not only because of the structure of invisibility that is imposed on it. Though it seeks out regularity, it also embodies the libidinal resistance to the *archē*, repressed under the more celebrated activities of *mente anomique* that aimed to displace *tektōn* from its ontological claims. If we can imagine *tektōn* not as a profession (engineering), not as the locus of a reimagined socio- (tradition) and not as moralized leverage against modernity (tectonics), but in all cases as the repressed we come closer to what is at stake in the history of "architecture" especially since Freud considered the repressed as a process inherent to social dynamics, as a sort of driving force of society. Brazilian philosopher Vladimir Safatle writes:

> In other words, the history of civilization itself is, to some extent, inseparable from something that in the course of a long process can only be assumed, without ever being totally exposed. Something that is internal to it, a mismatch that should be remembered within its tradition. Something that is not a merely external principle.[1]

Though the location of that repression was sited mostly in the hidden realities of vaults, foundations, and roofs, a specialized locus of the occupations of the *tektōn* come in the form of scaffolding. Giovanni Battista Piranesi (1720–8) aimed for the grand narrative, showing huge construction sites with tiny workers. He reveled in enormous beams and in precariously placed winches. Though the scaffolding structures were ostensibly temporary, they seem almost permanent, in fact, almost hopelessly permanent. Construction for him was in slow motion. The workers who made the huge scaffolding have

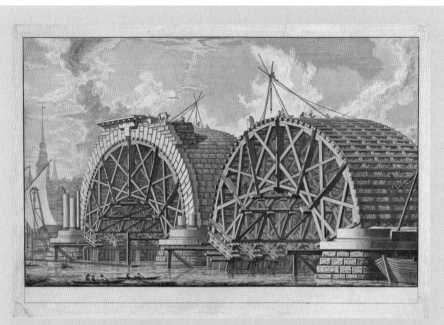

FIGURE 7.2.1 *A view of part of the intended Bridge at Blackfriars, London, Piranesi, c. 1764. The Elisha Whittelsey Collection, The Elisha Whittelsey Fund, 1962. The Metropolitan Museum of Art.*

themselves disappeared, leaving a few undermanned contractors the daunting task of completion. It is a rare glimpse into architecture's libidinal structure, a manifesto of the unrequited.

Nicola Zabaglia (1664–1750), master mason of the Fabbrica of St. Peter's and the director of the School of Practical Mechanics, gave scaffolding its more modern, utilitarian identity, designing variants depending on the type and scale of work that needed to be done. He championed the idea of flexible adaptability characterized by convenience, safety, and economy.[2] An example is his lightweight scaffolding for the tribune vault of S. Paolo fuori de mura. This scaffolding comes in easy-to-assemble parts that speak of the coefficient of time and the need to reduce the cost of labor. The *archē* in Zabaglia makes sure that the scaffolding's design conforms to proportional expectations, even if it becomes an aesthetic object in its own right. Ultimately Zabaglia's approach would win out. Here today, gone tomorrow.

* * * *

Although scaffolding can be just yet another part of the invisible in the grand dialectics of (in)completion, on occasion it rises to the level of an artwork, as here in Venice. This project made by an unknown contractor

FIGURE 7.2.2 *Scaffolding design by Nicola Zabaglia, 1743. (Scaffold for octagonal vault of St. Peter's Sacristy, Vatican. From* Castelli e ponti *1743: pl. XXVIII.)*

was composed of a corrugated metal tunnel, an interlocking armature of sticks, and plastic fabric mesh. Is the building not only now complete? Is this not perhaps what someone in the art world might call an "installation," a work of art that supplements the real?

* * * *

It was only in the twentieth century that we see scaffolding and its associated imaginaries begin to be deployed in architecture itself, first with the members of the Russian avant-garde. The Constructivists saw in the word "construction" the ethos of the newly forming industrial working class liberated from bourgeois control. But because Constructivists fought against the exclusion of art and imagination from the technical relation to reality, they were not always interested in construction per se, rather in its semiotic placement within the politics of disruption. Some designers did, however, take it into a more literal dimension. Iakov Chernikhov (1889–1951) incorporated the look of industrial cranes into one of his design proposals seeming to rise over something that looks like a steel mill. In another he perched a building on top of a large superstructure like what one might see at a port.

FIGURE 7.2.3 *Scaffolding, Venice (contractor/builder unknowm by author). Photograph by Mark Jarzombek.*

Whereas, normally, the constructed as construction is invisible (apart from some Piranesian exposé), it is here just the opposite. It is exciting, strange, and titillating, even if it is given an opportunity on the cultural stage that it neither sought out nor asked for as such. But Chernikhov's fascination with construction transcends the literal. "Construction" is designed to stand out, to express, and to even perform the presencing of labor. It is the "before" to the work of socialization. The *archē*, zooming through space, and the *tektōn*, lifting it from the ground, are each clearly identifiable, working in parallel, separating out white collar from blue collar, and administration from production. Its truth about the fracture in the discipline is a fiction, and yet in that fiction there is a truth that had never been tested out in architecture.

※ ※ ※ ※

The *tektōn* is not truly freed, even with the Constructivists. It was still expected to behave, in other words, to do the heavy lifting in a way that meets the expectations of what construction "should do." This was the mistake of most of the modernists as well who made an art of deploying structure structurally. The issue puts a different spin on the much-vaunted celebration of the engineer's aesthetic as described by Le Corbusier and others. According to Le Corbusier, engineers are "inspired by the law of Economy and governed by mathematical calculation." They put "us in accord with universal law." But Le Corbusier never wanted the engineer's aesthetic to be autonomous from the control of architecture or to be

FIGURE 7.2.4 Composition 26, *Iakov Chernikhov, 1929–31.*

expressed in open competition with it. "Finally, it will be a delight to talk of ARCHITECTURE after so many grain-stores, workshops, machines, and sky-scrapers. ARCHITECTURE is a thing of art, a phenomenon of the emotions, lying outside questions of construction and beyond them."[3] The conservatism of Le Corbusier has led any number of architects to treat "structure" as an aesthetic, projecting it as a form of tamed modernity, fully in line with Albertian expectations.

An example is the Modern Art Museum of Fort Worth, Texas, by Tadao Ando Architects and Associates. Elegant for sure, but an expression of architecture's symptomological compulsion to control the narrative. "Construction" is put on display in a way that silences its frictional presence in the discipline. There is admittedly a certain architectural pleasure that emerges in these situations, as it seeks out the erotics of sublimation more so than the logic of disenfranchisement. But the building fails to escape its disciplinary narcissism, removing from "structure" its potential vulgarity and presenting it to the public as submissive and dutiful. Here the reference is the caryatids of the Erechtheion on the Athenian acropolis who represented enslaved women. At the Fort Worth museum, the reference is presumably to men, each stoically holding up a roof. Not only has architecture without scare quotes won out, but so, too, the implied cult of masculinity in the chaste form of nudity without eroticism.

* * * *

The engagement with a messier tradition of exposed construction only began with Frank Gehry's Santa Monica Place (1979–81) and its chain-link front. What started as a fascination with low-tech construction-site materials, like plywood, cinderblocks, and chain link has become by now part of the aesthetic of trendy, high tech. That does not make it any less relevant to the

FIGURE 7.2.5 *Modern Art Museum of Fort Worth, Texas, Tadao Ando Architect & Associates, 2002. Photograph by Joe Mabel, 2007.*

conversation about "architecture," but whereas in the late 1970s it was part
of a movement to revisit the building site and to refamiliarize *archē* with the
everyday materials of the *tektōn*, it has now become an established part in
the upscale orientation of desire economy. Not too far from where I live, the
interior of a high-end coffee shop was designed completely with plywood.

※ ※ ※ ※ ※

The engagement in contemporary architecture with the semiotics of rafters,
beams, scaffolding moves into the space of monumental architecture with
Helmut Jahn's James R. Thompson Center in Chicago, originally the State
of Illinois Center (1985). The building masters the dialectics of (in)
completion without falling victim to projecting the libidinal energy of
construction as a form of Ersatz masculinity. Here its interior strikes one
immediately as unfinished and the elevator shaft as part of a construction-
site scaffolding. It is a masterpiece of "architecture" that has any number of
possible locations within the discourse. Its "structural" detailing was
designed not to overwhelm, but almost the opposite, to appear dangerously

FIGURE 7.2.6 *James R. Thompson Center (originally, State of Illinois Center),
Helmut Jahn, Chicago, 1985.*

minimal. The blue elements that represent "architecture" round out the conversation, both framed and framing.

∗∗∗∗

One place where we see *tektōn* as a semi-autonomous design element in the facade is in Frida Escobedo's La Tallera in Cuernavaca, Morelos, Mexico (2012), which has two billboards facing each other to frame the entrance piazza. If the facade of old was a way for power to express itself in the public domain—with determination and ostentation—screens, though compensating for the failure of modern architecture to develop a comparable public front, elevate the informal into the symbolic. One could easily imagine the building without them. Stark and austere, it would have been predictably modern. But with the screens, the building can now "speak" and because the billboards are visible as such, not pretending to be anything more, they themselves speak a truth—or at least a type of truth—that is no longer assumed for modern architecture. They aim to articulate not the alienated and alienating presence of power, nor the structurality of structure, but a more folksy "human touch." In other words, in a modern building where there can be, by definition, no facade, the *tektōn* in the form of scrim work is brought out of its normal hiding places to pronounce the presence of architecture as "architecture," something that it had rarely been allowed to

FIGURE 7.2.7 *La Tallera, Frida Escobedo, Cuernavaca, Morelos, 2012. © Rafael Gamo.*

do. The screens are here an afterthought that becomes a prologue to what architecture would like to say, but can only say it in that ever-so-thin sliver of reality between public and private space.

* * * *

Four Pancras Square in London stands as a counterexample, namely to fully repress the libidinal energy of the *tektōn* into a passive-aggressive position. Designed by Eric Parry Architects, it celebrates the steel framework as external references to its internal structure. Though clearly post-Miesian, the steel is exposed. But unlike Mies, where structure is embedded in a series of unstructural, pilaster-like elements, here *tektōn* stands dutifully to attention; it encases and yet is just as much a part of the outside as the inside. The building asks to be seen as "infrastructure," though here in exposed, exoskeletal form. The steel is allowed to rust to give it the patina of the nineteenth century, and with a massive, bridge-like, box truss at the base of the facade it references the early modern, and, one can say, masculinized, age of industrialization. Here the pride of workmanship is both real and fake. The grid is associated with modern architecture via engineering as if the honesty of engineering would make the grid appear cleansed of its association with bureaucracy and the excesses of neoliberal capitalism. The engineer is forced to play "the engineer." *Archē* here uses *tektōn* as an avatar of its modernity. *Tektonic* libidibalism becomes a convenient ersatz for the socio-.

* * * *

The Perot Museum of Nature and Science (2011) in Dallas, Texas, by Morphosis Architects was conceived as a large cube floating over a landscaped plinth. The tightly veiled building allows no visual access to its inner program,

FIGURE 7.2.8 *Four Pancras Square, Eric Parry Architects, London. Photograph Christine Matthews / Pancras Square, St Pancras, London / CC BY-SA 2.0.*

apart from the offices toward the top peeking out at the messy urban world from their remote and lofty perch. The lobby at the open corner is the only element that gives us a hint of an inner life. It is combined with a glassed-in rectangle along its flank that houses a 54-foot escalator and that pierces the southern flank of the building at a 30-degree angle. Although expressing the lobby is now expected of buildings that proclaim themselves as "public," the dramatic escalator is designed to speak about the dynamic interrelationship of machinery and humans in the manner inherited down from the Centre Pompidou in Paris. There is no doubt that the escalator is an exciting feature of the building, but here the libidinal attitude has been thoroughly aestheticized. It is neither disruptive nor fully expressed as "structure." As a design element, it becomes folded into the subversive nature of *mente animoque*, giving to the *tektōn* a pretend role in the theatrics of emancipation. Architecture (without scare quotes) here releases itself into the social function of the *tektōn* as a semiotic cover for its neoliberal abnegation of a concern for labor.

* * * *

Lebbeus Woods (1940–2012) was an American architect and artist known for his rich, yet mainly unbuilt work. Though often seen as a visionary or put into the camp of paper architects, he writes:

> I'm not interested in living in a fantasy world. All my work is still meant to evoke real architectural spaces. But what interests me is what the world would be like if we were free of conventional limits. Maybe I can show what could happen if we lived by a different set of rules.[4]

Woods first worked in the offices of Eero Saarinen as a field representative on the Ford Foundation building designed by Saarinen in New York City.

FIGURE 7.2.9 *The Perot Museum of Nature and Science, Morphosis Architects, Dallas, Texas, 2011. The Lyda Hill Texas Collection of Photographs in Carol M. Highsmith's America Project, Library of Congress, Prints and Photographs Division.*

After leaving Saarinen's office he was employed for a short period at the Champaign, Illinois firm of Richardson, Severns, Scheeler & Associates. He also produced paintings for the Indianapolis Art Museum during that period. In 1976 he turned exclusively to theory and experimental projects, developing a reputation as a refusenik:[5]

> Architecture and war are not incompatible. Architecture is war. War is architecture. I am at war with my time, with history, with all authority that resides in fixed and frightened forms. I am one of millions who do not fit in, who have no home, no family, no doctrine, no firm place to call my own, no known beginning or end, no "sacred and primordial site." I declare war on all icons and finalities, on all histories that would chain me with my own falseness, my own pitiful fears. I know only moments, and lifetimes that are as moments, and forms that appear with infinite strength, then "melt into air." I am an architect, a constructor of worlds, a sensualist who worships the flesh, the melody, a silhouette against the darkening sky. I cannot know your name. Nor you can know mine. Tomorrow, we begin together the construction of a city.[6]

FIGURE 7.2.10 The Hermitage, *Lebbeus Woods, sculpture, Rotterdam, 1998. Photograph by Gerardus.*

Though no *tektōn* of any stripe would ever speak like this, his drawings tell a different story. On the surface they portray the dialectic of anarchy and chaos protesting against the dull normalization of the building arts and their traditional association with law and order. But the structures that he portrays are not really anarchic. Rather they portray the *tektōn* unleashed from normalcy and literally coming out of the woodwork, to vault almost joyously across buildings and streets. Whereas before the *tektōn* had to hide in the rafters or adhere to the rationalized strictures of engineering, here it operates with a new sort of independence and a new sort of imagination speaking for generations of repression and what could have been had Alberti perhaps allowed the *tektōn* to speak.

* * * *

In 1988, Coop Himmelb(l)au completed a rooftop remodeling projected located on Falkestrasse in Vienna. The client was a law firm. Charles Jencks described the project as "a riotous mélange of twisted and warped shapes which resembles a dead pterodactyl that has crash-landed on the roof."[7] The project was also included as a part of the Deconstructivist Architecture exhibition held in the MoMA in New York in 1988. In his introduction essay to the exhibition, Mark Wigley states that the project "is clearly a form that has been distorted by some alien organism, a writhing, disruptive animal breaking through the corner. Some twisted counter-relief infects the orthogonal box. It is a skeletal monster which breaks up the elements of the form as it struggles out."[8]

I would proffer another interpretation. It is deconstructive not in what it looks like, but in how it speaks for an alternative language of an unrepressed *tektōn*. In the manner of Lebbeus Woods, this project unleashes the roof-making *tektōn* from its traditional obligations. It is, of course, still controlled by the magic of the masculinized *archē*, and perhaps might not be that far from Mies van der Rohe as it might seem, except that it is on the other end of spectrum when it comes to control. The Falkestrasse roof revisits the site of the repression—i.e., the roof—with its discomfort laid bare. It is neither the voice of the repressed per se, nor the revenge of the *tektōn*, but a monument—or perhaps even a memorial—by the *archē* to a lost world.

* * * *

We reach the outer limits of ambiguity with the facade of the drugstore Publicis in Paris (2004), designed by Hugh Dutton Associates with SAEE Studio.[9] Twenty-two meters high and lit by 17,000 LEDs it provides quite a spectacle at night. Though it falls prey to manufacturing the effect rather than the problem, its daytime appearance as a prosthetic to the dull modernist facade speaks to the ambivalent extremes of modernity's liberatory/incarceratory ethos. It is not clear whether the glass, the prototypical semiotic reference to modernity's promise of escape—as first expressed by Mies van der Rohe—is itself not that which is being incarcerated,

FIGURE 7.2.11 *Rooftop remodeling on Falkestrasse, Coop Himmelb(l)au, mixed media collage, Vienna, 1988. Collage by Ollybennett2.*

or whether, because of its innate pliability, it is being manipulated to the service of nocturnal entertainment.[10] Here the *tektōn* seems to enjoy its new-found capacity to mistreat the glass that for so long it had to quietly frame and support.

✳ ✳ ✳ ✳

In a backstreet of Harajuku, Japan, one can find the home of Design Festa that hosts a huge art and design event twice yearly. Several years ago, three local artists got together and reinvented the facade, adding paintings, and making a scaffolding that swarms over the building's front like some alien metal creeper.[11] Or perhaps it was smashed up by a big wind. The *tektōn* here is not portrayed as dutiful and powerful structure; it does not seek out some *archē*-induced, masculinized muscle-flexing, but unleashes itself from centuries of adherence to the standards of gravity and safety. No scaffolding contractor would ever show this as an example of good work on their website, and yet it asks fundamental questions about Before and After, bringing out of hiding the dialectics of (in)completion. Naturally, in a world that is biased toward *archē* and its disciplinary enforcements, such a work can only find its home in the liminal space of "art," or weirdness, rather than in the space of "architecture."

FIGURE 7.2.12 *Publicis, Hugh Dutton Associates with SAEE Studio, Paris, 2004.* © *Nicolas Janberg (Structurae).*

FIGURE 7.2.13 *Design Festa Gallery, Harajuku, Japan. Photograph by Bject.*

* * * *

At the more informal and esoteric end of ambiguity is the piece called "Mop and Scaffold" at Primary, Miami (January–March 2020), by Eva Robarts (b. 1982; lives and works in New York). After college, to pay her bills, Robarts worked in construction and some of that has rubbed off into her studio practice, such as this one. The work placed along two sides of a corner in the exhibition space featured a standard construction scaffolding with plain wooden planks. Along the walls, within the space of the squares and triangles, vibrant colors were painted that mimicked the geometry of the scaffolding. Some areas were left blank as if perhaps unfinished. The paint itself has the appearance of being brushed on rapidly. In some places there are gaps, in other places it drips. The *tektōn*, instead of seeking out is libidinal energy against the constraints of the *archē*, here performs its duty in its traditional capacity. But the tension between the scaffolding with all its predetermined, industrial precision and the sloppy paint job leads one to an uncertain condition. On the one hand, the colors speak of a childish playfulness with form that does not need to be "complete"—or even "artistic"—to be effective. In this case, they were not even painted by the artist, but by some local friends. On the other hand, the colors speak of the need to seek out "form" with the help of a prosthetic device, since art by itself—i.e., art on canvas and hung on a wall—would be unspeakably boring.

The status of the scaffolding is also uncertain. Though presumably used for the painting, its Duchampian presence seems to ask us to admire its joints and clamping mechanisms. But exposed and out of place, itself on exhibit, it is almost as if someone forgot to remove it. It serves more as a physical barrier to the art than as something that allows access. At the end of the show, the colors were painted over and the scaffolding packed up and returned to the rental company.

FIGURE 7.2.14 Mop and Scaffold, *Primary, Miami (January–March 2020), Eva Robarts.* © *Eva Robarts.*

The libidinal urge of scaffolding to seek permanence as "structure" or to at least play on the semiotics of impermanence is here doubled. On the one hand, its impermanence is accepted as part of the display. This is a temporary exhibit after all, so why bother making something complete or that even looks like it is complete? Here today, gone tomorrow. It is as if the artists missed the opening day or got called away for a lunch break and never came back. Is it really even art? And yet, as an artwork (for that it certainly is), it becomes permanent in another way, shifting from one medium to another as if seeking safety in the institutional guarantees that are part of the art world.

CHAPTER THREE

"Construction"

The word "construction" can all too easily imply a single process constituted within the parameters of a comprehensible epistemological range. But as Ralph W. Liebing, a teacher, engineer and Certified Professional Code Administrator in Ohio, points out,

> The process of delivering the finished project is simply called "construction." Those attuned wholly to the aesthetics and theory of architecture may well disdain this process, and look down upon it with less than understanding and respect. But if the truth be known, no architecture would exist without construction! The basic issue is that no matter what one's position in the professions or in the project work, there is a fundamental and unavoidable requirement to understand the whole of the process of delivering a project. One can be totally dedicated to one phase of the project, but understanding of all phases is imperative to successful execution of work in that one phase. But understanding and appreciating the totality of a project is virtually impossible to do, looking from just the one end, the inception.[1]

If we unpack construction into its constituent parts, we are only scratching the surface of its incomprehensibility. Take a steel beam. In and for itself it is not teleological in the conventional sense in that it does not "become" a building. But if we assume that it will be assembled in a grid of other beams and held together by bolts and that that grid will be designed in a way to accommodate human habitation and that the structure will be clad with glass and sheetrock and topped with a roof, then the beam is teleological, made so by the modern-day, corporate industrial complex. A vast array of facilitating mechanisms fuel this chain of causality. Banks and loan officers play their part, as do professional organizations of various types, laborers with a wide range of skills, not to mention taste-makers, political connections and so on. The range of interconnectedness is so vast that it would take volumes to write up the history of a single beam!

Today, we encounter the teleological focus that architecture brings into the economy not just with the beam, but also with the bolts, with the rubber gaskets, and with the sheetrock screws. It lurks even in the transparency of the plate glass, made ever more transparent by a slew of chemical additives. All architectural materials get conscripted into a grand machinery that is almost completely invisible—even to the architect. And yet, it is the architect who maximizes the energies of this teleological system and brings them into clear, immediate, and shameless visibility.

* * * *

The word "construction" seems to suggest a thing, when in reality it boxes together a vast array of activities: digging, pounding, grinding, hammering, contracting, hiring, firing, investing, risking, amortizing, renting, purchasing, borrowing, etc. The word "construction" cheats the system so that what is visible is first and foremost the teleology of completion.

There is no good and bad in all of this, but both good and bad depending on where one wants to look. The profession will see the great benefits the beam provides to society and celebrate the progress humans have made in making buildings taller and bolder. The complex intertwining of realities will be seen as the essential indicator of a healthy economy. The critics will point out that the ecological and human costs of making the beam into reality are profound and yet hardly known to any but the few and rarely make it into the news. The teleology of modernity hides such consequences in the success of its operations, glimmering on the outside, but dark and foggy on the inside.

* * * *

The whole could easily be rewritten in today's terms and go under the heading: Modern Architecture, a term that like so many others promises more than it can deliver. Modern Architecture tries to encapsulate the teleological, while overlooking its systemic failures. It is too facile to say that the so-called Modern Architecture of today is all the result of neoliberalism, even though neoliberalism is certainly the master of the teleological principle in the recent era. It wants the decision-making that links beginning and end (the animated "mind" with the instrumentalized "body") to flow with ever greater ease and with ever greater majesty as if it were the most natural thing in the world. Steel, concrete, rubber, and glass are now the architectural equivalents of staples—like rice and corn in the mythology of civilization. Computer programs, shipping manifests, cutting robots, automated cranes play their part.

* * * *

The "origins" of Modern Architecture's teleology are more or less unknown: whether they lie in the industrialization of steel, in the chemicalization of building products, in the pedagogies of the Bauhaus, or in the creation of dehumanized housing stock, or in all of the above and then some, is difficult to tell. But the architect sees only a future that by way of contrast is immanent and lies in the globally scaled, computationally organized networks of supply and production. The construction industry focuses on the maximization in the future.

The whole system seems almost weightless, but an equal part is played by the calculations of ignorance of how it all works. Indeed, teleology can *only* perform its magic as long as one does not look closely at its systems of production, finance, enforcements and exclusions.

* * * *

Can one decolonize architecture (without scare quotes) from its implicit teleological assumptions?

The answer, as I have tried to argue, lies, partially at least, in the magic of "architecture," a word that embraces its self-annihilatory meaning. Like a keyhole, it allows a glimpse into the strange inner workings of the otherwise boxed-in universe.

* * * *

The history of architecture (without scare quotes) is intimately tied not just to the history which has become codified in the normative History of Architecture, but also to the history of the construction industry. But we know so little about the construction industry even in historical times (at least in relationship to its importance) that other things rise to the surface: patronage, design, effect, style and so on. Just as importantly, since the History of Architecture became the history of its teleological ambition, the purpose of *archē* was to constrain and even dull what *can* be thought and what *can* be built and what *can* be history. This became the basic program for schools of architecture that began to proliferate from the middle of the nineteenth century onward. Some might think that the Bauhaus was the exception to this rule. It was not.

* * * *

Iron played a major part in setting up the foundations not just for the modern construction industry, but also for the disaggregation of epistemologies. Eugène Emmanuel Viollet-le-Duc, the late-nineteenth-century French designer and theorist, wrote:

> The nature of the metal and the forms in which it can be manufactured do not favor the construction of iron arches. But if we regard plate-iron as a material specially adapted for resisting tension, if the masonry in conjunction with it be so combined as to prevent distortion of the iron-work, if we consider iron as easy to employ and connect in straight pieces; and if of these separate pieces we form a kind of independent network, and on this network of girders we rest the vaulting in separate parts, we shall thus have contrived a system of iron framework consistent with the nature of the material, and a method for covering wide spaces by means of a series of distinct vaults.[2]

The change in tone is already noticeable in a book like Part 1 of *Building Construction and Superintendence* from 1897. Much of it might well have been comprehensible to builders even from the Roman age as it goes over familiar territory of how to make foundations, set walls, and lay courses of stone and brick except, of course, for the new parts that go over iron in Chapter 10 which begins:

> Although constructions of iron and steel do not properly come within the scope of this volume, there are so many places where metal work is used in connection with brick, stone and terra cotta that it has been thought desirable to briefly describe the most common forms of iron and steel construction used for supporting masonry walls, and the various minor details of metal work used in connection with the mason work.[3]

Unlike stone, brick, and wood, iron necessitated a complex supply chain that linked it not just to mines and manufacturing, but also to glass and everything that that entailed. The steel frames for skyscrapers required ever more coordination and planning, reaching deeper and deeper into corporate profits, national economies, and global exchanges. In fact, the very word "structure" that became common in the late nineteenth century would soon become a word to generically describe the systematization that was typical of steel.

* * * *

Construction Industry as a concept only emerged at the turn of the twentieth century. *Economics of the Construction Industry* (Washington, DC: Government Printing Office, 1919) was published by the US Department of Labor and had much to do with redefining the economy following World War I.[4] According to the authors of its Introduction,

> The building industry was the one great industry in the country which offered the greatest opportunities for expansion, it having been the one industry which had been especially suppressed during the war. Moreover, the building of homes adds both to the permanent wealth of the country and also has certain social features which are of inestimable value. I remember that you yourself once said: "A man was never known to hang the red flag of anarchy over his own hearthstone."[5]

Apart from prestige buildings that used iron or concrete, the building industry up until recently was, nonetheless, mostly quite local.[6] My house, built around 1900, has a foundation made of local field stones. The wood for the walls and floors probably came from Maine. Even the glass, which was comparatively expensive, was locally made as there were several regional manufacturers. The only elements that were metal were the nails and the cast-iron sewage pipes, both of which in those days were on the more "expensive" end, when it came to materials. A 1947 article of *Fortune*, entitled "The Industry Capitalism Forgot," notes that construction still had a "feudal character." It was, they argued "the one great sector of modern society that has remained largely unaffected by the industrial revolution."[7]

That has certainly changed. After mid-century, the everyday economy of architecture-making began to become more complex. First, there was the plastification of materials. The water and sewage pipes for a house are all plastic (PVC) and many of the metals in the appliances and even in the construction are coated in protective plastics. Then, there is chemicalization of materials. Glass is not just molten silicone (sand) but is made with a vast array of additives that guarantee its strength, durability, and transparency. Chemical additives are in the concrete, insulation, glues, and laminates. Then, there is metallification. Today metal, usually not found in domestic architecture, has been extraordinarily cheap and it will be found in the house's rebars, siding, railings, and walls. Then, there is computationalization of the design, production, and assembly. And finally, much underappreciated is the global transportation system that emerged with neoliberalism in the 1990s onward. Sheet glass today in the US takes one week from order to manufacture to delivery; but much of the materials in the house are global in nature, especially if one considers the various mines to various sites of production to its shipping and delivery. In total, in the US the industry has more than 680,000 employers with over 7 million employees and creates nearly $1.3 trillion worth of structures each year.[8]

* * * *

A test case of just how extensive the global footprint is of even a small modern house of today was developed by the Office of (Un)Certainty Research, exhibited in the Venice Biennale (2021).[9] Though they had documents from the architects and contractors, it turned out to be extremely difficult to develop a full map. Some parts of these stories are rendered invisible by the calculated manipulations of capital; some by the inadequacies of documentation (purposeful or not); some by core uncertainty of any attempt to "trace" the processes of production and labor.

Nonetheless, the house required mines in Africa, Asia, USA, and Canada. It required production streams that crossed the planet, using a full range of delivery mechanisms, ships, planes, trains, trucks, and cars. Some materials like glass were made almost exclusively by robots in factories that employ only five people, others like the metal stairs were made by hand by skilled craftsmen. The architects, though responsible in every professional way, were themselves oblivious of the nature and reach of these material productions.[10]

There were untold and unknown stories not just of labor and production but also of environmental degradation and human consequences: the insecticides used in the forests of Indonesia (for making the wood pulp in the laminate flooring), the sand particulates in the air that cause lung

FIGURE 7.3.1. *Construction site near Boston, Massachusetts. Photograph by Mark Jarzombek.*

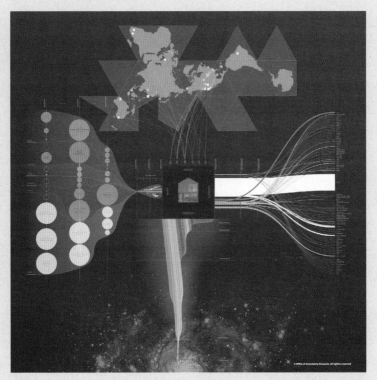

FIGURE 7.3.2. *Exhibition Diagram for House Deconstructed, Office of Uncertainty Research, Venice Biennale, 2021. © Office of Uncertainty Research (Mark Jarzombek and Vikramaditya Prakash); design by Paul Montie and Angie Door.*

problems in Wisconsin (for the making of the plate glass), the child labor used in the mining of cobalt (for the additive in the steel) in Africa, and so on. Recycled steel, much ballyhooed in the industry and used in the house in the name of sustainability, might well have gone through Chittagong in Bangladesh, where discarded ships by the hundreds are cut up releasing toxic chemicals and gases. The workers there are paid almost nothing and injuries are not compensated.

✳ ✳ ✳ ✳

We currently live in a "golden age" as far as the construction industry is concerned. Buildings can be designed on a computer, their materials and details worked out with the click of a button, and the parts ordered and manufactured using DocuSign. It will not last. What then?

✳ ✳ ✳ ✳

FIGURE 7.3.3. *Scene from* Ready Mix, *Lucy Raven, 2020. © Lucy Raven.*

Ready Mix (shown in the Dia Chelsea in New York in 2020) by Lucy Raven is one of the few works of art that thematize the construction industry.[11] The film follows the life cycle of concrete, from the extraction of gravel to large cast forms typical of post-9/11 barricades. The actors are the giant machines and processing sites where the concrete is produced. We see gravel pits, earthmovers, block-long dump trucks, even longer conveyor belts, immense chutes, and concrete-mixing trucks. All of these seem to operate on their own, without a person in sight until the very end. It is as if the whole is driven by the great teleological powers of construction itself. Though filmed on a sunstruck site in Idaho, one asks, on what planet are we? As art critic Roberta Smith explained,

> Close-ups take us inside the machines or look down in dazzling aerial views shot using a drone. We see masses of rocks and pebbles being mechanically sorted fill the screen. Different grades of gravel are sometimes still and nearly abstract; other times they rush past in a blur. Then the action jumps to a bird's-eye view as the camera wheels in sync

with the earth movers or conveyor belts. Either way, scale can become mutable, hard to measure, which is riveting.[12]

The work is not just about the processes of concrete but also about what happens when solids become liquids and then solids again as mineral aggregates and cement binders are churned into ready-mix concrete. In some instances, materials accumulate so quickly onscreen that the image becomes blurred to the point of seeming almost liquid leading to the end when we see huge building blocks hoisted into rows as if to wall out the world outside.[13]

* * *

It was not just the emergence of steel and then of concrete and glass and its overlays of engineering and extraction that set the stage for the teleology of the building industries. Another even more potent factor was the eradication at the end of the nineteenth century of the single-layer, load-bearing wall. It was a momentous event invisible in our history books. In an earlier age, walls were the site where the rules of geometry, quarrying, and chiseling prescribed well-known relationships between gravity and load. This changed not as the result of some innovation, but as a consequence of the proliferation of heating in French apartments at the end of the nineteenth century. Until then, heat was a luxury. The mansions of the rich had fireplaces that were costly to build and needed expensive wood to fuel. The less affluent had little stoves in individual rooms that were dangerous, sooty, and needed constant care. The development of centralized hot-water systems and the cast-iron radiators that became widespread by the end of the nineteenth century made heating a standard in bourgeois apartments.

But there was a problem: condensation. It would develop within the wall where it would lurk, creating mold and rot. Condensation endangered the life span of these new buildings and thus, of course, the financial investment that they represented. Though the problem was first noticed and studied by the French who were building thousands of apartments in Hausmann's Paris, it was in the northern climate of Berlin where condensation proved to be particularly vexing. It was thus natural that among the first scientists to address the problem was Adolf Wilhelm Keim (1851–1913), whose family name, by the way, means "germ." He argued that though dampness is brought into architecture because of the capillary nature of stone and brick, that in itself is not the problem. Stones and bricks had survived relatively well even in damp climates. What happens is that the dry heat on the inside sucks the moisture deeper into the building where it no longer dries out in the summer. In the lingering encounter with lime and cement, this moisture creates corrosive chemical discharges that Keim called *Mauerfrass*, literally a "wall-eating" disease that was, in Keim's mind's eye, similar to cancer eating at the tissue of a living body.

To protect against *Mauerfrass*, Keim argued that the wall needed to be ventilated from within so that the flow of air would remove the moisture. The

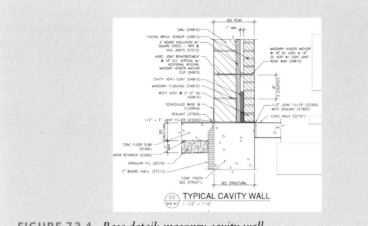

FIGURE 7.3.4. *Base detail: masonry cavity wall.*

wall, therefore, needed to be separated into two component layers, a structural wall and a type of skin or internal surface separated from the structural wall by about an inch. To keep moisture in that air corridor from entering through the bricks, Keim added that it was beneficial to give the inner surface of the tiles a coat of asphalt. This would leave the surface facing the room permanently dry so that it could be coated with plaster, which can then be painted or papered. Wallpaper, which had become common in bourgeois houses, and which had also become quite costly, was now safe from the damp.

In Keim's world, architecture, in facing the crisis of industrialization, needed to be rethought from the inside out without having to give up its appearance of unity. His metaphor was thus appropriately biological. Structure had to be separated from skin by an air slot that served as lung. The structure could then do the heavy lifting, the interior wall could work as backdrop for the decorative embellishments in the room, and the lung could guarantee the whole a long and healthy life. Here we see the first true separation of interior design from architecture, and architecture from environmental engineering. It is perhaps here that the full instrumentalities of *archē-tekton* take shape.

Needless to say, Keim's solution has been used in architecture ever since, except that by the early twentieth century tar paper was preferred, and by the mid-twentieth century special types of plastic sheathing like Tyvek, known to every home-builder in the United States, became the norm.

✳ ✳ ✳ ✳

The end result of construction is not an object otherwise known as a building, but an After to its process, a semiotic referent *to* construction.

✳ ✳ ✳ ✳

FIGURE 7.3.5. *Construction site near Boston, Massachusetts. Photograph by Mark Jarzombek.*

FIGURE 7.3.6. *Casa Sperimentale, Giuseppe Perugini, Uga de Plaisant, and Raynaldo Perugini, Fregene, Italy, 1968 and 1975. Photography by FRENCH+TYE.*

Any number of modernist architects saw an opportunity to isolate construction from architecture, to turn a field of integrated operationality into something more literal. One building that plays on the theme of "construction site" particularly well is the Casa Sperimentale designed by Giuseppe Perugini with Uga de Plaisant and Raynaldo Perugini, between 1968 and 1975. It is located on a corner plot in the coastal resort town of Fregene, Italy, and was built for weekend occupation. The living area was elevated up off the ground within a set of exposed columns and beams with some elements left deliberately in an unfinished state.

FIGURE 7.3.7. *García-Abril House, Las Rozas, Spain. Courtesy, Ensamble Studio.*

FIGURE 7.3.8. *García-Abril House, Las Rozas, Spain. Courtesy, Ensamble Studio.*

Despite its unusual and creative take on the problem, a much overlooked gem of modern architecture, Casa Sperimentale remains a rather traditional exposition of *archē-tekton*, where each side is recognizable. The *tektōn* produces the framework and the *archē* the habitable areas. More complex is the house designed in Las Rozas, Spain, by Antón García-Abril, a Madrid architect. Here we see the dislocation of "construction" from its conventional cultural and semiotic settings. The building features huge Vierendel and Warren beams weighing some 50 tons that were originally intended to be part of a bridge, and the troughs a part of an irrigation canal. The initial idea was to recycle the beams that had been discarded due to fabrication issues or minor defects. However, the manufacturer did not agree to let the architects use these for liability reasons, so finally the architects worked with them using their standard molds to fabricate the elements.

The apparent simplicity of the move required, in fact, complex calculations to manage the pre-stressing and post-tensioning of the steel rods that sew the web of the beams together. Once the parts were set in place, the structure—or is it a "structure"—was basically enclosed in glass, with the whole thing taking only about seven days to complete. The beams were not just a convenience. García and his partner "were thinking about how to start our new life."[14] And so, it seemed for them reasonable to think about the basic origins of architectural space. In this case, those origins did not come from within the discipline, but from its borderlands in engineering.

The teleology of the construction industry is here creatively misapplied. The beams, recontextualized, live an alien life that displaces disciplinary certainty. As semiotic references to the construction industry they do not belong in the normative world of architecture with its powerful alliances with the world of social appropriateness. It is as if the *tektōn* here holds the *archē* hostage in the pronouncements of its (mis)appropriated finality.

❊ ❊ ❊ ❊

At the negative end of this teleology is the Morpheus Hotel at the City of Dreams in Cotai, Macau by Zaha Hadid Architects (2018) where a free-form, high-rise exoskeleton is composed as a pattern of structural members that progress upwards to a less dense grid of lighter members at its summit.

FIGURE 7.3.9. *City of Dreams in Cotai, Macau. Photography by Fitsimz Gucoartem.*

FIGURE 7.3.10. *Architectural garbage at a construction site in Venice, 2021. Photograph by Mark Jarzombek.*

The interior surface is now a "skin" of glass, thus freeing the interior from the problematics of wall and its residual attraction to the decorative.[15] The structure, like a bridge to nowhere, expresses its infinite pliability, taking on the decorative as its transcendent location. But there is another element at play. According to one of the designers, a "comprehensive parametric model combined all of the hotel's aesthetic, structural and fabrication requirements."[16] The messy, repressed world of the building industries has been wiped clean behind a utopian fantasy of sweatless labor. Here architecture (without scare quotes) rises to the summit of its disciplinary narcissism.

FIGURE 7.3.11. *Matter Design,* Cyclopean Cannibalism, *Seoul Biennale of Architecture and Urbanism, 2017. Courtesy of Brandon Clifford.*

* * * *

The US Department for Energy calculates that US office buildings have an average life span of seventy-three years. When a building comes to the end, there is no method for reusing the material in new buildings; instead all constructions today require virgin material. The result: 200 million tons of architecture is thrown away each year in the US. Construction waste accounts for 40 percent of landfill in the United States. Construction of a typical 2,000-square-foot home contributes 8,000 pounds of waste. Based on rough estimates, 2016 was the first year where there exists more than one trillion tons of concrete on earth. More than the total weight of living trees on the planet.[17]

* * * *

Brandon Clifford has proposed a technique for computationally arranging materials after the demolition and unmaking of architecture. Rather than downcycling concrete into low-value aggregate or melting glass into bottles, he takes these materials, indexes and remachines them into new assemblies for some future use. These new bits are "holding patterns," keeping buildings afloat in a wasteful world. Brandon's book, *The Cannibal's Cookbook: Mining Myths of Cyclopean Constructions* (2021), which starts with a picture of a demolition hammer,

> is a manual for the hungry, for those who are not satiated by the careless building practices of the present. With one foot in the past and another in the present, the cookbook bridges the realities of our ancestors and ourselves. We propose a series of architectural "recipes" after dining on this body of past expertise.[18]

We have here post-teleology of new sort. Instead of rehab, we have the redigesting of buildings that come to live in a different form altogether—a tektōn of new order, one that is not just architecture's "dead weight" but now its form-giving essence.

De-Positioning

Archē(non)tektōn creates a subject that at the very start is split, broken, and combined, composed of affirmations, negations, and posturings. It comes in parts, not in completions, first through the aristocratizing interplay of *ratio et via* and *mente animoque* and then through its augmented attachment to the "instrumentalized" labor of the skilled worker and then through the disciplinary tortures of *archē²* and its search for that ever-so-elusive socio-. We have to see these splittings, now in their fully indoctrinated state, not as an expression of the discipline's interiority, but just the opposite, as an expression of its worldliness, a worldliness of a particular sort, one not fashioned by it over a long period of reasoned speculation, but that was bestowed upon it almost accidentally by disinterested philosophers. Had Socrates been less obsessed by the overly exalted nobility of the Self, and Plato less obsessed by geometries of governance, the whole conversion in our field might well be different.

It is impossible to square the anamorphic history of *archē(non)tektōn* with the idea of Self, that John Locke back in the seventeenth century succinctly and ever so brutally defined as "that conscious thinking thing," and that is now so fundamental to the modern worldview.[1] *archē(non)tektōn* posits a modernity of a very different sort.

* * * *

Archē(non)tektōn is not a dualism, but an integrative/disintegrative system within the slippery domain of disciplinary contestations and yet it lies outside of disciplinary capture. This history—though it is certainly not a history in any classic linear sense—fed by the energy of production and power, of commissions and clients, and of a complex culture war about the nature of space-making, thrives in a world of the contracts and deliverables that are generated from within the teleological and post-teleological relationship between *archē* and *tektōn*. *Archē(non)tektōn* brings out of hiding the multiplicities of these (dis)locations—though usually quite unwillingly.

The absence—the *non*—is key to the operative nature of the discipline that came to be known as architecture (without scare quotes). That discipline and much of its associated history and theory—with its support structure from various philosophers—sees no gap—no violation—at all, for what discipline could possibly go forth in a self-annihilating posture? It sees just a clear and unambiguous field of operation, and yet it is the absence of the negation that allows the discipline the space of its operation.

Archē and tektōn are thus not concepts that should be discussed on the basis of some sort of presumed etymological security that can now be "applied" neo-teleologically in the search for some sort of meaning and depth. They are rather the signifier of signification. Each composing element, though diverted and torn from its center, brings the object of its semiotic referent into direct relationship to the center which is, however, absent. Each is a difference that differentiates the center as a theater of permutations.

* * * *

Architecture does not thereby cease to be a mode of creativity even if its disciplinary enablers protect its sense of purposefulness by means of its silencing mechanisms.

* * * *

The decisiveness of a building, its gravitational hold on the earth, its self-imprisonment in the pretend social contract of "design" and "program," the residual manifestation of the modernized archē and its deceptions, belies the tangled and largely invisible web of realities that made it happen. While the possibility of intelligibility is presented throughout (promised in the very idea of modernity and its disciplinary liberations from presumably "past" modes of being and understanding), the "architecture" of a building seeks to preserve the secret that is at its core—at the core of its very sense of modernity—the repressed violence/productivity that makes it possible. For that reason, we need to always remind ourselves of the strange inversion that is in play as we approach that thing called architecture which is always some variant of not-architecture.

And yet a building as it stands in the landscape is not a contradiction. On the contrary, it speaks unambiguously. But about what? The more one studies a building, or better yet, fights against its foreclosures, the more one realizes it has an almost magical place in contemporary culture. But if in one breath it is magical, in the next it is scandalous.

* * * *

The profession, as architecture's administrative body (architecture without scare quotes), does its best to ignore, critique, disparage, or control "architecture" in places where the two encounter each other. The profession reaches back to its formation at the end of the nineteenth century when it wanted carpenters to no longer call themselves "architects," in essence fulfilling Alberti's goal and bringing the conversation to an end. Perhaps one can say in a reversal of expectations that architecture's administrative body operates theoretically (since all professional structures are metaphysical in nature), whereas the disciplinary body of "architecture" operates historically, meaning not that it has "a" history, but that it operates through the contingencies of time out of which it can never escape. Like a fractured skeleton within the body of the profession, the disciplinary structure of *archē(non)tektōn* is only visible in X-ray form of which this text is its preliminary diagnostic. It has no surface appearance, and furthermore, the professional body has forgotten its ancient trauma and has naturalized its modus operandi.

The architectural discipline, meaning its professional agencies, its academic institutions, and even the libraries attempt to all cover over the split, to either ignore it, diminish it, or accommodate it.

To evoke the imaginary of pure handcraft, though always something to be valued in the age of advanced industrialization, does not solve the problem of how to locate "architecture"—whether in practice or in theory—in the cultural/ontological firmament. To evoke some "theory of architecture" as if those words could have some form of stability is itself preposterous. A phenomenological or existential clarification is also impossible since the architect has to acknowledge not only the conscription of the unrecognized other within the strategies of identity, but also its cross-purposed, theoretical orientations.

* * * *

The beginning point of the issue is not in the debates about modernity, or in the development of industrialization, or in the emergence of a professional class, but in the ancient (Eurocentric) formation of architecture's nomenclatural history. The distinction between *archē* and *tektōn* (and its long list of associated concepts like mind and body and creativity and work, etc.) gave to architecture the imprint of a modernity that cannot be resolved even in our so-called modern times. It is in some conditions visible as an artifice, but no less resolvable.

* * * *

Archē(non)tektōn is a compressed grammar, the background of which is practically unknowable, but the "future" of which is always being rewritten.

Archē(non)tektōn will not liberate architecture from the scare quotes, but rather promises (but does not deliver) a possible practice.

* * * *

What then is the status of the architect in all of this? Yes, the profession today removes the threat of scare quotes, but that safety position only applies to the instruments of accreditation, not to the broader field of its productions. The architect is the embodiment of the discipline. As the bearer of its insignia, the architect carries the imprint of its weight and guilt in equal relationship to its potential. From that point of view, the architect can have no oceanic feeling of coherence, no quiet space of interior contemplation, no pure "artistic" urge, no happily intimate intensity of thought. The architect can never escape the bottomless divisibility of the discipline despite the modernist and Enlightenment attempts to harness subjectology and tame its incompletions into acceptable professional behaviors.

The silent (*non*) is the point of the in-between that collapses a presence that becomes an absence. It is a spacing between the shallow ontological space of the architect and the deep de-ontological space of the *faber*, a spacing that exists prior to its unfolding in the figural proliferations of practice.

The architect can never fully liberate its Self from its desire to imperialize the Other and thus carries the awkward and mutually contaminating traces of that relationship where ever it goes.[2] Perhaps only now we can address the lingering, and corrosive, institutionality of the Socratic *banausos*.

* * * *

The architect—today—does not produce the modern, but operates *within* a pre-modern modernity—a pretzel of time and space—a residue of something that is ancient, but that has no conventional originary moment.

The architect—today—is a strange figure, outside of the conventions of modernist subjectology.

The architect—today—is constructed of haunted, silent, and repressed voices that speak (~~speak~~) through its operations in ways that both construct and falsify its consciousness.

* * * *

The architect—as the carrier of the discipline—opens a door to a type of ontology that, despite its professionalization, is still the *after* to "architecture" that is produced *through* the discipline. In this, it is different—if I may speak generally—from a musician and an artist, who are usually thought of as having ontologies that begin before the discipline. One cannot be a born architect.

The architect—as the carrier of the discipline—sits within the modalities of its social construction, its logic first set out by Plato then mobilized into disciplinary formation by Alberti that grounded itself on the disappropriation of the subject, constituted not as a splitting apart—as in terms of opposition (even though this is often how it gets reduced)—but rather as a splintered stability that works to create its disciplinarity nonetheless.

Postscript

Roland Barthes once wrote that a discourse is nothing but a long sentence. This book might well prove that, or at least be an approximation. It did not start that way. I began to puzzle over Alberti's claim—"it is no carpenter that I would have you compare to the greatest exponents of other disciplines"—only a few years ago. Many scholars have made note of it, but they mostly framed it within Alberti's broader writings and theories. I wanted to treat the sentence like a sip of wine, savoring its aftereffects. And so, the book, as a type of "extended reading," came about slowly, first as a single slide in a lecture that I gave for my seminar Thinking about Architecture, then as a paragraph, then as an essay, and finally, as more pieces came into focus, as a book. Perhaps the book could have been even more experimental, but I did not want to lose the story that was embedded in that sentence, the story of something that is almost impossible to tell.

Unlike other books I have written, where I am assumed to be a "scholar" or an "architectural historian and theorist"—as if such categories are self-explanatory—a book like this might demand a more transparent exposition of where I stand and where I come from. And I admit that, based on my biography, I have a strong sympathy for the *tektōn*. Perhaps because my father was not only a person whom we today would call a "maker," but also a man who in any given year might say three sentences. I came to always want to fill in the gaps of silence. But I did not want this book to be a celebration of the maker/craftsman/contractor, much less an elevation of that world over and against some notion of loss. As an architect, I was just as sympathetic to the academic and professional aspects of the discipline. The way out was to see the *tektōn* as a figure semiotically entrapped in the onto-politics of the discipline, as an internal exile, and in that my argument has the aura of a political problem, even if I wanted to suggest it with the lightest of brushes. The socio-philosophical heroics that are associated with the issue of labor in the modern industrial world overshoot by far the humbler problem of how to understand the role of the *tektōn* and all its avatars within the arc of its disciplinary entrapments. We can, of course, follow Henri Lefebvre and think of the issue of "space"—as in his *La production de l'espace* (1974)—as the place on this planet where we live and build, as the next frontier of a critique of Late Capitalism, one that displaces the older crisis of labor-and-the-factory. But as valuable as that optimism is, Lefebvre misses the fact that the making of that "space" cannot be seen as simply a transparent extension of industrial/capitalist operations. Yes, buildings are the result of processes of production that are governed by a means of control, and hence of domination and of power, but his critique gets stuck in the grating machinery of "architecture" as a *constructum* of a very unique type. In that sense, I wanted to slow our observational energy down almost to a crawl, to get to a place where we end more or less where we started, where perhaps we need not a more vigorous critique, but a new set of words, a new way to not say architecture.

NOTES

Foreword

1   Paul Valéry, *Dialogues*, trans. William McCausland Stewart (New York: Pantheon Books, 1956), 110, 109.

Part One

1 Preface

1   Leon Battista Alberti, *On the Art of Building in Ten Books*, trans. Joseph Rykwert, Neil Leach, and Robert Tavernor (Cambridge, MA: The MIT Press, 1988), 3.

2   Vitruvius, in the open of his treatise, says that the architect needs to combine knowledge of making with a more explicatory form of knowing (*fabrica et ratiocinatione*). Alberti's distinction is quite different as he is not speaking about the ontology of the architect, but about two different classes of men. Nowhere in his treatise does Vitruvius discuss the architect's relationship to the contractor or builder. Furthermore, when Alberti does speak about the ontological make-up of the architect, he approaches it quite differently.

3   The word *carpentarii* came into use during the late Roman Empire when, because of its famous roads, there was a high demand for carriages, mostly made, presumably, by enslaved Gauls. With the breakdown of the empire, *carpentarii* moved into house construction. Though the word made its way into normative Spanish, French, and English during the Middle Ages, it had not yet become common in Italy by the time of Alberti.

4   *Tignum*: Proto-Italic *tegnom*, from Proto-Indo-European *teg-nom*, from *(s)teg-* ("beam, stake"). It is also the root for τέκτων (*tektōn*).

5   "Introduction," *Architectural Magazine* 1 no. 1 (March 1834): 5.

6   At some moment in time, the accusative singular of *faber*, namely *fabrum*, became *fabbro* in Italian and designated ironworker.

7   Mary Hollingsworth, "The Architect in Sixteenth-Century Florence," *Art History* 7 (December 1984): 385.

8   Mari Yoko Hara, *Places of Performance: Baldassarre Peruzzi (1481–1536)—a Renaissance Painter-Architect* (PhD diss., University of Virginia, 2015), 19.

9   Because interest rates during the fifteenth century were so low, the rich invested their wealth in socially productive efforts, like building palaces and churches or in art. On the topic, see especially R. A. Goldthwaite, *Wealth and the Demand for Art in Italy 1300–1600* (Baltimore: Johns Hopkins University Press, 1993).

10   Julian Brooks, "Introduction," in *Taddeo and Federico Zuccaro: Artist-Brothers in Renaissance Rome* (Los Angeles: Getty Publications, 2007), 2; quoted in Elisabeth Merrill, "The Professione di Architetto in Renaissance Italy," *Journal of the Society of Architectural Historians* 76 no. 1 (March 2017): 29. For a general discussion of architecture as an emerging profession during the Renaissance, see Elisabeth Merrill, "The Professione di Architetto in Renaissance Italy," *Journal of the Society of Architectural Historians* 76 no. 1 (March 2017): 13–35.

11   The term in ancient usage was frequently contrasted with an ironworker, or smith (χαλκεύς: kalkeus: worker in copper) and the stoneworker or mason (λιθολόγος, [lithologos] λαξευτής [laxeftís—sharpener]).

12   Leon Battista Alberti, *L'Architettura [De re aedificatoria]*, Vol. 2, trans. Giovanni Orlandi (Milan: Edizioni il Polifilo, 1966), X.2, 881.

13   Derrida defined grammatology as the study of the way in which thoughts as recorded in writing affect the nature of knowledge.

14   Though the term "autopoiesis" (literally, self-creation) was coined by Humberto Maturana, the German philosopher Niklas Luhmann transposed it into the domain of social theory. Needless to say, what follows is a critique. For Luhmann, all contingency is met by the argument that everything is "communication." For him, the communicative actions of people are constituted by society, and society is constituted by the communicative actions of people: society is people's environment, and people are society's environment.

15   Jacques Derrida, *Psyche: Inventions of the Other*, Vol. 2, ed. Peggy Kamuf and Elizabeth Rottenberg (Stanford: Stanford University Press, 2008), 119.

16   I am not discussing what happens when artists take on architecture as the subject matter of their work. This has become a genre in its own right, especially with the emergence of "site-specific" art that often deals with or incorporates buildings, spaces, and cities. Exhibitions such as *Psycho Buildings: Artists Take on Architecture*, Hayward Gallery (2008); *Automatic Cities: The Architectural Imaginary in Contemporary Art*, Museum of Contemporary Art San Diego (2010), and others have added heft to this approach. And, of course, there are the architects who have embraced the art world such as Diller + Scofidio, Zaha Hadid, and Frank Gehry. For an excellent introduction to that question, see *Art About Architecture: A Strange Utility*, ed. Isabelle Loring Wallace and Nora Wendl (Burlington, VT: Ashgate, 2013). In general, in my view, the distinction between art and architecture is so devoid from relevance—except perhaps in museological domains—that even to theorize that distinction is to fall in the death spiral of semiotic tautologies.

17   Gayatri Chakravorty Spivak, *Outside in the Teaching Machine* (New York: Routledge, 1993), 121.

2 Arche-Tekton

1   Jacques Derrida, "No (Point of) Madness—Maintaining Architecture," in *Psyche: Inventions of the Other*, Vol. 2, ed. Peggy Kamuf and Elizabeth Rottenberg (Stanford: Stanford University Press, 2008), 90.

2   Ibid., 91. On the changing nature of *oikos*, see Gregory Cameron, "Oikos and Economy: The Greek Legacy in Economic Thought," *PhaenEx* 3 no. 1 (spring/summer 2008): 112–33. Though I am applying deconstructive ideas in my interpretation, I am not interested here in Derrida's "theory of architecture." That topic has been discussion by various scholars including Francesco Vitale in his *The Last Fortress of Metaphysics: Jacques Derrida and the Deconstruction of Architecture*, trans. Mauro Senatore (SUNY series, Intersections: Philosophy and Critical Theory, 2018).

3   Ibid., 90–1.

4   We are forced to forgive Derrida of the Eurocentric assumption that architecture (without scare quotes) is a universal, even though, when he was writing in 1986, the problems of Eurocentrism were becoming ever more apparent.

5   Ibid., 91.

6   Robert Stuart, *A Dictionary of Architecture*, Vol. 1 (Philadelphia: A. Hart, Late Carey and Hart, 1851), 263.

7   In the *Statesman*, the Eleatic Stranger (ξένος, xenos), not Socrates, plays the more dominant role. It is difficult to attribute the views put forward by the Eleatic Stranger to Plato, beyond the difficulty inherent in taking any character to be an author's "mouthpiece."

8   See, in particular, David Roochnik, *Of Art and Wisdom: Plato's Understanding of Techne* (University Park, PA: Pennsylvania University Press, 1996), 17–88.

9   258e. This distinction is new in the writings of Plato and differentiates his later writings from earlier ones.

10   259e–260a.

11   Aristotle, *Metaphysics*, bk. 1, sections 981a and 981b, trans. Hugh Tredennick (Cambridge, MA: Harvard University Press; London: William Heinemann Ltd., 1933, 1989).

12   The student learns his profession first from a teacher (guru), but later from various specialists. Takşaka (□□□□) or "carpenter" is stated to know the Veda, and be skilled in his craft of wood-joinery. The word derives from Sanskrit *Taksh*: to plane, chisel, cut, divide, fashion, etc.

13   Discussed in Isabella Nardi, *The Theory of Citrasutras in Indian Painting, A Critical Re-evaluation of Their Uses and Interpretations* (London: Routledge, 2006), 28.

3 Shell Games

1   In Homer, the *tektōn* is described as holding a *státhmi* (stathmi) or a level.

2   Pausanius, *Description of Greece*, trans. W. H. Jones (Cambridge, MA: Harvard University Press: Loeb Classical Library, 1918), 5.16.1: https://www. theoi.com/Text/Pausanias5B.html.

3   See *Vitruvius, De architectura,* Book X, preface.

4   *The Landmark Herodotus: The Histories*, ed. Robert B. Strassler; trans. Andrea L. Purvis (New York: Anchor Books, 2009), 3.60.

5   The Egyptian hieroglyph for "overseer of builder" was pronounced "mr— iqdw" (myhr—ik-due). "Mr" was represented as a cow's tongue because of the sacredness of the cow and its reference to divine power that was embodied by the overseer. Iqdw was written in the shape of a rectangular plan of a stone building with a laborer standing next to it. Though the Greek addition of *archē* to *tektōn* followed the pattern set out by "mr—iqdw", *tektōn* shifts the narrative to the woodworker since in ancient Greece the temples were obviously of wood and not stone. The emphasis was also, obviously, on joinery, rather than on geometry as it was for the Egyptians. Furthermore, whereas in Egypt, the principle of "Mr" lies in its ancient authority, perhaps one can say preceding the idea of building in stone, in Greek the situation is reversed. *Archē* came to be added to *tektōn* only later.

6   By the time Corinthians was written in the middle of the first century CE, the word *architektōn* had become normative for what we would call "master builder." "According to the grace of God given to me, like a skilled [σοφὸς (sophos)] master builder [ἀρχιτέκτων (architektōn)] I laid a foundation, and someone else is building upon it. Let each one take care how he builds upon it" (1 Cor. 3:10).

7   Jonas Holst, in "The Fall of the *Tektōn* and The Rise of the Architect: On the Greek Origins of Architectural Craftsmanship," *Architectural Histories*, 5 no. 1 (2017), sketches out the history of the term *tektōnēs*.

8   Richard Sennett, *The Craftsman* (New Haven: Yale University Press, 2008), 22.

9   Dana Henriques, "Bernie Madoff, Architect of Largest Ponzi Scheme in History, Is Dead at 82," *The New York Times*, April 14, 2021.

10   Even in Japanese, the word *takumi* (匠), or "artisan," means not just "skill" but also "cleverness" and "trickery."

11   "Tel Aviv Museum of Art Amir Building / Preston Scott Cohen," *ArchDaily* (November 11, 2010), https://www.archdaily.com/87739/tel-aviv-museum-of-art-amir-building-preston-scott-cohen.

12   The measurements are extrapolated from a surviving original section drawing and may be slightly different from the real artifact. In the rebuilding of the pavilion in 1986, the architects built a solid concrete roof 20 centimeters thick, assuming that that was what Mies "wanted."

13   Emil Kaufmann, "Étienne-Louis Boullée," *The Art Bulletin* 21 no. 3 (1939): 223–4.

14   Cumbria is in the northwest of England.

15   "Serpentine Pavilion 2019: Japan's Great Conjuror Falls Foul of Health and Safety," *The Guardian* (June 18, 2019), https://www.theguardian.com/artanddesign/2019/jun/18/.

16 David McManus, "MIT Media Lab Building Boston by Fumihiko Maki," *e-architect* (March 20, 2010), https://www.e-architect.com/boston/mit-media-lab-building.

Part Two

1 Befores and Afters

1   F. E. Davidons, "Co-operation Between Architecture and Contractors," *The Architect and Engineer* 68 no. 3 (March 1922): 80.

2   Robert Stuart, *Cyclopedia of Architecture* (New York: A. S. Barnes, 1854), 261.

3   "The Rights and Obligations of the Contractor," *Carpentry and Building* 19 (January 1897): 23.

4   Miriam and Lidia start with a precise analysis of a project. After having gone over the plans in detail with the architects, they choose the main angles they will work on. The duration of a project can go from three months to a year, with the first pictures usually show the shell or the initial state. The building project shown here in Berlin-Kreuzberg (Germany) was designed by the architects FLACKE+OTTO from Berlin and constructed between 2018 and 2019.

5   Latin writers tended to use the masculine form *animus* to refer to intellect, and the feminine form *anima* to refer to emotional or spiritual qualities, even though the two sets of meaning often overlapped.

6   Vasari, *Lives*, 65.

7   Francesco di Giorgio Martini (1439–1501), in his *Trattati di architettura, ingegneria e arte militare*, used both those words. For discussion, see Pari Riahi, *Ars et Ingenium: The Embodiment of Imagination in Francesco di Giorgio Martini's Drawings* (New York: Routledge, 2015), 87.

8   Alberti, *On the Art of Building*, 194.

9   Alberti, *On the Art of Building*, 315.

10 Cook County (IL) Board of County Commissioners, *Official Proceedings . . .* (1906), 239.

11 Karl Joseph Geiger, *Der Mensch und sein Beruf* (Vienna: M. R. Toma, 1835–41).

12 Charles E. White, *Successful Houses and How to Build Them* (New York: Macmillan Co., 1912), 401.

13 Report, *Sessional Papers Great Britain. Parliament. House of Commons*, Vol. 22 (1974), 223.

14 Frank Forrest Frederick, *Architectural Rendering in Sepia* (New York: William T. Comstock, 1892), 12.

15 James O'Brien, "Las Vegas Today: Rome in a Day: Corporate Development Practices and the Role of Professional Designers," *Journal of Architectural Education* 54 no. 2 (2000): 68–79.

16   Cary Provost, *High Stakes* (New York: Penguin, 1994), 72.

17   For more, see Nick Gelpi, *The Architecture of Full-Scale Mock-Ups: from Representation to Reality* (New York: Routledge, 2020).

18   "The History of the First Stone of an Aedifice," *The Builder* (June 26, 1888): 788.

19   "The First Cornerstone Architect of the Capitol," accessed April 20, 2021, https://www.aoc.gov/explore-capitol-campus/buildings-grounds/capitol-building/first-cornerstone.

20   The Latin translation was commissioned by the Hungarian king Matthias Corvinus. The work was done by Antonio Bonfini, born in the Italian town of Ascoli, who had moved to the Hungarian court in 1486. Bonfini was a professor of Latin, Greek, grammar, poetry, and rhetoric. Bonfini sythensized and edited Filarete's treatise, reducing its length to almost half.

21   Wilhelm Günther Bleichrodt, *Architektonisches Lexikon, oder allgemeine Real-Encyclopädie der gesammten architektonischen und dahin einschlagenden Hilfswissenschaften* (Weimar: Bernhard Friedrich Voigt, 1840), 106 (translation by author).

22   "The Sicilian Art of the Incomplete—Sicily Inside & Out," accessed April 10, 2021, https://sicilyinsideandout.com/2013/12/11/the-sicilian-art-of-the-incomplete/.

23   Moste cunnynge woorkemen theare weare prepared, Withe spediest ordynaunce for eauery thynge, Nothynge expedyent was theare oughtis spared That to the purpose myght bee assistynge; One thynge (chieflye) this was the hynderynge, The woorkefolke for lack of goode ouerseers Loytered the tyme, like false tryfelers.

24   *The Carpenter* 19 no. 2 (February 1899): 1.

25   Stephen M. Pollan and Mark Levine, "All About Renovation: The Big Fix," *New York Magazine* (June 10, 1991): 38.

26   John V. Robinson, "The 'Topping out' Traditions of the High-Steel Ironworkers," *Western Folklore* 60 no. 4 (Autumn, 2001): 243–62.

27   "'Topping out,'" *The American Art and Building News* 61 no. 1176 (July 9, 1898): 16.

28   *Carpenter* (United Brotherhood of Carpenters and Joiners of America, 2001), 13.

29   "Museum Honors History with Two Major Mile Stones," *Centered* IV (2007), https://www.ilholocaustmuseum.org/filebin/PDF/NEWSF07.pdf.

30   "Architecture Illinois Holocaust Museum and Education Center," accessed April 20, 2021, https://www.ilholocaustmuseum.org/pages/about/architecture/. Illinois Holocaust Museum & Education Center, *Chicago Architect Stanley Tigerman Describes Illinois Holocaust Museum's Symbolic Design*, 2018, https://www.youtube.com/watch?v=ewenIjAJKno&t=345s.

31   David Chappell, *Professional Practice for Architects and Project Managers* (New York: John Wiley & Sons, 2019), 345.

32   Private communication. See Hanno Wolfensberger, *Architektendämmerung: 10 Abgesänge auf einen Berufsstand* (Frankfurt am Main: Campus-Verlag, 1993).

33 Marc-Antoine Laugier, *An Essay on Architecture*, trans. Wolfgang and Anni Hermann (Los Angeles: Hennessey & Ingalls, 1977), 8, 7.

34 Ibid., 7.

35 Cee Donohue, "How to Christen a Room | Homesteady," *HomeSteady*, accessed March 15, 2021, https://homesteady.com/13412185/how-to-christen-a-room.

36 The building was designed by Shepley, Rutan, and Coolidge, with the contractors Norcross Brothers. It still exists, today known as the Flour and Grain Exchange Building, and is located at 177 Milk Street, Boston, MA.

37 *Ceremonies Connected with the Opening of the Building of the Boston Chamber of Commerce* (January 20 and 21, 1892), 43.

38 Viollet-le-Duc, *The Story of a House*, trans. George M. Towle (Boston, MA: James R. Osgood and Co., 1874), 273, 277.

39 An excellent book is Hilary Sample, *Maintenance Architecture* (Cambridge, MA: The MIT Press, 2016).

40 Adolf Loos, *Vom armen reichen Manne*. "*Neues Wiener Tagblatt*," April 26, 1900, reprinted in August Sarnitz, *Adolf Loos, 1870–1933, Architect, Cultural Critic, Dandy* (Cologne: Taschen, 2003), 20–1.

2 Dialectics of (In)completion

1 The "completion of work" was first developed in the engineering fields in the late nineteenth century mostly around projects that required public expenditure, and slowly gravitated into architecture by the mid-twentieth century.

2 "Contracts and Permits," *History of Architecture, Architectural Design, Specifications* (Scranton: International Textbook Co., 1903), 37.

3 Dyschronometria is a condition of cerebellar dysfunction in which an individual cannot accurately estimate the amount of time that has passed (i.e., distorted time perception). It is associated with cerebellar ataxia.

4 Frank Lloyd Wright and Bruce Brooks Pfeiffe, *The Essential Frank Lloyd Wright: Critical Writings on Architecture* (Princeton: Princeton University Press, 2008), 358.

5 Peter Macapia and Alejandro Zaera-Polo, "Consistency: A Conversation with Alejandro Zaera-Polo," *Log* no. 3 (2004): 37.

6 "5 Keys to Consistent Architecture Firm Branding," ARCHMARK | Architect Marketing, accessed April 10, 2021, https://www.archmark.co/blog/an-architects-guide-to-brand-consistency-and-branding.

7 "Architectural Design," *History of Architecture, Architectural Design, Specifications* (Scranton: International Textbook Co., 1903), 1–2.

8 Henry Sanoff, *Methods of Architectural Programming* (London: Routledge, 2016), 4.

9 "An examination of the design theory behind Seattle Central Library by OMA," Double Stone Steel, August 14, 2020, https://www.doublestonesteel.

com/blog/architecture/an-examination-of-the-design-theory-behind-seattle-central-library-by-oma/.

10 Rem Koolhaas et al., "2 Architects 10 Questions on Program," *PRAXIS: Journal of Writing + Building* no. 8 (2006): 14.

11 John Locke, *An Essay Concerning Human Understanding . . . With the Notes and Illustrations of the Author, and an Analysis of His Doctrine of Ideas. Thirty-First Edition. Carefully Revised, and Compared with the Best Copies, Etc.* (William Tegg & Company, 1853), 24.

12 John Locke, *Two Treatises on Civil Government* (G. Routledge and Sons, Limited, 1887), 241.

13 The Seattle Central Library was designed by OMA/LMN with Rem Koolhaas and Joshua Prince-Ramus the principal architects, and Magnusson Klemencic Associates the structural engineer with Arup.

14 https://www.doublestonesteel.com/blog/architecture/an-examination-of-the-design-theory-behind-seattle-central-library-by-oma/.

15 It was located at 8604 West Brown Deer Road, Milwaukee, Wisconsin.

16 James Wines, *De-Architecture* (New York: Rizzoli, 1987), 150.

3 Post-Teleology

1 https://www.epa.gov/smm/sustainable-management-construction-and-demolition-materials.

2 See the insightful account by Stefan Tanaka, "Discoveries of the Hōryū ji," in Kai-wing Chow, Kevin M. Doak, and Poshek Fu, eds., *Constructing Nationhood in Modern East Asia* (Ann Arbor, 2001), 117–48.

3 See Shabnam Yazdani Mehr, *Analysis of 19th and 20th Century Conservation Key Theories in Relation to Contemporary Adaptive Reuse of Heritage Buildings Heritage*, Vol. 2 (2019), 920–37.

4 Leon Battista Alberti, *On the Art of Building in Ten Books*, trans. Joseph Rykwert, Neil Leach, and Robert Tavernor (Cambridge, MA: The MIT Press, 1988), 358.

5 Ibid., 320.

6 Filarete, *Filarete's Treatise on Architecture: Being the Treatise by Antonio Di Piero Averlino, Known as Filarete*, Vol. 1, trans. John R. Spencer (New Haven: Yale University Press, 1965), 12.

7 Jim Locke, *The Well-Built House* (Boston: Houghton Mifflin, 1988), 88.

8 "Keep Moisture Out of Your Buildings," *Buildings*, accessed April 21, 2021, https://www.buildings.com/articles/34202/keep-moisture-out-your-buildings.

9 George G. Bruntz and John Bremer, *American Government* (Boston, MA: Ginn and Co., 1965), 147.

10 "Home Maintenance Checklist | How to Maintain Your Home," accessed April 21, 2021, https://www.improvenet.com/a/home-maintenance-checklist.

11 "MIT 2030 | Addressing Deferred Maintenance," accessed March 15, 2021, http://web.mit.edu/mit2030/themes/renovation-renewal-stewardship/addressing-deferred-maintenance.html.

12 Otero-Pailos studied architecture at Cornell University, holds a PhD from MIT, and was a founding faculty member of the School of Architecture at the Polytechnic University of Puerto Rico. He is professor and Director of Historic Preservation at GSAPP at the Columbia School of Architecture.

13 The museums are Museum of London; Ulster Museum, Belfast in Northern Ireland; Whitworth Art Gallery at the University of Manchester; The Glynn Vivian Art Gallery in Swansea; Kelvingrove Art Gallery and Museum, and The People's Palace, Glasgow.

14 5 Essential Tools for Facility Managers," *eLearning Industry*, August 23, 2017, https://elearningindustry.com/5-essential-tools-for-facility-managers.

15 https://www.dirtymaintenancenation.com/apartment-maintenance-technician-jobs/.

16 Cinzia Talamo, "Knowledge Management for Facility Management (FM) Services: a Rising Demand Within a Growing Market," *Knowledge Management and Information Tools for Building Maintenance and Facility Management*, ed. Cinzia Talamo and Marcella Bonanomi (Zurich; Springer, 2015), 2–3.

17 https://www.treehugger.com/truly-maintenance-free-house-4856752.

18 Rizzi graduated from the Politecnico di Milano and obtained a Masters in Restoration from the Institute of Advanced Architectural Studies at the University of York. He began working in India as an assistant to Sir Bernard Feilden and then in Bahrain where he followed the first restoration work on the Portuguese fortress. Subsequently he continued to deal with the recovery of historic buildings working on various conservation and restoration projects both in Italy and abroad. As a consultant to UNESCO, the World Monument Fund, and ICCROM, he has collaborated on projects on archaeological sites in France, Jordan, Syria, Lebanon, and Pakistan.

19 Private communication with the author.

20 Some first steps in a more dynamic understanding of renovation are, for example, Albena Yaneva, "How Buildings 'Surprise': The Renovation of the Alte Aula in Vienna," *Science & Technology Studies, special issue: Understanding Architecture, Accounting Society* 21 no. 1 (2008): 8–28. Yet here, too, the issue revolves around a renovation, not around a broader question of the cultural ontology of a building.

21 Alois Riegl, *Der moderne Denkmalkultus, seine Wesen und seine Entstehung* (Vienna, 1903). English translation by Kurt Forster and Diane Ghirardo, "The Modern Cult of Monuments: Its Character and Its Origins," in *Oppositions* no. 25 (Fall 1982): 21–51.

22 See, for example, Daniel M. Abramson, *Obsolescence, an Architectural History* (Chicago: The University of Chicago Press, 2016). There is a growing body of literature on post-completion issues. Robert Kronenburg, *Flexible: Architecture That Responds to Change* (London: Peter King, 2007); Stephen Cairns and Jane M. Jacobs, *Buildings Must Die: A Perverse View of*

Architecture (Cambridge, MA: The MIT Press, 2014; Mohsen Mostafavi and David Leatherbarrow, *On Weathering: The Life of Buildings in Time* (Cambridge, MA: The MIT Press, 1993); Architecture Post Mortem *The Diastolic Architecture of Decline, Dystopia, and Death*, ed. Donald Kunze, David Bertolini, and Simone Brott (New York: Routledge, 2014).

23   Columbia GSAPP, *Architecten De Vylder Vinck Taillieu*, 2018, https://www.youtube.com/watch?v=ZQfhBOSecNo.

24   James H. Myers and William H. Reynolds, *Consumer Behavior and Marketing Management* (Boston: Houghton Mifflin, 1967), 46.

25   Private communication with the author.

Part Three

1 The Curse of Socrates

1   Giorgio Vasari, *The Lives of the Most Excellent Painters, Sculptors, and Architects*, trans. by Gaston Du C. De Vere (London: MacMillan and Co., 1914), https://web.archive.org/web/20171110202413/http://members.efn.org/~acd/vite/VasariFil.html.

2   Filarete, *Filarete's Treatise on Architecture*, Vol. 1, 12.

3   Neither he nor his immediate contemporaries ever referred to the manuscript as a Trattato, though it is usually now called that. The book contains twenty-five parts, most of which were written between 1461 and 1462 during his stays in Milan. The version dedicated to Francesco Sforza was destroyed in World War II. An excellent copy with illustrations, that was finished in Florence probably by 1464 and dedicated to Piero de Medici, is the parent version of later copies.

4   Filarete, *Filarete's Treatise on Architecture*, Vol. 1, 5.

5   Filarete, *Filarete's Treatise on Architecture*, Vol. 1, 64.

6   According to one ancient source, Socrates father, Sophroniscus, was by trade a stonemason or sculptor, but several scholars question the authenticity of that claim, mainly on the grounds that the earliest extant sources of the story are comparatively late and that it is unmentioned by more reliable sources. See Nicholas Smith and Thomas C Brickhouse, *The Philosophy of Socrates* (Boulder, CO: Westview Press, 1999), 17.

7   For discussion, see Alison Burford, *Craftsmen in Greek and Roman Society* (Ithaca, NY: Cornell University Press, 1972).

8   We encounter the concept also in the Bible in various places as in John 10:32: "Πολλὰ ἔργα ἔδειξα ὑμῖν" [Many good works have I shewed you].

9   Anonymous, "To Hephaestus," *Anonymous. The Homeric Hymns and Homerica with an English Translation by Hugh G. Evelyn-White* (Cambridge, MA: Harvard University Press; London: William Heinemann Ltd., 1914).

10   M. M. Austin and P. Vidal-Naquet, *Economic and Social History of Ancient Greece* (Berkeley: University of California Press, 1977), 108.

11 *The History of Herodotus*, trans. G. C. Macaulay (London and New York: Macmillan and Co., 1890).

12 Nicholas Lobkowicz, *Theory and Practice: History of a Concept from Aristotle to Marx* (Notre Dame: University of Notre Dame Press, 1967), 19. See also Robert Garland, *The Eye of the Beholder: Deformity and Disability in the Graeco-Roman World* (Ithaca, NY: Cornell University Press, 1995); E. Hall, "Hephaestus the hobbling humorist: the club-footed god in the history of early Greek comedy," *Illinois Classical Studies* 43 no.2 (2018): 366–87.

13 Xenophon, *Oeconomicus*, trans. Carnes Lord (Ithaca, NY: Cornell University Press, 1970) 4, 2.

14 The term *banausos* largely disappeared in philosophy, but not the attitude. The word returned to use in the nineteenth century with the revival of humanistic learning. Today in German *Banause* is used to mean an uncouth person indifferent to high culture.

15 Plutarch, *The Life of Pericles: The Parallel Lives*, Vol. 3, trans. Bernadotte Perrin (Cambridge, MA: Harvard University Press, Loeb Classical Library, 1916), 153– 2, paragraph 1.

16 For discussion, see Elspeth Whitney, "Paradise Restored: The Mechanical Arts from Antiquity through the Thirteenth Century," *Transactions of the American Philosophical Society* 80 no. 1 (1990): 1–169.

17 Peggy Deamer, "Introduction," *The Architect as Worker, Immaterial Labor, the Creative Class, and the Politics of Design*, ed. Peggy Deamer (London: Bloomsbury, 2015), xxix.

18 *The Architectural Magazine* 1 no. 5 (July 1834): 186.

19 Karl Marx reversed the position of the *banausos* in respect to society, but he was interested in industrial labor, and since, in architecture, industrial labor played only a small part until recently, it is still fair to say that specialized craft labor remained undertheorized even by leftist philosophers.

20 Immanuel Kant, *Kant's Critique of Judgement* (London: Macmillan, 1914), 183.

21 Konstantinos Stefanis, "Nathaniel Hone's 1775 Exhibition: The First Single-Artist Retrospective," *Visual Culture in Britain* 14 no. 2 (2013): 131–53.

22 *Louis I. Kahn: In the Realm of Architecture*, exhibition at the Museum of Modern Art, New York, June 14 to August 18, 1992; accessed April 10, 2021, https://www.moma.org/calendar/exhibitions/371.

23 *History of Architecture, Architectural Design, Specifications* (Scranton: International Textbook Co., 1903), 1–2.

24 Le Corbusier, *Towards a New Architecture*, trans. Frederick Etchells (London: J. Rodker, 1931), 19.

25 Ibid., 153.

26 Le Corbusier, *Vers une architecture* (1923; repr. Paris: Editions Flammarion, 1995), 187.

27 John Ruskin, *The Stones of Venice, Vol. 2: The Sea Stories* (New York: Cosimo Classics, repr. ed., 2007), 167.

28 Richard Saul Wurman, ed., *What Will Be Has Always Been: The Words of
    Louis I. Kahn*, (New York: Rizzoli, 1986), 205.

29 Sarah Williams Goldhagen, "ON ARCHITECTURE: Extra-Large," *The New
    Republic* (July 2006).

30 Constant Nieuwenhuys, manuscript of lecture at the ICA, London, November
    7, 1963, quoted in Mark Wigley, *Constant's New Babylon: The Hyper-
    Architecture of Desire* (Rotterdam: Witte de With, Center for Contemporary
    Art: 010 Publishers, 1998), 8.

31 Exhibition catalogue: *Space, Time, Existence* (Venice: European Cultural
    Centre, 2021), 368–9.

32 Jacques Lacan, *The Seminar of Jacques Lacan. Book III: The Psychoses
    1955–1956*, ed. Jacques-Alain Miller, trans. Russel Grigg (New York:
    W.W. Norton & Co., 1993), 185, 190.

33 "Zaha Hadid on Worker Deaths in Qatar: 'It's Not My Duty As an Architect'"
    ArchDaily, accessed April 20, 2021, https://www.archdaily.com/480990/
    zaha-hadid-on-worker-deaths-in-qatar-it-s-not-my-duty-as-an-architect.

34 Greg Lynn, *Animate Form* (New York: Princeton Architectural Press, 1999).

2 Occupationality

1   باب النجار مخلع My thanks to Nasser Rabbat for this reference.

2   Labor historians have traditionally been inclined to focus on the development
    of the factory, arguing that the complex division of labor, the subjection of
    labor to the rhythm of the machine, and the new opportunities for surveillance
    and discipline combined to create an alienated and proletarianized labor force.
    The building trades do not fit this model, or at least not very neatly.

3   https://www.bls.gov/ooh/construction-and-extraction/carpenters.htm#tab-1.

4   See Raphael Pumpelly, *Report on the Mining Industries of the United States
    (exclusive of the Precious Metals)* (Washington, DC: Government Printing
    Office, 1886), 814.

5   Review of S. T. Averling, *Carpentry and Joinery: A Useful Manual for Many*
    (London: F. Warne and Co., 1871), in the *Illustrated Carpenter and Builder* 2
    no. 35 (April 5, 1878): 215.

6   "Some Sound Advice," *The Carpenter* 37 no. 2 (February 1917): 51.

7   Ibid.

8   The issue of expertise deals only with the high end of occupationality. And yet
    even in 2006 we read, "while (expertise) lies at the intersection of core issues
    involving learning, skill, knowledge, and experience, it has rarely attracted
    explicit philosophical attention." Evan Selinger and Robert P. Crease, eds.,
    "Introduction," *The Philosophy of Expertise* (New York: Columbia University
    Press, 2006), 1.

9   David Gerstle, *Running a Successful Construction Company* (Newtown, CT:
    Taunton Press, 2002), 7.

10 The Christian Saint Joseph was a carpenter who brought up his son, Jesus, and trained him in the art of carpentry. Among Catholics of today, Saint Joseph is seen as a model for all fathers and working individuals today. In Europe, different regions had different patron saints for carpentry. In Regensburg, Germany, it is St. Wolfgang, a tenth-century monk and bishop. He can be invoked against internal bleeding, paralysis, stomach diseases, and strokes. In art he is usually depicted holding a cathedral, dressed as a bishop, or forcing Satan to help him construct a church. Another referent is St. Paul, who was often sermonized around the theme of master builder. See, for example, Edward Payne, *The Foundation of a Master-Builder: A Sermon* (London: Bell and Daldy, 1855).

11 Charles William Pearson, *The Carpenter Prophet*; *A Life of Jesus Christ and a Discussion of His Ideals* (Chicago: Herbert S. Stone and Co., 1902), 33.

12 Pierre Bélanger, "A 38-Point Design Manifesto," http://www.opsys.net. Bélanger is Associate Professor of Landscape Architecture at the Harvard Graduate School of Design, Co-Director of OPSYS.

13 The advent of advanced technology in the twentieht century placed architecture more centrally into the ideologies of capitalism, but it did little to change the normative occupationality of the building trades.

14 Plutarch, *Life of Pericles*, Modern Library edition (New York: Random House, 1984), 191–2.

15 "Arbitration Clauses in Construction Contracts," *Murdock Law, S. C.* (blog) January 14, 2019 at 2:34 p.m., and "Are Oral Construction Contracts Enforceable?" *Murdock Law, S.C.* (blog), June 16, 2018, https://www.murdock-law.com/2018/06/16/are-oral-construction-contracts-enforceable/.

16 "About Us," accessed March 15, 2021, https://www.agc.org/about-us.

17 Johann Beckmann, *Anlietungzur Technologie* (Göttingen: Verlag der Wittwe Vandenhoeck, 1777).

18 *Home Study for the Building Trades* Vols. 1–3, ed. W. Scott-Collins (Scranton, PA: The Colliery Engineer Co., 1898).

19 Grace Palladino, *Skilled Hands, Strong Spirits, A Century of Building Trades History* (Ithaca, NY: Cornell University Press, 2005), 15, 19.

20 Nathaniel Ruggles Whitney, *Jurisdiction in American Building Trades Unions* (Baltimore: Johns Hopkins University Press, 1914).

21 "Report of Frank Duffy, General Secretary of the United Brotherhood of Carpenters and Joiners of America," *Proceedings of the Biennial Convention of the United Brotherhood of Carpenters and Joiners of America* Vols. 15–16 (1908): 70.

22 E. H. Neal, "Theory and Theorists," *The Carpenter* 35 no. 5 (May 1915): 8.

23 Though architectural firms can be complex in their disciplinary make-up, they do not reflect the realities of occupationality. Perhaps one of the few firms to acknowledge the potential of its complex networks is MASS (Model of Architecture Serving Society) based in Boston, Massachusetts, and Kigali, Rwanda. It was founded on the belief that the best architecture is a team effort

and that it must be created with input and labor from the community. Its roster of employees includes not just architects, landscape architects, and engineers, but also builders, furniture designers, and makers.

24 C. Christiansen, "Defining Lives: Occupation as Identity: An essay on competence, coherence and the creation of meaning," *American Journal of Occupational Therapy* 53 (1999): 547.

25 Vladimir B. Skorikov and Fred W. Vondracek, "Occupational Identity," in *Handbook of Identity Theory and Research*, ed. Seth J. Schwartz, Koen Luyckx, and Vivian L. Vignoles (Berlin: Springer Science+Business Media, 2011), 693–714.

26 One of the few attempts to give an overview of the sociology of the construction worker is Herbert Applebaum, *Construction Workers, U.S.A.* (Westport, CT: Praeger, 1999).

27 Philip A. Korth, *Craftsmanship and the Michigan Union Carpenter* (Bowling Green, OH: State University Popular Press, 1991), 107.

28 Albert H. Jenkins, "Don't pass up Deductions," *Signalman's Journal* 39 no. 3 (March 1958): 87.

29 "Preface" of *The Illustrated Carpenter and Builder* 6 (London: John Dicks, 1880).

30 Mark Erlich, *With Our Hands, The Story of Carpenters in Massachusetts* (Philadelphia: Temple University Press, 1986), xi.

31 Erlich, *With Our Hands*, xv.

32 Erlich, *With Our Hands*, 19.

33 "Must explain to Customers Difference Between Good Work and Cheap Work," *American Builder* (American Carpenter and Builder Company, 1916): 72.

34 "Our Sermon," *The Builder* 1 (1842): 3; http://archive.org/details/gri_33125006201749.

35 Jim Locke, *The Well-Built House* (Boston: Houghton Mifflin, 1988), 3.

36 Jacob Paskins, *Paris Under Construction: Building Sites and Urban Transformation in the 1960s* (New York: Routledge, 2015) is one of the few books that looks at urban history from the perspective of the building site. Another book of note is Linda Clarke, *Building Capitalism: Historical Change and the Labour Process in the Production of the Built Environment* (New York: Routledge 1992).

37 Melnikov (1890–1974) was a Russian architect who rose to eminence in the Soviet Union in the 1920s. Though his work has been associated by some with Constructivism, he was more connected with the Productivists, who saw themselves as anti-artistic Constructivist technicians. He is best known for his Workers' Factory Clubs in Moscow and for his own house in Moscow that consisted of two interlocking cylinders (1927–9).

38 Thanks to Danilo Udovicki for this information.

39 "Michigan Laborers Union," accessed March 15, 2021, https://www.mi-laborers.org/.

40 "Construction Worker Memorial—MASS—NYS Laborers Union," accessed March 15, 2021, http://www.nysliuna.org/latest-news/construction-worker-memorial-mass/.

41 "Construction Workers in London Commemorate International Workers' Memorial Day," BWI—Building & Wood Workers' International, accessed March 15, 2021, https://www.bwint.org/cms/construction-workers-in-london-commemorate-international-workers-memorial-day-1398.

42 *Life and Labor of the People in London*, 5, ed. Charles Booth, (London: Macmillan and Co., 1895), 31.

43 "What It Means to Be a Female in the Construction Industry?," *Boston Real Estate Times* (blog), March 6, 2020, https://bostonrealestatetimes.com/what-it-means-to-be-a-female-in-the-construction-industry/.

44 A rare insight into this world is provided by Kris Paap, *Working Construction: Why White Working-Class Men Put Themselves—and the Labor Movement—in Harm's Way* (Ithaca, NY: Cornell University Press, 2018).

45 Sylveste Augustus, *Hammering Through, Resisting Racial Prejudice, Systemic Biases, and Discriminating Setbacks in the Construction Industry in the USA* (xlibris.com, 2020), 17–18.

46 "First female carpenter to represent N.J. in national skills competition" (June 22, 2018; Jan. 30, 2019,) https://www.nj.com/mercer/2018/06/female_carpenter_at_mcts_wins_1st_place_in_local_c.html.

47 Xinhua, *Global Times* (August 16, 2021), https://www.gettyimages.com/detail/news-photo/aug-14-2021-xinhua-beatrice-nanyangwe-a-female-carpenter-news-photo/1234690326.

48 https://www.yesmagazine.org/economy/2013/09/27/less-than-two-percent-of-carpenters-are-women-meet-master-builder.

49 Charles S. Johnson, "Negro Workers in Skilled Crafts and Construction," *Opportunity: Journal of Negro Life* 11 no. 10 (October 1933): 296–300. In another article, Johnson writes that the number of carpenters per thousand of the population has actually declined since 1910 with "few chances for apprenticeship in the new field of steel working." See Charles S. Johnson, "The New Frontier of Negro Labor," *Opportunity: Journal of Negro Life* 10 no. 6 (June 1932): 170. Johnson also authored "The New Frontage on American Life," *The New Negro, An Interpretation*, ed. Alain Locke (New York: Albert and Charles Boni, 1925), 278–98.

50 Robert C. Weaver, "Experiments in Negro Labor," *Opportunity* 14 no. 10 (October 1936): 298.

51 Larry Haun, *A Carpenter's Life, As Told by Houses* (Newtown, CT: Taunton Press: 2011), 189.

52 John Michael Vlach, *By the Work of Their Hands: Studies in Afro-American Folklife* (Charlottesville: University Press of Virginia, 1991), and *The Afro-American Tradition in Decorative Arts* (Athens, GA: University of Georgia Press, 1990). I want to thank Hampton Smith for this reference.

53 Jim Postell and Nancy Gesimondo, *Materiality and Interior Construction*, 1st ed. (Hoboken, NJ: John Wiley & Sons, 2011), 229.

3 Faber Ingenium

1   Brian Green, "Social Mobility and Construction: Building routes to opportunity," ciob.org (December 19, 2016), https://www.ciob.org/industry/research/Social-Mobility-Construction-Building-routes-opportunity.

2   Lionel March, *Architectonics of Humanism: Essays on Number in Architecture* (London: Academy Editions, 1998), xii.

3   Leon Battista Alberti, *On Painting*, trans. John R. Spencer (New Haven: Yale University Press, 1956), 63, 64.

4   Vasari, *Lives*.

5   Ibid., 63.

6   Elizabeth M. Merrill, "The Trattato as Textbook: Francesco di Giorgio's Vision for the Renaissance Architect," *Architectural Histories* 1 no. 1 (2013): 1.

7   Ibid., 2.

8   Filarete wrote "your devoted and *filareto* architect, Antonio Averlino, Florentine," using the term as an adjective in the dedication to Piero de' Medici in 1465. It is not known when he began to call himself Filarete. See also Helena Guzik, "Measuing and Making the World: Self-Promotion, Cosmology in Filarete's Libro Architettonico," *Imago Temporis. Medium Aevum* XV (2021): 387–412.

9   The work did not appear as a conventional single-volume treatise. Book IV was first published in Paris in 1545; Book V also in Paris in 1537. The first five books were then published together in Venice in 1584 under the title *Tutte l'opere d'architettura et prospecttiva*. It was then translated into Dutch (1606) and English (1611).

10   Sebastiano Serlio, *Five Books of Architecture* (repr. of the English ed. of 1611, New York: Dover, 1982), 160.

11   Andrea Palladio, *The Four Books of Architecture*, trans. Issac Ware (repr. of English ed. published by Issac Ware, 1738, New York: Dover, 1965), preface p.n.n.

12   Palladio, 2, 3,4.

13   Alberti (bk 2, ch. 13), 58.

14   Andrea Palladio, *The Four Books of Architecture*, preface p.n.n.

15   *Serlio*, 1.

16   Given his orientation to stereometry, Delorme aligns himself not with the model of a primitive hut, a model that came through Vitruvius, but with the relationship between geometry and divinity. And by divine proportions, as he explains in the foreword, he means those that were first recorded in the Old Testament for the construction of the Ark of Noah, the Ark of the Covenant, and the Temple of Solomon. Delorme claims that these models have not been known, studied, nor put into practice neither by ancient nor modern architects. He announced that he would cover the topic in a second volume, yet that *Second Tome de l'Architecture* never appeared. Delorme died in January 1570, a little more than two years after the *Premier Tome* was published in 1567. See Sara Galletti, "Philibert Delorme's Divine Proportions

and the Composition of the Premier Tome de l'Architecture," *Architectural Histories* 2 no. 1: 12. DOI: http://doi.org/10.5334/ah.bh.

17 José Calvo-López, *Stereotomy: Stone Construction and Geometry in Western Europe 1200–1900* (Zurich: Springer, 2020); Giuseppe Fallacara, *Stereotomy: Stone Architecture and New Research,* (Paris: Ponts Chaussees, 2013), 585.

18 Hans Straub, *Die Geschichte der Bauingenieurkunst* (Basel: Birkhäuser. 1992), 151.

19 Little is known of his biography apart from that he was from an ancient family of Kent. He participated in Wyatt's rebellion against Mary. He was opposed to Catholicism and to Spanish interference. His motivations are uncertain and afterwards his land was removed as punishment for treason. Digges's *Prognostication*, published in 1553, apparently to earn money after his estate was lost, and then reprinted frequently, was an almanac with, among other things, astronomical information on how to determine the hour at night from the stars, and information about instruments for observation. More info at: http://galileo.rice.edu/Catalog/NewFiles/digges_leo.html.

20 For example, Anthony Fitzherbert's *Book of Surveying* appeared in 1523 and Sir Richard Benese's *The Manner of Measuring* in 1537.

21 Wyatt Papworth, "On the Superintendents of English Buildings in the Middle Ages; with an Especial Reference to William of Wykenham," *The Builder* 18 no. 890 (February 25, 1860): 115.

22 *History of Architecture and the Building Trades of Greater New York*, 1 (New York: Union History Company, 1899), 103–4.

23 Peter Clark, "Migration in England during the Late Seventeenth and Early Eighteenth Centuries," *Past & Present* 83 (May 1979): 6.

24 Wilhelm Günther Bleichrodt, *Architektonisches Lexikon, oder allgemeine Real-Encyclopädie der gesammten architektonischen und dahin einschlagenden Hilfswissenschaften* (Weimar: Bernhard Friedrich Voigt, 1840), 871.

25 Thomas Kelley, *The New Practical Builder, and Workman's Companion* (London: Weed and Rider, 1823).

26 Kevin Ireton, "Introduction," *Framing Roofs* (Newton, CT: Taunton Press, 2002), 3.

27 Morris Williams, "Further Comments on Laying out Face Mold for Stair Rail," *Carpentry and Building* 24 no. 3 (March 1902): 70.

28 *Carpentry and Building* 1 no. 1 (January 1879).

29 Robert L. Self and Susan R. Stein, "The Collaboration of Thomas Jefferson and John Hemings," *Winterthur Portfolio* 33 no. 4 (1998): 233–48.

30 Studies of builder's manuals and pattern books, especially in the US, has been quite thorough. See Daniel D. Reiff, *Houses from Books: Treatises, Pattern Books, and Catalogs in American Architecture, 1738–1950, A History and Guide* (University Park, PA: Pennsylvania University Press, 2000).

31 H. Misson, *Memoirs and Observations in his Travels over England* (London, 1719 ed.), 200. See also Lawrence Stone, *The Crisis of the Aristocracy, 1558–1641* (Oxford: Oxford University Press, 1965).

32   For a discussion, see Valérie Nègre, "Craft Knowledge in the age of
     encyclopedism," *Crafting Enlightenment, Artisanal Histories and
     Transnational Networks*, ed. Lauren R. Cannady and Jennifer Ferng
     (Liverpool: Liverpool University Press, 2021).

33   Antoine Quatremère de Quincy, *Encyclopédie Méthodique: Architecture* 2
     (Paris: Chez Mme. veuve Agasse, 1802–20), entry: "Conucteur," 56.

34   "Guitarde—Beautiful French Dormers," accessed April 21, 2021, http://www.
     historicalcarpentry.com/guitarde---beautiful-french-dormers.html.

35   "(3) School of Practical Stereotomy—École Pratique de Stéréotomie—Posts |
     Facebook," accessed April 21, 2021, https://www.facebook.com/
     thestereotomist/posts/3622164604538587.

36   "Sept ans de travail et un chef-d'œuvre," *SudOuest.fr*, accessed April 21, 2021,
     https://www.sudouest.fr/2012/05/05/sept-ans-de-travail-et-un-chef-d-
     oeuvre-706253-1776.php.

37   The attempt to revitalize skill trades in carpentry has taken root in several
     places around the world; in the US with the United Brotherhood of Carpenters
     and Joiners of America (https://www.carpenters.org); in Singapore (https://
     www.indesignlive.sg/articles/in-review/reviving-a-trade); in Bosnia and
     Herzegovina (https://www.ebrd.com/news/2019/reviving-artisanal-woodwork-
     in-bosnia-and-herzegovina.html). As much as I support these efforts, this book
     does not focus on these badly needed activities, but rather on the disciplinary
     (dis)locations of carpentry and related structural knowledges.

38   "What Math Classes Do Architects Take in College?" *Education—Seattle PI*,
     accessed March 15, 2021, https://education.seattlepi.com/math-classes-
     architects-college-1107.html.

39   Diane Simpson, who lives and works in Chicago, was born in Joliet, Illinois, in
     1935. She constructs sculptures that deploy a broad range of materials and
     sources, often addressing issues of gender and abstraction. She writes that
     architecture has had a strong influence on her work. "When looking at
     architecture, I isolate a section of a building (a chimney, a window, a roof
     shape) that interests me. In the same way, I concentrate on a particular section
     or detail of clothing (a turn of a collar; the shape of a sleeve). I am interested
     in the seamless shifting from body to architectural form in the melding of the
     wearable with the structural un-wearable."

40   Benedetta Tagliabue studied architecture at the Istituto di Architettura di
     Venezia (IUAV) and is director of the Barcelona-based architecture firm Miralles
     Tagliabue EMBT, founded in 1994 in collaboration with Enric Miralles.

Part Four

1 "Architecture"

1   Victor Hugo, *Notre-Dame of Paris*, trans. John Sturrock (New York: Penguin
     Books, 2004), 190.

2   Richard Wittman, "The Hut and the Altar: Architectural Origins and the Public Sphere in Eighteenth-Century France," *Studies in Eighteenth Century Culture* 36 no. 1: 235–59 (253). See also Neil Levine, "The Book and the Building: Hugo's Theory of Architecture and Labrouste's Bibliothèque Ste-Geneviève," in *The Beaux-Arts and Nineteenth-Century French Architecture*, ed. Robin Middleton (London: Thames & Hudson, 1982), 138–73.

3   It is widely agreed that the two bays on the right of the facade were added in a second phase and were, therefore, probably not Alberti's design. For the sake of this argument, it matters little as to when it was built.

4   The chair has been studied over the centuries; the last time it was removed from its niche in the Bernini altar was a six-year period from 1968 to 1974 during which studies pointed to a chair whose oldest parts date to the sixth century.

5   Andrew Russeth, "Constant Displacement: Pierre Huyghe on His Work at Skulptur Projekte Münster," *ARTnews.Com* (blog), June 26, 2017, https://www.artnews.com/art-news/artists/constant-displacement-pierre-huyghe-on-his-work-at-skulptur-projekte-munster-2017-8602/.

6   "Benjamin H. D. Buchloh on Some Means and Ends of Sculpture at Venice, Münster, and Documenta—Artforum International," accessed March 22, 2021, https://www.artforum.com/print/201707/benjamin-h-d-buchloh-on-some-means-and-ends-of-sculpture-at-venice-muenster-and-documenta-70461.

2 Anamorphic Realism

1   Leon Battista Alberti, *On Painting*, trans. John R. Spencer, (New Haven: Yale University Press, 1956), 63.

2   Private correspondence with the artist. Nowadays the work has totally disappeared, covered by umbrellas and potted plants. Jan Dibbets and others have also used anamorphism in compelling ways.

3   Andrea Palladio at his Il Redentore (1592) in Venice had already rolled out the grand column as a white, plastered surface apart from the lowermost socle of stone.

4   Mies van der Rohe, *Architectural Forum* 92 no. 1 (January 1950): 76.

5   In the original design, the altar was separated by a wall from the sacristy. The roof drainpipe would have descended in that wall. When the plan to build the chapter house that was next door fell through, the chapel had to be extended about 2 feet to the rear to accommodate the bathrooms. The altar and the wall were also moved up about 2 feet or so, leaving the pipe "free standing" and visible as it is today.

6   Trinh T. Minh-ha, *Woman, Native, Other* (Bloomington: Indiana University Press, 1989).

Part Five

1 Arche-Socio(~~Arche~~)ology

1   Filarete, 206.

2   Filarete, 195.

3   Alberti, *On the Art of Building*, 8.

4   Filarete, 10.

5   Alberti, *L'architettura*, 2, 451.

6   Alberti, *On the Art of Building*, 23.

7   Ibid., 7.

8   "Finding Shelter in the Paleolithic," *Architect Magazine*, accessed March 22, 2021, https://www.architectmagazine.com/design/finding-shelter-in-the-paleolithic_o.

9   https://www.moma.org/momaorg/shared/pdfs/docs/press_archives/3348/releases/MOMA_1964_0135_1964-12-10_87.pdf?2010.

10   Alison and Peter Smithson, *Without Rhetoric: An Architectural Aesthetic, 1955–1972* (London: Latimer, 1975), 6.

2 Arche-²

1   Wolfgang Herrmann, *Laugier and Eighteenth Century French Theory* (London: A. Zwemmer, 1962), 6.

2   Richard Wittman, "The Hut and the Altar: Architectural Origins and the Public Sphere in Eighteenth-Century France," *Studies in Eighteenth Century Culture: Studies in Eighteenth Century Culture* 36 no. 1 (January 2007): 235–59.

3   Laugier, 2–3.

4   Jean-Jacques Rousseau, *A Dissertation on the Origin and Foundation of the Inequality of Mankind*, in *Social Contract & Discourses*, trans. with introduction by G. D. H. Cole (New York: E. P. Dutton, 1913), 7.

5   Quoted in Christopher Kelly, "Taking Readers as They Are: Rousseau's Turn from Discourses to Novels," *Eighteenth-Century Studies* 33 no. 1 (Fall 1999): 88.

6   Critiquing superficiality became one of the long-standing tropes of post-Enlightenment bourgeois philosophers. In the opening chapter of *Postmodernism, or, The Cultural Logic of Late Capitalism* (1991), the "enormous glass surfaces" of building epitomize the "flatness" and "depthlessness" of contemporary society. While this may be an excellent sound bite, it reduces the critique of capitalism to the critique of its effect rather than to the question of production. It also assumes an "art object" status to architecture, one that is conditioned by the magic of its making and the unified framework of perception, in this case by an audience of naives, namely you

and me, who as "superficials" fail to register our complicity in the scheme. My discussion does not touch on the "art object" status of architecture since I argue that *archē*(non)*tektōn* has destroyed architecture's capacity to be read as "object" at the very moment the discipline was formed.

7   Johann Joachim Winckelmann, *Johann Joachim Winckelmann on Art, Architecture, and Archaeology*, trans. David Carter, (Woodbridge: Boydell & Brewer, 2013), 42.

8   Quoted in Lasse Hodne, "Winckelmann's Depreciation of Colour in Light of the Querelle du coloris and Recent Critique," *Konsthistorisk tidskrift/Journal of Art History* 89 no. 3 (2020): 199.

9   Dennis Sharp, *The Illustrated Encyclopedia of Architects and Architecture* (New York: Whitney Library of Design, 1991), 145.

10 Semper was born into a well-to-do industrialist family in Altona, Germany, and went to Paris to work for the architect Franz Christian Gau. He traveled to Italy and Greece in order to study the architecture and designs of antiquity, participating for four months in archaeological research at the Acropolis in Athens. During this period, he became very interested in the polychromy debate, which centered on the question whether buildings in ancient Greece and Rome had been colorfully painted or not.

11 As quoted by Robert Vuyosevich in "Semper and the Two American Glass Houses," in *Reflections: The Journal of the School of Architecture, University of Illinois at Urbana-Champaign* (Champaign: Universtiy of Illinois Press, 1987), 6.

12 Gottfried Semper, *Wissenschaft, Industrie und Kunst: Vorschläge zur Anregung nationalen Kunstgefühles, bei dem Schlusse der Londoner Industrie-Ausstellung* (Braunschweig ed., 1852), 4; translated by the author.

13 "The Pan-European Living Room: OMA addresses the legacy and value of cross-border design," *Design Pulse, Knoll*, accessed August 19, 2020, https://www.knoll.com/knollnewsdetail/pan-european-living-room.

14 Peter Eisenman, *Lateness* (Princeton: Princeton University Press, 2020), 99.

3 Laugier's Haunts

1   Marc-Antoine Laugier, *An essay on architecture in which its true principles are explained, and invariable rules proposed, for directing the judgement and forming the taste of the gentleman and the architect, with regard to the different kinds of buildings, the embellishment of cities* (London: T. Osborne and Shipton, 1755).

2   See also Hanaa Dahy, "'Materials as a Design Tool' Design Philosophy Applied in Three Innovative Research Pavilions Out of Sustainable Building Materials with Controlled End-Of-Life Scenarios," *Buildings* 3 no. 9 (2019): 11–12.

3   https://www.urdesignmag.com/design/2017/12/11/gilles-retsin-pavilion-tallinn/.

4   Jean Baudrillard, *Architecture: Truth or Radicalism*, trans. David L. Sweet (Los Angeles: semiotext(e), 2007), 7.

5　Ibid., 25.

6　Ibid., 16.

7　"I'm Lost In Paris," *ICON Magazine*, accessed March 22, 2021, https://www. iconeye.com/icon-075-september-2009/im-lost-in-paris. "Lostinparis," accessed March 22, 2021, https://www.new-territories.com/lostinparis.htm.

8　François Roche, DSV and Sie, "Situation," *Quaderns* 217 (1997): 97.

9　https://www.markmack.com/furniture-83/k4h6nk4danlcswvnl522asfg5ucgo8.

10　Sudarshan Khadka, Jr., is principal architect of I.Incite, Inc. Alexander Eriksson Furunes has a practice in Norway. He and Khadka Barangay Engkanto formed Framework Collaborative to design this pavilion, called "Structures of Mutual Support."

11　https://themixedculture.com/2013/09/25/filipinos-bayanihan/.

12　https://www.sofn.com/blog/how-norways-evolving-dugnad-tradition-keeps-the-pandemic-in-check/.

Part Six

1 Tekton-Topia

1　Louis F. Allen's *Rural Architecture: being a complete description of Farm Houses, Cottages and Out Buildings, Carriage Houses . . . Stables . . . Smoke and Ash Houses . . . Sheds for Cattle. Etc.* (New York: C. M. Saxton, 1852), 9.

2　This history can be found in Mary N. Woods, *From Craft to Profession: The Practice of Architecture in Nineteenth-Century America* (Berkeley: University of California Press, 1999), and Dell Upton, *Architecture in the United States* (New York: Oxford University Press, 1998).

3　Quoted in Michael J. Lewis, "Owen Biddle and 'The Young Carpenter's Assistant,'" *American Architects and their Books to 1848*, ed. Kenneth Hafertepe and James O'Gorman (Amherst, MA: University of Massachusetts Press, 2001), 150–1.

4　Ibid., 153.

5　"Review," *Genesee Farmer* 7 no. 8 (August 1846): 194.

6　Chas. D. Lakey, "Prefatory," *Woodworker* 1 no. 1 (1879): 2.

7　*The Builder* 30 no. 21 (July 1, 1843): 249.

8　Catherine W. Bisher, "Jacob W. Holt: An American Builder," *Common Places: Readings in American Vernacular Architecture*, ed. Dell Upton and John Michael Vlach (Athens, GA: University of Georgia Press, 1986), 447–81.

9　Ibid., 450.

10　William Robert Ware, *An Outline for a Course in Architectural Instruction* (Boston, MA: John Wilson and Sons, 1866), 11.

11 Ernest Newton, "Architects and Surveyors," *Architecture a Profession Or an Art Thirteen Short Essays on the Qualifications and Training of Architects* (London: John Murray, 1892), 91–5.

12 John Thomas Micklethwaite, "Architecture and Construction," *Architecture a Profession Or an Art Thirteen Short Essays on the Qualifications and Training of Architects* (London: John Murray, 1892), 25.

13 "Seaside Architecture," *Architecture and Building* 13 no. 8 (August 23, 1890): 90.

14 T. G. Jackson, "Introduction," *Architecture a Profession Or an Art Thirteen Short Essays on the Qualifications and Training of Architects* (London: John Murray, 1892), xiii–xiv.

15 *The Liverpool Mercury*, cited in Glen Huntley, "Jerry Builder: Origin of the term," https://theprioryandthecastironshore.wordpress.com/2017/07/06/jerry-builder-origin-of-the-term/.

16 *The Builder* 45 (December 16, 1843): 544.

17 Quoted in David van Zaten, *Designing Paris: the Architecture of Duban, Labrouste, Duc, and Vodoyer* (Cambridge: The MIT Press, 1987), 117.

18 *The Iconographic Encyclopaedia of the Arts and Sciences: Architecture*, ed. and trans. W. N. Lockington (Philadelphia: Iconographic Publishing, 1888), 19.

19 "Why Architects Are Not 'Engineers!" *Arch2O.Com*, accessed March 22, 2021, https://www.arch2o.com/architects-not-engineers/. https://www.arch2o.com/architects-not-engineers/.

20 "Architects and Engineers: Working Together to Design Structures—Lesson," *TeachEngineering.org*, accessed April 12, 2021, https://www.teachengineering.org/lessons/view/cub_intro_lesson03.

21 Letter to Frederick W. Taylor, November 6, 1914, p. 2 (Freeman Papers, Box #41, MIT Archives).

22 Craig Taylor, *New Yorkers: A City and Its People in Our Time* (New York: W.W. Norton & Co., 2021), 230.

23 Durand was trained to become an architect and he started his career under the influences of the French Revolution in 1789. He was hired to teach at the École Polytechnique in 1794. The *Précis* was the summary of the content of his courses at the École.

24 Jean-Nicolas-Louis Durand, *Précis of the Lectures on Architecture: With Graphic Portion of the Lectures on Architecture* (Los Angeles: Getty Publications, 2000), 15.

25 Alberto Pérez-Gómez and Alberto Pérez Gómez, *Architecture and the Crisis of Modern Science* (Cambridge, MA: The MIT Press, 1983), 302, 311.

26 For context of how the grid came to be used, see L Jeroen Goudeau, "The Matrix Regained: Reflections on the Use of the Grid in the Architectural Theories of Nicolaus Goldmann and Jean-Nicolas-Louis Durand," *Architectural Histories* 3 no. 1: 9, 1–17.

27 Cristopher Alexander, *The Timeless Way of Building* (Oxford: Oxford University Press, 1979), xvi.

28 Ibid., 8.

29 Ibid., 26.

30 The book was adopted by the University of Oregon as part of its campus planning, which it defines as "a framework of patterns and principles defining the qualities inherent to a functional, beautiful campus and sets forth how those qualities will be preserved and expanded with new construction." https://cpfm.uoregon.edu/campus-plan.

31 Christopher Alexander, *A Pattern Language: Towns, Buildings, Construction* (Oxford: Oxford University Press, 2018), front book flap.

32 The legacy continues under the banner of urban morphology. Representatives are Saverio Muratori from the 1940s, who attempted to develop historical analysis as the basis for the new architectural works in the syntax of the urban tissue. In England, M. R. G. Conzen, a geographer, developed a technique called "town-plan analysis" that studied streets and their arrangement into systems. See Anne Vernez Moudon, "Urban morphology as an emerging interdisciplinary field," *Urban Morphology* (1997): 1, 3–10.

33 John Ruskin, *Praeterita*, ed. A. O. Cockshut (Edinburgh: Edinburgh University Press, 2012), 86.

34 Edward S. Prior, "The Ghosts of the Profession," *Architecture a Profession Or an Art Thirteen Short Essays on the Qualifications and Training of Architects* (London: John Murray, 1892), 103.

35 See Junko Habu and Clare Fawcett, "Jomon Archaeology and the Representation of Japanese Origins," *Antiquity* 73 (1999): 587–93.

36 W. Edwards, "Buried discourse: the Toro archaeological site and Japanese national identity in the early postwar period," *Journal of Japanese Studies* 17 no. 1 (1991): 3.

37 In this book I am not setting out to praise those many architects who learn best practices from vernacular conditions. Though important and necessary, and something I personally admire, I am not trying to "solve" the problem of the architect-builder, but rather trying simply to stay close to the wound as set out by Socrates and reinforced by Alberti and its subsequent Enlightenment and modernist reinforcements.

38 By the first decade of the twenty-first century, scholars working in the field were well aware of the complexity of the term and its disciplinary realities, whether overtly or covertly expressed. See, for example, Nezar AlSayyad's *Traditions: The "Real," the Hyper, and the Virtual in the Built Environment* (New York: Routledge, 2014). In the Introduction, AlSayyad writes: "Because of all of these contradictions about what tradition really means in different cultures and how it may be deployed in the making of built environments, it becomes impossible to generate a singular universal narrative about tradition and built form" (p. x).

39 See Yasuyuki Yoshida, "Archaeological Craft Work 2020: Ethnography of Archaeology at Suwahara Site, Hokuto City, Yamanashi 2020," *The Hiyoshi Review of the Humanities* no. 36 (2021): 61–2.

40 Eugène Emmanuel Viollet-le-Duc, *Dictionnaire raisonné de l'architecture française du XIe au XVe siècle* (1854–68). *The Foundations of Architecture, Selections from the Dictionnaire raisonné*, trans. Kenneth D. Whitehead (New York: George Braziller, 1990), 105.

41 I would like to thank Timothy Hyde for pointing this out. See also Timothy Hyde, "'Well Built, But Poorly Roofed': Notes on The Remains of Architectural History," *Architectural Theory Review* 22, no. 2: 210–32.

42 Ibid., 214.

43 Frank Chodorov, "The Radical Rich," *Mises Daily Articles* (March 21, 2011) Mises Institute.

44 https://www.wikihouse.cc/About.

45 Ibid.

46 Gaston Bachelard, *The Poetics of Space* (Boston, MA: Beacon Press, 1994), 7, 46.

47 David Lang, *Zero to Maker* (San Francisco: Maker Media Inc., 2017), 10.

Part Seven

1 Master Builder

1 Hal Foster, *Design and Crime (And Other Diatribes)* (London: Verso, 2002).

2 Ibid., 24.

3 Theodor Adorno, *Aesthetic Theory*, trans. C. Lenhardt (New York: Routledge, 1984), 307, 308.

4 Adorno, *Aesthetic Theory*, 319.

5 Critical Theory conventionally aims to position architecture—or at least a *possible* architecture—in opposition to the seductions of capitalism. This is certainly worthwhile and important, though it is sometimes difficult to tell when the critique of capitalism is an academic trope deployed as a way to "look good" among like-minded peers and when it cuts closer to the bone of reality. The central problem rotates around the difficulty of how to connect action and work, the former self-generating around a particular theoretical platform, and the latter ostensibly operating in a way that should seem to be natural and productive and not the product of some artificial, mental artifice. The problem compounds itself in the failure of Critical Theory to adequately deal with race, feminism, and aboriginality, not to mention the digital revolution and its impact on capitalism. In this text, I am trying to imagine a *predecessor* critique to Critical Theory, one that does not engage the leviathan of capital in any frontal way—where the interweaving forces, whether violent or peaceful, of action and work leave traces of each other through the entire fabric of the discipline. The potential for a full separation of self and the world—that so concerned Horkheimer and that is at the heart of Critical Theory's attempt at reconciliation—is at the far end of possibility within the grammatology of *archē*(~~non~~)*tektōn*, but it is an extreme that transcends the theoretical play of signifiers since the two poles are actually never separate. This means that "architecture" can never—even under the right circumstances and in the right hands—penetrate through all the

illusions, for that like capitalism it is grounded in its self-contesting illusions. The word "architecture" expresses the nonidentity between concept and object.

6   As quoted in Kenneth Frampton, *Studies in Tectonic Culture: The poetics of construction in nineteenth and twentieth century architecture* (Cambridge, MA: The MIT Press, 1995), 4.

7   Herrmann, *Gottfried Semper: In Search of Architecture*, 141.

8   Frampton, *Studies in Tectonic Culture*, 377.

9   Brennan Buck, "What Plastic Wants," *Log* 23 (Fall 2011): 36. See Kenneth Frampton, "Rappel a l'ordre: The Case for the Tectonic," *Architectural Design* 60 nos. 3–4 (1990). Reprinted in Frampton, *Labour, Work, and Architecture* (London: Phaidon Press, 2002), 99.

10   Marc Angelil, "The Architecture of Making in Search of a Critical Theory of Building," *Oz* 7 no. 4 (1985): 15.

11   Herrmann, *Gottfried Semper*, 144.

12   Whereas European and American theorists used the word "tectonics" to focus on how things are put together, Russian writers during the avant-garde period used the word more metaphorically. In 1922, Aleksi Gan, a Russian artist and graphic designer, authored a book called *Konstruktivzm* (Construction) in which he proposed a radical transition from bourgeois sensibilities to a Marxist one based on the principles of industry. He outlined three interconnected terms, *tektonika, faktura* (texture), and *konstruktsiya*, words that were popular among the avant-garde during this period. In the text he does not define the terms apart from saying, somewhat ambiguously: "Tectonics is synonymous with the organicness of thrust from the intrinsic substance . . . Texture is the organic state of the processed material . . . Construction should be understood as the collective function of constructivism." In the so-called "Productivist Manifesto" by Alexander Rodchenko and his wife Varvara Stephanova, *tektonika* "is derived from the structure of communism and the effective exploitation of industrial matter." Nonconstructivists also used the term. Aleksandr Shevchenko, for example, argued that a tectonic composition meant the "continual displacement and modification of tangible forms of objects until the attainment of total equilibrium on the picture's surface." See discussion in J. E. Bowlt, *Russian Art of the Avant-Garde: Theory and Criticism 1902–1934* (London: Thames & Hudson, 1988), 216–17.

13   According to Mitchell Schwarzer, tectonics is "a rejection of any ideology of blind progress or global homogenization." Mitchell Schwarzer, "Tectonics of the Unforeseen," *ANY: Architecture 14: Tectonics Unbound: Kernform and Kunstform Revisited!* (1996): 62–5.

14   Robert Maulden, *Tectonics in Architecture: From the Physical to the Meta-Physical* (Masters Thesis, MIT 1986), 73.

15   "The (Non) Pop Art of Jim Dine," accessed March 22, 2021, https://fineartmultiple.com/blog/jim-dine-tools-heart-bathrobes-pop-art/.

16   The Hammer Museum in Haines, Alaska, opened to the public in 2002 and portrays the complex history of the tool. It has over 2,000 artifacts on display, and roughly 8,000 more in storage.

17 Richard Deacon, *After*, 1998, wood, steel, aluminum and resin, acquired by the Tate, London, 2002, accessed March 15, 2021, https://www.tate.org.uk/art/artworks/deacon-after-t07867.

18 Bhuvanesh Gowda, in *Artspace*, accessed March 15, 2021, https://www.artspace.com/artist/bhuvanesh_gowda.

19 The work of Abesti Gogora III also comes to mind, but these are too much in line with Abstract Expressionism. Gowda's work has a cultural/narrative component that among other things speaks to the cultural location of *tektōn*.

20 Tomà Berlanda, "Ground Control: The Zoma Museum by Meskerem Assegued and Elias Sime," *Architectural Review* (blog), February 10, 2020, https://www.architectural-review.com/buildings/ground-control-the-zoma-museum-by-meskerem-assegued-and-elias-sime. The walls consist of a bamboo frame stitched with strings, upon which walls are crafted and infilled with mud and straw. Water is then added to ferment the mud and straw which is mixed every three days. The houses are covered by plastic tarpaulin to protect them from the rain until they turn a richer dark brown. After approximately a month, the mud becomes gluey and then like rock. Then the walls are coated with flour, lime, and cactus juice to make them naturally waterproof.

21 The idea of a Post-critical—as championed by Robert Somol and Sarah Whiting among others—emerged in the late 1990s as a critique of Critical Theory with its emancipatory promises that derived from the left-leaning discourses of the Frankfurt School. Though Critical Theory in architecture hardly dominated the discourses of theory as is sometimes portrayed, it did set up the appearance of a profound gap between academe and practice that troubled many, particularly those looking in on academe. Though both camps saw themselves in opposition to large global firms, post-criticalists in architecture championed the restrained progressivism of the small practice. In this, they were closer to the realities of the contractors, seeing themselves as working *with*—rather than in theoretical opposition *to*—the techniques and aesthetics of production and making. They were thus opposed to practices that might be considered purposeful disruptive like collage or montage. See Robert Somol and Sarah Whiting, "Notes Around the Doppler Effect and Other Moods of Modernism," *Perspecta* 33 (2002): 72–7.

22 NADAAA is a Boston-based architecture and urban design firm led by principal designer Nader Tehrani, in collaboration with partners Katherine Faulkner and Daniel Gallagher.

2 Tekton Libidinalism

1 Safatle, Vladimir. 2010. Políticas da Forma: Aula 5. Manuscript. P. 3. As quoted in and translated by Lilian Campesato, "The Paradox of Music Transgressions: Noise as a Libidinal Energy," *Cuadernos de Música, Artes Visuales y Artes Escénicas* 14 no. 1 (2019): 103–14.

2 *Castelli e Ponti di Maestro Nicola Zabaglia*, 1743: pl. XX; copperplate engraving; drawing by Francesco Rostagni, engraving by Michele Sorello.

See Nicoletta Marconi, "Nicola Zabaglia and the School of Practical Mechanics of the Fabbrica of St. Peter's in Rome," *Nexus Network Journal* (July 2009): 187.

3   Le Corbusier, *Towards a New Architecture*, 36.

4   William Yardley, "Lebbeus Woods, Unconventional Architect, Dies at 72," *The New York Times*, accessed April 12, 2021, https://www.nytimes. com/2012/11/01/arts/lebbeus-woods-unconventional-architect-dies-at-72.html.

5   Woods never received a degree in architecture nor was he ever licensed to practice. But from the perspective of the long trajectory—and tragedy—of "architecture" it makes little difference if he has a degree or not.

6   Lebbeus Woods, *War and Architecture* (New York: Princeton Architectural Press, 2002), 1.

7   Frank Werner, *Covering + Exposing: Coop Himmelblau* (Basel: Birkhäuser, 2000),

8   Museum of Modern Art Fact Sheet, March 1988, https://www.moma.org/ momaorg/shared/pdfs/docs/press_archives/6526/releases/ MOMA_1988_0029_29.pdf?2010.

9   SAEE STUDIO was founded in Los Angeles, California, by Michele Saee in 1985.

10 3D techniques were used to design and mold the glass into rounded forms, cylindrical and conical surfaces, hybrid panels interlocking with one another and fusions of complex shapes.

11 Simon Richmond, "Design Festa Gallery: Harajuku," *WhereInTokyo.com*, accessed March 15, 2021, https://whereintokyo.com/venues/25082.html.

3 "Construction"

1   Ralph W. Liebing, *Construction of Architecture, From Design to Built* (New York: John Wiley & Sons, 2011), ix. Liebing is currently a Senior Architect/ Group Leader with Lockwood Greene, Engineers, in Cincinnati, Ohio. He is a registered architect and a Certified Professional Code Administrator. He has taught architecture at the University of Cincinnati School of Architecture and architectural technology at ITT Technical Institute, as well as serving as building commissioner for Ohio's Hamilton County in the Cincinnati area.

2   Eugène Emmanuel Viollet-le-Duc, *Discourses on Architecture*, trans. Benjamin Bucknall (New York: Grove Press. 1959) Lecture XII, 89.

3   F. E. Kidder, *Building Construction and Superintendence*, Part 1, (New York: William T. Comstock, 1897), 301.

4   The document listed three matters of concern: 1) to ameliorate the shortage of housing and of other private buildings; 2) to deal with the deficiency in number of schools, hospitals, roads, etc.; and 3) to furnish employment to demobilized soldiers and industrial workers (p. 9).

5   Roger W. Babson, "Letters of Transmittal," *Economics of the Construction Industry* (Washington, DC: Government Printing office 1919), 7.

6   In 1994, there were 620,852 firms in the industry. Only 7 percent of these had more than 20 employees. Sixty-five percent had only one to four employees.

Most of them also worked within a relatively narrow geographical range. See Herbert Applebaum, *Construction Workers, U.S.A.* (Santa Barbara: ABC-CLIO, Inc., Contributions in Labor Studies Series, 1999), 118.

7   "The Industry Capitalism Forgot," *Fortune* 36 (August 1947): 61–7.

8   "Construction Data," *Associated General Contractors of America*, accessed March 22, 2021, https://www.agc.org/learn/construction-data.

9   The Office of (Un)Certainty Research was founded by Mark Jarzombek and Vikramadytia Prakash in 2019. https://www.officeofuncertaintyresearch.org.

10 For a test case of just how extensive the global footprint is of even a small modern house today, see *House Deconstructed* by the Office of (Un)Certainty Research, exhibited in the Venice Biennale (2021). https://www.officeofuncertaintyresearch.org.

11 Born in Arizona, Raven's work considers the complex histories of this region's formation and depiction, as well as its contemporary role in global commerce, communication, and development. Incorporating moving images, photography, sculpture, and sound, her immersive installations address issues of labor, technology, and the hidden mechanisms of power.

12 https://www.nytimes.com/2021/04/15/arts/design/dia-chelsea-reopens-review.html?auth=login-email&login=email.

13 https://www.vogue.com/article/dia-chelsea-lucy-raven.

14 Andrés Cala, "Raise High the Bridge Beam for a House in Spain," *The New York Times*, November 11, 2010, sec. Great Homes & Destinations, https://www.nytimes.com/2010/11/11/greathomesanddestinations/11location.html.

15 In this, it perpetuates, of course, the Miesian tradition—now fully adopted almost everywhere—of glass as an invisible.

16 "Morpheus Hotel / Zaha Hadid Architects," *ArchDaily*, accessed March 22, 2021, https://www.archdaily.com/896433/morpheus-hotel-zaha-hadid-architects.

17 Daniel Marshall, Caitlin Meuller, Brandon Clifford, and Sheila Kennedy, "Computational Arrangement of Demolition Debris," *Detritu* 11 (July 2020): 3.

18 Brandon Clifford, *The Cannibal's Cookbook: Mining Myths of Cyclopean Constructions* (Novato, CA: ORO Editions, 2021).

De-Positioning

1   John Locke, *An Essay Concerning Human Understanding* (bk II, ch. 27, p. 19). https://www.gutenberg.org/files/10615/10615-h/10615-h.htm#link2HCH0005.

2   I am not pointing to the classic, disruptive avant-gardist positions like Dada and Fluxus that use collage and montage to convey the artistic mistrust of their own medium. These practices, as important as they are in exposing the fetishization of the "artwork" as a singular object of study and presentation, remain nonetheless artworks themselves and are thus ultimately subject to the

disciplinary predilection to place them within a particular slot of operation. Furthermore, they adopt a one-dimensional posture of aggression toward some presumed normative which is usually associated with capitalism and institutionalism. The aggressive element implied in *archē(non)tektōn*, though it can be overt, is a passive-aggressive position, in which disciplinarity, capitalism, and institutionality can themselves be seen as the aggressors.

LIST OF CREDITS

Frontispiece Rear view of a building mockup, Watertown MA, 2022, Builder Unknown, Photo by Mark Jarzombek.

Figure 1.2.1. Diagram of Derrida's argument. Diagram by Mark Jarzombek.

Figure 1.2.2. Diagram of *technē* in Plato's *Statesman*. Diagram by Mark Jarzombek.

Figure 1.3.1. The Aronson Building, San Francisco, 1903, 2018. Photograph by Mark Jarzombek.

Figure 1.3.2. Dome of Les Invalides, Jules Hardouin-Mansart, 1670s, Paris. Jules Hardouin Mansart, cross-section, illustration from *Denkmaeler der Kunst* (Monuments of Art), by Wilhelm Luebke and Carl von Luetzow, 3rd edition, Stuttgart 1879, volume 2, steel engraving by H. Gugeler. INTERFOTO / Alamy Stock Photo.

Figure 1.3.3. Tel Aviv Museum of Art, Herta and Paul Amir Building, Tel Aviv: View of it under construction in 2010. Photograph by Mark Jarzombek.

Figure 1.3.4. Tel Aviv Museum of Art, Herta and Paul Amir Building, Tel Aviv, 2010. ..‫טייקר צילום: ד"ר אבישי‬

Figure 1.3.5. Partial section of Barcelona Pavilion, drawing by author. Diagram by Mark Jarzombek.

Figures 1.3.6–7. Barcelona Pavilion, Ludwig Mies van der Rohe, 1929, 1986, Barcelona. Right: with roofline altered by author. Ralf Roletschek, photographer © 2021 Artists Rights Society (ARS), New York / VG Bild-Kunst, Bonn.

Figure 1.3.8. Section: Design for the French National Library, Étienne-Louis Boullée, Drawing, 1785–8. © Bibliothèque Nationale de France.

Figure 1.3.9. Perspectival drawing: Design for the French National Library, Étienne-Louis Boullée, Drawing, 1785–8. © Bibliothèque Nationale de France.

Figure 1.3.10. Serpentine Pavilion, Junya Ishigami, London, 2019. Images George Rex, London, England.

Figure 1.3.11. Exterior: Nana Harbor Diner, Takeshi Hazama, Okinawa, 2006. Photograph by Mark Jarzombek.

Figure 1.3.12. Section: Statue of Liberty, Liberty Island, Manhattan, New York, 1875. American Engineering Record, National Park Service, Library of Congress, 1875.

Figure 1.3.13. MIT Media Lab, Maki and Associates, Cambridge, Massachusetts, 2010. Photograph by Sayamindu Dasgupta.

Figure 1.3.14. MIT Media Lab under construction, Cambridge, Massachusetts, 2008. © Bond Brothers, Inc.

Figure 2.1.1. *San Agustín*, Baltasar del Águila, Oil on Panel, 1564. Museum of Fine Arts of Córdoba.

Figure 2.1.2. LU7 – Project Berlin-Kreuzberg, Flake + Otto Architkten, 2018–19. © Lidia Tirri and Miriam Otte by Baudoku Berlin www.baudokuberlin.de.

Figure 2.1.3. Loggia of the palace of Agostino Chigi, Rome. Photograph by Mark Jarzombek.

Figure 2.1.4. *Der Architect etc.* from the series *Der Mensch und sein Beruf*, *c.* 1840, by Karl Joseph Geiger. Wien Museum, Vienna.

Figure 2.1.5. Page from William and John Halfpenny, *The Modern Builder's Assistant*, 1757: p. 23. © Getty Research Institute.

Figure 2.1.6. Architect's rendering of the new ESO Headquarters Extension (daytime), Garching, Germany. ESO/Auer+Weber (https://www.eso.org/public/images/eso1215a/).

Figure 2.1.7. A mock-up for a planned building along Riverway, Jamaica Plain, Boston, Massachusetts. Photograph by Mark Jarzombek.

Figure 2.1.8. *Capitol Cornerstone Ceremony*, 1793; Allyn Cox; Oil on canvas applied to the wall, 1973–4; Hall of Capitols, Washington DC. © Architect of the Capitol.

Figure 2.1.9. Architecture, *Libro Architettonico*, Filarete, *c.* 1488–9. © Biblioteca Nazionale Marciana, Venice. On permission of Biblioteca Nazionale Marciana, Venice. Reproduction is strictly forbidden.

Figure 2.1.10. Building Work (work being carried out on a building at a 16th-century construction site), 1558. © Rischgitz / Stringer, 51246516, Hulton Archive.

Figure 2.1.11. An incomplete building in Sicily (contractor/builder unknown by author). Photograph taken October 16, 2005. © incompiuto siciliano.

Figure 2.1.12. Photo of the Palacio Legislativo, now the Monumento a la Revolución, Mexico City, Guillermo Kahlo, 1912. © Revista Imagenes.

Figure 2.1.13. A construction site being prepared in Brooklyn, New York. Photograph by Mark Jarzombek.

Figure 2.1.14. The architect David Chipperfield standing in front of the James Simon Gallery, Berlin, July 10, 2019. Photo: Christoph Soeder/dpa. – Berlin/Berlin/Germany. © AGE Stock Photo / Picture-Alliance.

Figure 2.2.1. Dining Room, Country Cottage, Max Schemel, near Bremen, H. Licht Architect, *c.* 1890.

Figure 2.2.2. Tugendhat House, Brno, Czech Republic. View of study and living room. 1928–30. Silver-gelatin print, 6 1/8 x 9 1/8" (15.6 × 23.2 cm). Mies van der Rohe Archive. Digital Image © The Museum of Modern Art / Licensed by SCALA / Art Resource, NY.

Figure 2.2.3. Interior, Mike Osean, Real Estate Agent, Newport, Rhode Island, 2019.

Figure 2.2.4. Frontispiece, *Examples of Gothic Architecture*, Augustus Pugin, 1836.

Figure 2.2.5. *Bâtiment qui contiendroit les Académies* (Building that would house the Academies), Marie-Joseph Peyre, Plan. 1756.

Figure 2.2.6. Rolex Learning Center, SANAA, Lausanne, 2010. Photograph by Bernard Vogel.

Figure 2.2.7. Deloitte Building, Christchurch, New Zealand. Photograph by Michal Klajban.

Figure 2.2.8. Diagram, Seattle Library, OMA, 2004. Image courtesy of OMA.

Figure 2.2.9. SITE: BEST Showroom: Inside/Outside Building, Milwaukee, Wisconsin, 1984. © I-Beam Architecture and Design.

Figure 2.3.1. *Architectural Ruins, a Vision*, Joseph Michael Gandy, Watercolor on Paper, 1798. © Sir John Soane's Museum, London.

Figure 2.3.2. *The Little Bridge*, Jacob Isaacksz van Ruisdael (Netherlands, b.1628–9, d.1682), 1650–5. Etching, 19.5 x 28 cm. Art Gallery of New South Wales. Bequest of Tom Roberts, 1931. Photo: AGNSW. 62.1998.

Figure 2.3.3. Abandoned barn north of Boston, Massachusetts (contractors/builders unknown by author). Photograph by Mark Jarzombek.

Figure 2.3.4. Street advertisements for various contracting services, New York City. Photograph by Mark Jarzombek.

Figure 2.3.5. Diagram of post-teleology. Diagram by Mark Jarzombek.

Figure 2.3.6. Indoor mold on the head jamb of the inner window in multistory building, Russia, 2018. Photograph by Alexander Davronov.

Figure 2.3.7. Man on ladder cleaning house gutter from leaves and dirt, *c.* 2018. Photograph by ronstik. Getty Images / iStockphoto.

Figure 2.3.8. Black & Decker advertisement, 1950s. Neil Baylis / Alamy Stock Photo.

Figure 2.3.9. *Cleaning a Gerrit Rietveld Building*, Job Koelewijn, Amsterdam, 1992. Thanks to E. v. d. Boom. © Job Koelewijn.

Figure 2.3.10. *The Ethics of Dust*, Westminster Hall, London, 2016. Commissioned and produced by Artangel. Photograph by Marcus J. Leith. © Jorge Otero-Pailos.

Figure 2.3.11. "Tap Left On," Alison Elizabeth Taylor, 2010, wood veneer, shellac (71 × 75 × 48 inches). © Alison Elizabeth Taylor.

Figure 2.3.12. Maintenance-Free House, Denmark, Arkitema Architects, 2014. © Arkitema Architects. Photograph by Niels Nygaard.

Figure 2.3.13. Prosthesis for a beam, Gionata Rizzi, 2021. Photograph by Mark Jarzombek.

Figure 2.3.14. Detail of wall support, Venice (contractors/builders unknown by author). Photograph by Mark Jarzombek.

Figure 2.3.15. Arch, Venice (contractor/builder unknown by author). Photograph by Mark Jarzombek.

Figure 2.3.16. Detail of door support, Venice (contractors/builders unknown by author). Photograph by Mark Jarzombek.

Figure 2.3.17. Italian church under restoration (contractors/builders unknown by author). Photograph by Joanbanjo.

Figure 2.3.18. Church building under restoration, near Barcelona (contractors/builders unknown by author). Photograph by Mark Jarzombek.

Figure 2.3.19. House Sanderswal, De Vylder Vinck Tallieu, Belgium, 2015. © architecten de vylder vinck taillieu. Photograph by Filip Dujardin.

Figure 2.3.20. Mark Jarzombek inside the Cinthia Marcelle installation, San Francisco Museum of Modern Art, 2019. Photograph by Mark Jarzombek.

Figure 2.3.21. Destroyed House in Gaza. © Marjan Teeuwen, Courtesy Bruce Silverstein Gallery.

Figure 2.3.22. Makoko Floating School, Lagos, NLÉ, 2013. Image by NLÉ.

Figure 2.3.23. Makoko Floating School, Lagos, after its collapse, 2016. Photograph by Allyn Aglaïa.

Figure 2.3.24. Sheetrock advertisement, 1923. Courtesy of Historic New England.

Figure 2.3.25. *Mural*, Diller + Scofidio, Whitney Museum of American Art, New York, 2003. © Elizabeth Diller.

Figure 2.3.26. *Mural*, Diller + Scofidio, Whitney Museum of American Art, New York, 2004. © Elizabeth Diller.

Figure 3.1.1. A 13th-century drawing showing the construction of a church. Possibly drawn by Matthew of Paris. © Culture Club / Getty Images.

Figure 3.1.2. Diagram of Immanuel Kant's organization of the arts. Diagram by Mark Jarzombek.

Figure 3.1.3. Construction workers on a building site in Mexico. © Tomas Castelazo, www.tomascastelazo.com.

Figure 3.1.4. *New Babylon*, Constant Niewenhuys, 1963 (ink on paper). *Lithografieën in kleur: New Babylon, rechtsonder gesigneerd "Constant."* Collection Het Nieuwe Instituut, ABAM1211+.

Figure 3.1.5. Project for the Cardiff Bay Opera House competition, Greg Lyynn, 1996. © Greg Lynn.

Figure 3.2.1. Carpenter's tools used by William Martin Knudsen in the building of the Minnesota State Capitol, St. Paul, *c.* 1900. © Minnesota Historical Society.

Figure 3.2.2. Masonry: Illustration. Plate 276. Masonry. *Encyclopédie*. Edited by Denis Diderot (1713–84) and Jean Le Rond d'Alembert (1717–83). © Lanmas / Alamy Stock Photo.

Figure 3.2.3. *Trades Practiced in Bologna*, Etching (*Virtù et arti essercitate in Bologna*, Plate 6), Francisco Curti, Italy, *c.* 1603–70. © Los Angeles County Museum of Art (LACMA), M.69.7.1g / public domain.www.lacma.org.

Figure 3.2.4. Electrician at work, *c.* 2018. Ken Altmann Electric.

Figure 3.2.5. Barn Raising. Construction workers, Massachusetts, late 19th century. Courtesy of Historic New England.

Figure 3.2.6. Soviet Pavilion in Paris under construction, March 1925. © Melnikov House archive, State Museum of Konstantin and Viktor Melnikov. Inv. 581/25, neg. 2.

Figure 3.2.7. *The Building Worker*, Alan Wilson, London, 2006. Photograph by Glyn Baker.

Figure 3.2.8. Contruction Workers in Duala, Cameroon. Photograph by Minette Lontsie.

Figure 3.2.9. Portrait of an African American bricklayer (between 1860 and 1870). Platt, A. C. (Alvord C.), 1828–84, photographer. Library of Congress, Prints and Photographs Division, The William Gladstone Collection of African American Photographs [reproduction number, LC-DIG-ppmsca-11288].

Figure 3.2.10. A visible concrete pour line in a building in Berlin. Photograph by Mark Jarzombek.

Figure 3.2.11. The Bruder Klaus Chapel, Euskirchen, Germany, 2007. Peter Zumthor (Architect); Hermann-Josef and Trudel Scheidtweiler (Developers).

Figure 3.2.12. Detail of the Bruder Klaus Chapel, Euskirchen, Germany, 2008. Peter Zumthor (Architect); Hermann-Josef and Trudel Scheidtweiler (Developers).

Figure 3.2.13. Detail of Pavillon Le Corbusier (Heidi Weber House), Zurich, 1967. Photograph by Frederik Kaufmann.

Figure 3.2.14. *Beam Drop*, Chris Burden, Netherlands, 2009. Photograph by Funkyxian.

Figure 3.2.15. Construction site in Cambridge, Massachusetts, 2022. Contractor: John Moriarty & Associates. Photograph by Mark Jarzombek.

Figure 3.3.1. Skew arch opening in an inclined curved wall, Philibert de L'Orme, *Premier tome de l'architecture* (Paris, 1567) fol. 79v.

Figure 3.3.2. Frontispiece, *Iesu Christi Dei Domini, Salvatoris Nr̄i Infantia, c.* 1600. © Artokoloro / Alamy Stock Photo.

Figure 3.3.3. Baby Jesus helping his father Joseph, *Iesu Christi Dei Domini, Salvatoris Nr̄i Infantia, c.* 1600. © BTEU / RKMLGE / Alamy Stock Photo.

Figure 3.3.4. Frontispiece, *Tectonicon*, Leonard Digges, 1634. Columbia University Libraries.

Figure 3.3.5. Page 1, *The Building Trades Pocketbook*, 1905.

Figure 3.3.6. Frontispiece, *The Art of Sound Building*, William Halfpenny, 1725.

Figure 3.3.7. Plate 1, *Useful Architecture: Being the Last Work in this Kind of William Halfpenny, Architect and Carpenter, in Twenty-five New Designs with Full and Clear Instructions, in Every Particular, for Erecting Parsonage-houses, Farm-houses, and Inns*, William Halfpenny, 1760.

Figure 3.3.8. Plate 9, *The City and Country Builder's and Workman's Treasury of Designs*, Batty Langley, 1745 (page 417).

Figure 3.3.9. Plate 11, The City and Country Builder's and Workman's Treasury of Designs, Batty Langley, 1745 (page 421).

Figure 3.3.10. Roof Framing Plan, Plate 50, *The Carpenter and Joiner's Companion in the Geometrical Construction of Working Drawings*, Peter Nicholson, 1826.

Figure 3.3.11. Kakasd Community Center, Imre Makovecz, 1987–91. Photograph by Dr. János Korom, 2008.

Figure 3.3.12. 360 Newbury Street, Frank Gehry, Boston, Massachusetts (built 1918; renovated 2005). Photograph by Pi.1415926535.

Figure 3.3.13. Stair Case Landing, George Ball House, Galveston, Texas (Harry L. Starnes, Photographer April 9, 1936). Historic American Buildings Survey, Library of Congress Prints and Photographs Division, Washington, DC.

Figure 3.3.14. Construction drawing for a stair railing, *Carpentry and Building*, March 24, 1902, p. 70.

Figure 3.3.15. *Guitardes*: 49 rue des Beaumonts; rue du Faubourg-Saint-Jean, Orléans. Mazzhe; Bertrand Pierre (charpentier).

Figure 3.3.16. Detail of a drawing by François Guillon from the Romanèche-Thorins school of draft, 1892.

Figure 3.3.17. *Drawings For Cape (B)*, Diane Simpson, 1990. Simpson, Diane (b. 1935) © The Art Institute of Chicago / Art Resource, NY.

Figure 3.3.18. *Party Wall*, Caroline O'Donnell, New York, 2013. Photograph by Zachary Tyler Newton. © Caroline O'Donnell.

Figure 3.3.19. Santa Caterina Market, Benedetta Tagliabue, Barcelona, 2005. Photograph by Zhicheng Xu.

Figure 3.3.20. Santa Caterina Market, Benedetta Tagliabue, Barcelona, 2005. Photograph by Samuel Dubois.

Figure 4.1.1. Plan and detail: Santa Maria delle Grazie, Milan. Photograph by Mark Jarzombek.

Figure 4.1.2. Exterior elevation and detail view: Palazzo Rucellai, Florence. Photograph by M-i-k-e-v.

Figure 4.1.3. Elevation drawing: Palazzo Rucellai, Florence. Drawing by Mark Jarzombek.

Figure 4.1.4. Panel pilaster, Santa Maria presso San Satiro, Milan. Drawing by Mark Jarzombek from "Pilasters," *Thresholds* 58.

Figure 4.1.5. Cathedra at the Basilica of St. John Lateran, Rome. Photograph by BrettLewis88.

Figure 4.1.6. Original Altar of Chair of St. Peter, Bernini, Vatican City, alongside Altar of Chair of St. Peter, as altered by author.

Figure 4.1.7. Bawa House, Deshamanya Geoffrey Manning Bawa, Colombo. Left: Plan of second floor showing locations of the missing column and the column hidden in the closet. Right: Plan of roof terrace. Drawing by Mark Jarzombek.

Figure 4.1.8. Roof terrace, Bawa House, Deshamanya Geoffrey Manning Bawa, Colombo. Drawing by Mark Jarzombek.

Figure 4.1.9. *After ALife Ahead*: Pierre Huyghe, Münster, 2017. Skylight view. © 2021 Artists Rights Society (ARS), New York / ADAGP, Paris.

Figure 4.1.10. *After ALife Ahead*: Pierre Huyghe, Münster, 2017. Floor detail. © 2021 Artists Rights Society (ARS), New York / ADAGP, Paris.

Figure 4.2.1. Altarpiece of San Esteban, Jaime Serra, 1385. National Art Museum of Catalonia, Barcelona. © J. Enrique Molina / Alamy Stock Photo.

Figure 4.2.2. *Un carré pour un square*, Jean-Max Albert, Paris, 1988.

Figure 4.2.3. Borromini Corridor, Palazzo Spada, Rome, *c.* 1635. Photograph by Livio and Ronico 2013.

Figure 4.2.4. Plan: Borromini Corridor, Palazzo Spada, Rome. © Relevé d'architecture.

Figure 4.2.5. Interior altar of San Carlo alle Quattro Fontane, Francesco Borromini, Rome, *c.* 1635. Photograph by Livio and Ronico 2013.

Figure 4.2.6. Palazzo dei Conservatori, Michelangelo Buonarotti, Rome, 16th century. Image courtesy of https://www.michelangelo.org/.

Figure 4.2.7. Interior: Sant'Andrea al Quirnale, Gian Lorenzo Bernini, Rome, 1670. © F1online digitale Bildagentur GmbH / Alamy Stock Photo.

Figure 4.2.8. San Carlo alle Quattro Fontane, Francesco Borromini, as modified by author. Photograph and modifications by Mark Jarzombek.

Figure 4.2.9. Interior Perspective, Mies van der Rohe, *Architectural Forum*, January 1950, p. 76. Drawing by Mies van der Rohe.

Figure 4.2.10. Plan based on the drawing by Mies van der Rohe. Plan by Mark Jarzombek.

Figure 4.2.11. Robert F. Carr Memorial Chapel of St. Savior, Mies van der Rohe, service in progress, Illinois Institute of Technology, Chicago, *c.* 1950s, with pictorial additions by author. © HB-16676-B, Chicago History Museum, Hedrich-Blessing Collection.

Figure 4.2.12. Plan and roof and section: Robert F. Carr Memorial Chapel of St. Savior, Mies van der Rohe, Illinois Institute of Technology, Chicago. Section by Mark Jarzombek.

Figure 5.1.1. Drawing, *Libro Architectonico*, Filarete, Book 1, folio 5r.

Figure 5.1.2. Drawing, *Libro Architectonico*, Filarete, Book 1, folio 5v.

Figure 5.1.3. Author stocking up at The Home Depot. Photograph by Mark Jarzombek.

Figure 5.1.4. Diagram: Marc-Antoine Laugier. Diagram by Mark Jarzombek.

Figure 5.1.5. Oslo Opera House, Snøhetta, Oslo, 2007. Photograph by Chuthulu975.

Figure 5.1.6. Panthéon, Paris, 1790, with additions by the author. Diagram by Mark Jarzombek.

Figure 5.1.7. Royal Institute of British Architects insignia as stamped on a leather book cover. © Royal Institute of British Architects.

Figure 5.1.8. Diagram: Pan-European Living Room, OMA. Diagram by Mark Jarzombek.

Figure 5.1.9. Diagram: Peter Eisenman. Diagram by Mark Jarzombek.

Figure 5.1.10. Autographed page of *Five Books of Architecture*, Peter Eisenman. Photograph by Mark Jarzombek.

Figure 5.2.1. Frontispiece, *An Essay on Architecture*, Samuel Wale, 1755. Courtesy of archive.org, accessed October 9, 2020, at https://archive.org/details/essayonarchitect00laugrich.

Figure 5.2.2. Frontispiece: *Essai sur l'architecture*, Charles-Dominique-Joseph Eisen, 1755.

Figure 5.2.3. Interlocking Shell: Biomimetic Research Pavilion 2018. Bachelor thesis of Arzum Coban and Victoria Ivanova, supervised by Prof. Dr.-Ing. Arch. Hanaa Dahy. Photograph by Coban, Ivanova, BioMat@ITKE/University of Stuttgart. © Arzum Coban and Victoria Ivanova.

Figure 5.2.4. Tallinn Architecture Biennale Pavilion, Gilles Retsin Architecture, 2017. Photograph by NAARO.

Figure 5.2.5. Diagram: Jean Baudrillard. Diagram by Mark Jarzombek.

Figure 5.2.6. General view: *Perimeters/Pavilions/Decoys*, Mary Miss, Nassau County Museum, Roslyn Harbor, New York, 1978. © Mary Miss.

Figure 5.2.7. Interior: *Perimeters/Pavilions/Decoys*, Mary Miss, Nassau County Museum, Roslyn Harbor, New York, 1978. © Mary Miss.

Figure 5.2.8. Study for Tower in *Perimeters/Pavilions/Decoys*, 1977. Pencil, colored pencil, and correction fluid on paper. 18 1/4 × 22 1/4" (46.4 × 56.5 cm). Digital Image © The Museum of Modern Art/Licensed by SCALA / Art Resource, NY. Gift of the Gilbert B. and Lila Silverman Instruction Drawing Collection, Detroit.

Figure 5.2.9. A reconstruction of a pit house at the Step House ruins in Mesa Verde National Park, Colorado. Photograph by Elisa Rolle.

Figure 5.2.10. The Green Corner Building, Anne Holtrop, Muharraq, Bahrain, 2019–20. © Studio Anne Holtrop.

Figure 5.2.11. Franklin Court Museum, Robert Venturi, Philadelphia. Photograph by Elisa Rolle.

Figure 5.2.12. Restored CMU block chair, Mark Mack, 1983. © Mark Mack. Photograph by Mark Jarzombek.

Figure 5.2.13. CMU block chair, Mark Mack, 1983. © Mark Mack. Photograph by Mark Jarzombek.

Figure 6.1.1. Postcard showing the Carpenters' Hall, Philadelphia, 1905.

Figure 6.1.2. Two Men and a Boy with Outside Calipers, Backsaw, Square, and Frame Saw, 1860s. Tintype with applied color. Metropolitan Museum of Art, New York.

Figure 6.1.3. Street sign in Warrenton, North Carolina, commemorating the work of Jacob W. Holt.

Figure 6.1.4. *The Architectural Magazine*, 1834.

Figure 6.1.5. Sheet of drawings, *Partie graphique des cours d'architecture faits à l'École Royale Polytechnique depuis sa réorganisation* [. . .], Jean-Nicolas-Louis Durand, orig. ed. Paris 1821. Reprint Unterschneidheim: Uhl Verlag, 1975: pl. 3.

Figure 6.1.6. Reconstruction of Jomon hut, Goshono Archaeological Site, Japan. Photograph by Qurren.

Figure 6.1.7. Reconstructed Thoreau Cabin, Walden Pond, Concord, Massachusetts. Photograph by RhythmicQuietude.

Figure 6.1.8. Diagram: Martin Heidegger. Diagram by Mark Jarzombek.

Figure 6.1.9. Diagram: The primary zones of *tekton*-topia. Diagram by Mark Jarzombek.

Figure 7.1.1. Exterior: Marin County Civic Center, California, Frank Lloyd Wright, 2008. Photograph by Fizbin.

Figure 7.1.2. Column detail: Marin County Civic Center, California, Frank Lloyd Wright, 2008. Photograph by Mark Jarzombek.

Figure 7.1.3. Column detail: Marin County Civic Center, California, Frank Lloyd Wright, 2008. Photograph by Mark Jarzombek.

Figure 7.1.4. Mortensrud Church, Oslo, Jensen & Skodvin Arkitekter AS, 2002. © Jan Olav Jensen.

Figure 7.1.5. Corner detail: S. R. Crown Hall, Illinois Institute of Technology, Chicago, Mies van der Rohe, *c.* 1955, with changes by author. Photographs and additions by Mark Jarzombek.

Figure 7.1.6. Ceiling detail: McCormick Tribune Campus Center, Illinois Institute of Technology, Chicago. Photograph by Mark Jarzombek.

Figure 7.1.7. *Seven White Hammers*, Jim Dine, 2008. Etching, aquatint and drypoint, with hand-coloring in acrylic and charcoal. © 2021 Jim Dine / Artists Rights Society (ARS), New York.

Figure 7.1.8. *Born from Each Other*, Bhuvanesh Gowda, 2016. Image courtesy of Chemould Prescott Road, Mumbai, India. © Chemould Prescott Road and Bhuvanesh Gowda.

Figure 7.1.9. Zoma Museum, Addis Ababa, Elias Sime, 2002–9. © Zoma Museum.

Figure 7.1.10. *Concrete Drops*, Zach Cohen, 2017. © Zach Cohen.

Figure 7.1.11. Mistake House? Photograph by Mark Jarzombek, with alterations.

Figure 7.1.12. Telephone pole near Boston, Massachusetts (contractors/builders unknown by author). Photograph by Mark Jarzombek.

Figure 7.1.13. Sketch of elevation: Telephone pole near Boston, Massachusetts. Drawing by Mark Jarzombek.

Figure 7.1.14. John H. Daniels Faculty of Architecture, Landscape, and Design Addition, Toronto. © Nic Lehoux, Daniels Faculty.

Figure 7.2.1. A view of part of the intended Bridge at Blackfriars, London, Piranesi, *c.* 1764. The Elisha Whittelsey Collection, The Elisha Whittelsey Fund, 1962. The Metropolitan Museum of Art.

Figure 7.2.2. Scaffolding design by Nicola Zabaglia, 1743 (Scaffold for octagonal vault of St. Peter's Sacristy, Vatican. From *Castelli e ponti* 1743: pl. XXVIII.)

Figure 7.2.3. Scaffolding, Venice (contractor/builder unknowm by author). Photograph by Mark Jarzombek.

Figure 7.2.4. *Composition 26*, Iakov Chernikhov, 1929–31.

Figure 7.2.5. Modern Art Museum of Fort Worth, Texas, Tadao Ando Architect & Associates, 2002. Photograph by Joe Mabel, 2007.

Figure 7.2.6. James R. Thompson Center (originally, State of Illinois Center), Helmut Jahn, Chicago, 1985.

Figure 7.2.7. La Tallera, Frida Escobedo, Cuernavaca, Morelos, 2012. © Rafael Gamo.

Figure 7.2.8. Four Pancras Square, Eric Parry Architects, London. Photograph Christine Matthews / Pancras Square, St Pancras, London / CC BY-SA 2.0.

Figure 7.2.9. The Perot Museum of Nature and Science, Morphosis Architects, Dallas, Texas, 2011. The Lyda Hill Texas Collection of Photographs in Carol M. Highsmith's America Project, Library of Congress, Prints and Photographs Division.

Figure 7.2.10. *The Hermitage*, Lebbeus Woods, sculpture, Rotterdam, 1998. Photograph by Gerardus.

Figure 7.2.11. Rooftop remodeling on Falkestrasse, Coop Himmelb(l)au, mixed media collage, Vienna, 1988. Collage by Ollybennett2.

Figure 7.2.12. Publicis, Hugh Dutton Associates with SAEE Studio, Paris, 2004. © Nicolas Janberg (Structurae).

Figure 7.2.13. Design Festa Gallery, Harajuku, Japan. Photograph by Bject.

Figure 7.2.14. *Mop and Scaffold*, Primary, Miami (January–March 2020), Eva Robarts. © Eva Robarts.

Figure 7.3.1. Construction site near Boston, Massachusetts. Photograph by Mark Jarzombek.

Figure 7.3.2. Exhibition Diagram for House Deconstructed, Office of Uncertainty Research, Venice Biennale, 2021. © Office of Uncertainty Research (Mark Jarzombek and Vikramaditya Prakash); design by Paul Montie and Angie Door.

Figure 7.3.3. Scene from *Ready Mix*, Lucy Raven, 2020. © Lucy Raven.

Figure 7.3.4. Base detail: masonry cavity wall.

Figure 7.3.5. Construction site near Boston, Massachusetts. Photograph by Mark Jarzombek.

Figure 7.3.6. Casa Sperimentale, Giuseppe Perugini, Uga de Plaisant, and Raynaldo Perugini, Fregene, Italy, 1968 and 1975. Photography by FRENCH+TYE.

Figure 7.3.7. García-Abril House, Las Rozas, Spain. Courtesy, Ensamble Studio.

Figure 7.3.8. García-Abril House, Las Rozas, Spain. Courtesy, Ensamble Studio.

Figure 7.3.9. City of Dreams in Cotai, Macau. Photography by Fitsimz Gucoartem.

Figure 7.3.10. Architectural garbage at a construction site in Venice, 2021. Photograph by Mark Jarzombek.

Figure 7.3.11. Matter Design, *Cyclopean Cannibalism*, Seoul Biennale of Architecture and Urbanism, 2017. Courtesy of Brandon Clifford.

INDEX